KALPA SŪTRA
of
Bhadrabāhu Svāmī

LALA SUNDARLAL JAIN RESEARCH SERIES

VOLUME XIII

KALPA SŪTRA
of
Bhadrabāhu Svāmī

Translation and Notes by
KASTUR CHAND LALWANI

MOTILAL BANARSIDASS PUBLISHERS
PRIVATE LIMITED • DELHI

2nd Reprint : Delhi, 2014
First Edition: Delhi, 1979

ISBN: 978-81-208-0856-0

MOTILAL BANARSIDASS
41 U.A. Bungalow Road, Jawahar Nagar, Delhi 110 007
8 Mahalaxmi Chamber, 22 Bhulabhai Desai Road, Mumbai 400 026
203 Royapettah High Road, Mylapore, Chennai 600 004
236, 9th Main III Block, Jayanagar, Bengaluru 560 011
Sanas Plaza, 1302 Baji Rao Road, Pune 411 002
8 Camac Street, Kolkata 700 017
Ashok Rajpath, Patna 800 004
Chowk, Varanasi 221 001

Printed in India

by RP Jain at NAB Printing Unit,
A-44, Naraina Industrial Area, Phase I, New Delhi–110028
and published by JP Jain for Motilal Banarsidass Publishers (P) Ltd,
41 U.A. Bungalow Road, Jawahar Nagar, Delhi-110007

In memoriam

Sri Sunderlalji Jain

who lived a dedicated life
in the propagation of Indology

CONTENTS

LIST OF ILLUSTRATIONS

FOREWORD

A translation of the *Kalpa Sūtra* into English needs justification, since during the past few years several such translations have appeared in the market. The pioneering work by Hermann Jacobi remains a classic to this day, while in recent translations the writers have exercised a freedom which is hardly justified. The present translation not only claims complete authenticity, but, like the translation of a few other Jaina texts by the same writer, it also strictly follows the prakrit text in prose as well as verse so that the reader through the English medium may enjoy a taste of the original. The translation has also been checked with Jacobi's work on the one hand and an authentic Bengali translation by Basanta Kumar Chattopadhyaya published by the Calcutta University on the other, and slight inaccuracies noticed in these two works have been carefully weeded out. Jacobi's translation being addressed primarily to the Western readers does not provide the prakrit text, while the text as well as translation in Chattopadhyaya's work is printed in Bengali script so that its use can at the most be very limited to the Bengali readers who have an appetite for a Jaina text. These difficulties have been done away with in the present work. An Appendix at the end provides alternative readings for a few passages, followed by Sūtra-wise Notes based on commentaries and an Index of Proper Nouns (names) appearing in the text.

Bhadrabāhu's *Kalpa Sūtra*, writes Jacobi, "has been held in high esteem by the Jainas for more than a thousand years." If Bhadrabāhu be the author of this work, then it should be about 2300 years' old. If, however, its date be reckoned from the time of its writing, which took place at a meeting of the second Jaina Council at Ballabhi in A.D. 513, under the inspiring presence and leadership of Devardhi Kṣamā-Śramaṇa, even then it must be 1500 years' old. We are, however not much bothered about a controversy, if any, about the author and the exact date of its writing, which are issues to be thrashed out by scholars. It is enough for us that the work exists, and that it is a very old work, the oldest available, on the life of the Tīrthaṅkaras, and has a fairly long list of names of men who had been the leaders of the Jaina church till the time of writing, and who, in fact, were the founders of innumerable denominations called *gaṇas kulas*, *gacchas* and *śākhās* into which the Jaina church got itself fragmented, both vertically and horizontally, over several centuries, before Jainism as a powerful religion, particularly in the eastern region and in the deep south, was knocked off its pedestal and perhaps it will not be wrong to add that it has not regained its original position to this day, but is a religion of a small minority group.

As the earliest account of the life of the Tīrthaṅkaras, the 24th 23rd, 22nd and 1st,—since the arrangement of the text moves back in time,—*Kalpa Sūtra* should in the fitness of things, occupy a unique position. Scholars have divided this work into three parts as Tīrthaṅkaras, Church Leaders and Parjuṣaṇā, the last one being a code for the monks during the rainy season. For the present translation, however, the work has been divided into seven parts as follows: Śramaṇa Bhagavān Mahāvīra, Arhat Pārśva, Arhat Ariṣṭanemī, twenty other Tīrthaṅkaras, Arhat Ṛṣabha, Church Leaders and Parjuṣaṇā. Parjuṣaṇā in this text seems to have a wider connotation spreading as it may over the entire rainy season and is not just restricted to a few days during this season.

Among the *Āgamic* texts, *Kalpa Sūtra* belongs to a group called *Cheda Sūtras*. It is, however, not known what the word *cheda* stands for. Going by the contents of these texts, it would appear that they contain rules about personal behaviour and organisational discipline to be observed by the monks. How a work on the biographies of the Tīrthaṅkara entered into this group is anybody's guess. Among the *Cheda Śūtras*, three names usually go together which are *Dasā-Kappa-Vavahāra* (दसा-कप्प-ववहार) and they are compiled into one text called *Śruta Skandha*. *Kalpa Sūtra* is the eighth chapter of the *Dasā* text.

The word *kalpa* stands for the mode of some religious practice, usually a sacrifice; but in the Jaina context, it should mean the code of conduct of the monks during religious festivities. For the word *sūtra*, we have the following definition:

स्वल्पाक्षरमसन्दिग्धं सारवत्-विश्वतोमुखम् ।
अस्तोभमनवद्यं च सूत्रं सूत्रविदो विदुः ॥

(Precise, beyond doubt, substantial, universally true, collected into a single thread, beautiful prose.)

If precision be a criterion, it is doubtful if the description rightly applies to the Jaina texts in general, and the *Kalpa Sūtra* in particular. The Jaina *Sūtras* are not precise texts nor terse formulae, except the *Tattvārtha*, but are very elaborate and exhaustive. But undoubtedly they are master-pieces, full of substance, and works by great masters, believed by the Jainas to be universally true.

As it struck the translator, the first three accounts about Mahāvīra, Pārśva and Ariṣṭanemi use the same diction, with only the names of personalities changing. This indeed facilitated the work of the writer and the orthodox explanation would, perhaps, be that since all the three came with the same maturity and mission, their earthly experience could not have been dissimilar. It is not certain if an explanation like this would satisfy a rational mind or the requirements of history.

In one respect, however, even on the authority of the *Kalpa Sūtra*, Bhagavān Mahāvīra stands somewhat apart not only from the other two immediately preceding him, but from the whole lot. This is his strong Brahmanical association of which at least two items have been noticed even in the *Kalpa Sūtra*. They are, 1. descent from heaven into the womb of a Brahmin lady, and 2. all his Gaṇadharas being Brahmins versed in Vedic learning. As to the first, the mistake, somewhat unusual, was detected in time and rectified through a marvel in surgery at that date but as to the second, nothing could be done, and it is somewhat unusual that none of his Gaṇadharas was a Kṣatriya. Subsequent biographers of Bhagavān Mahāvīra have noticed a few more Brahminical associations with his life, like a Brahmin beggar receiving one half of his robe at the time of his initiation and following him for the whole year to receive the other half, a Brahmin making him the first offer after he became a truly homeless, and so on, but we overlook them as being less authentic. In the case of other Tīrthaṅkaras there was no association whatsoever with a Brahmin on important occasions of their life. What was the Kṣatriya reaction in general to this, particularly reaction from within his own clan, may be an appropriate subject for research, but the reaction of the Kṣatriya youth Jamālī to Mahāvīra's doctrines, as against the reverence of Skandaka who was a Brahmin and Vedic scholar, both of whom had joined the order of monks under Bhagavān Mahāvīra (vide *Bhagavatī Sūtra*) stands out as the most typical of the Kṣatriya attitude.

Another thing in the life of Bhagavān Mahāvīra which struck the translator more than anything else is Bhadrabāhu's brief account of the last day on which Bhagavān Mahāvīra's earthly mission was to close. According to Bhadrabāhu, it was the *divālī* day, which happened to be the last day of the month of Kārttika when the rainy season was to formally end and when Bhagavān Mahāvīra was to enter into liberation, that 18 Malla and Licchavi kings from the Licchavi Confederacy, all his kinsmen, and 18 rulers from the Kāśi-Kośala region, in all 36, mustered strong at Pāvā. No sooner did Bhagavān Mahāvīra's soul discard its mortal frame than, writes Bhadrabāhu, these rulers declared,

The Light of Intellect being out,
let us lit the earthen lamps.

At this point, Bhadrabāhu abruptly ends his narrative without offering any comment, and subsequent *ācāryas* have preferred to keep silent over what had happened on that fateful day.

Looking back in a dispassionate spirit, the above looks like a determination on the part of the Kṣatriya rulers to participate in and determine succession to the spiritual seat of Bhagavān Mahāvīra even when he was still alive. Other events like the removal of Indrabhūti Gautama from Pāvā and Bhagavān Mahāvīra's entering into a long recital of some texts are no less significant of the fact that he preferred to be indifferent at what was going on at this moment. It is true that remaining at a distance Indrabhūti attained omniscience on this fateful day, but that was no disqualification for him against Sudharman to succeed to the chair of Bhagavān Mahāvīra. Be it noted that Sudharman attained omniscience long after this event. Indrabhūti was alive for a few more years after this event, but only as one of the many monks in the order and not as its leader. In this respect the Digambara belief about Indrabhūti, and not Sudharman succeeding Bhagavān Mahāvīra as the leader of the church does not appear very convincing, since in that case the *Āgamic* texts would not have later been issued in the name of Sudharman. It was perhaps in desperation that the Digambaras declared the Jaina texts as having been lost and they stick to this belief to this day. The disorder in the Jaina church at the liberation of Bhagavān Mahāvīra has its corroboration from the Buddhist sources as well. It is thus beyond doubt that the Kṣatriya kings turned an occasion of deep mourning into an occasion of festivity at their apparent success, and celebrated it as the Festival of Light, as is done even to this day, and on this day every year, a section of the Jainas even now rush to Pāvā to 'worship' Vītarāga Bhagavān Mahāvīra with sweet balls (*laddu*), a symbolic reminiscence of what the Kṣatriyas did on that day two thousand five hundred years' ago. Most other Jainas, however, observe the day as the day of fast. The translator invites research on the events on this fateful day on the basis of the Jaina and other contemporary texts.

The next twenty Tīrthaṅkaras, till Arhat Ajita, second in succession, have been lumped together into a single chapter, as if nothing special need be said about them, except putting them on record, and the time-difference between the one and his predecessor has been indicated in astronomical figures. The implication seems to be that these twenty had no dissimilar experience and all of them came down to fullfil the same earthly mission, which they effectively did. In the use of astronomical figures, however, the Jainas do not stand apart from the rest in this country where such figures have been freely used in the sacred texts of all religions, including Hinduism, to establish their respective antiquity. If, however, we bear in mind the time difference between the last three Tīrthaṅkaras, the 24th, 23rd and 22nd, which was no bigger than a few centuries, and superimpose this model for the rest, then the date of Arhat Ṛṣabha may go somewhere near the sixth or fifth century B.C., which was about the date when Indian civilization might have had its genesis. The account of this chapter is so dull and dry that Jacobi has preferred to restrict it to a single printed page, though, for this translation, the complete rendering of the original text has been included, since any abridgement would tantamount to a distortion, and hence be counted as a sacrilege.

Arhat Ṛṣabha, the first Tīrthaṅkara, stands somewhat apart from the rest since he has been viewed by the Jainas as the founder of the Indian civilization. He started the system of marriage outside one's immediate family, established a monarchy, created a social organisation, taught arts and crafts including farming and provided a script for writing named after one of his two daughters, Brāhmī. It may be interesting to recall that the script has been used in Aśokan Edicts. He had one hundred sons, of whom the eldest, Bharata, became the first emperor and the country took her name from him. The other ninetynine were also settled as rulers over different territories before Ṛṣabha courted the life of a monk after having "lived as a prince for 20,00,000 *pūrvas* and as a monarch for 63,00,000 *pūrvas*." His exit from home, the long procession that took him to a park where he initiated himself into monkhood and changed over from a householder into a homeless mendicant and other chain of events are, however, not dissimilar from those of his successors. He was now destined to provide a church, create its four segments, monks, nuns, male followers and female followers, and provide the necessary texts, including the code of conduct, that go in in the making of a religion. He also named his Gaṇadharas who were the heads of the constituent units of the church. All these one comes across in the life of each Tīrthaṅkara who by virtue of these activities becomes the organiser of the *tīrtha* or order. It appears that between one Tīrthaṅkara and another, the order created by the former faded out so that on each occasion it had to be re-created. It is, however, intersting to note in parenthesis that although during the past two thousand five hundred years, no Tīrthaṅkara has appeared on the scene, the need for one has perhaps not been felt during this entire period. It may be added that the life of Ṛṣabha as recorded in a Hindu Purāṇa, Śrīmad Bhāgavata, in several chapters (Skandha 5 Chapters 3-6) is more elaborate than any existing in the Jaina texts, including the *Kalpa Sūtra*. Therein he has been described as the eighth incarnation of Viṣṇu (1.3.13) and attributed with the creation of a new type of religion based on total detachment and tranquilisation of sense organs and mind (1.7.10). This shows the amount of esteem in which he was held in this country. Still more interesting is that he has been noticed in one of the early Vedas. Cf.

> ऋषभं मासमानानां सपत्नानां विसासहीम् ।
> हंतारं शत्रुणां कृधि विरजं गोपितांगवाम् ॥
>
> *Ṛg Veda* x.12.166.

(Oh Divinity! Do thou produce amongst us, of high descent, a great god like Ṛṣabha, who by becoming an *arhat*, which is the epithet of the first world teacher, may become the destroyer of enemies.)

Equally dull-reading is Part Six which contains an almost non-ending account of the senior monks and church leaders till the time of Devardhi Kṣamā-Śramaṇa who lived in the early part of the sixth century A.D. One also gets in this Part an early glimpse of the gradual disintegration of the Jaina church into *gaṇas*, *gacchas*, *kulas*, *etc.*, during a millennium after the liberation of Bhagavān Mahāvīra. Since then the thread appears to have been lost and even though the medieval period produced excellent scholars like Hemacandra, no effort was ever made to pick it up again. The present-day denominations of the church had their genesis towards the last phase of the medieval period, including some which were added in our living memory, and hardly anyone of these sects can establish a definite genealogical link with the traditional church as it existed at the time of Devardhi Kṣamā-Śramaṇa.

Part Seven contains an exhaustive prescription about the conduct of the Jaina monks during the four months of the rainy season loosely called Parjuṣaṇā. It is the personal opinion of the writer that this part is not particularly relevant for a work which purports to be an account of the Tīrthaṅkaras and church leaders, and must have been added at a later period when the reading of the *Kalpa Sūtra* became popular with certain sects of the Jainas during the Parjuṣaṇā. As not a few, but many, prescriptions about conduct were liable to diverse interpretation, they must have been crucial in promoting schisms, in which each break-away group claimed purity to itself, calling into question the *bona fides* of the parent group, the latest to occur like this has been with the Terāpanth Sect of the Jainas.

For those who are not familiar with the Jaina spiritual festivities, it may be worthwhile to add a few lines. The period during which they are celebrated usually falls in the month of Bhādra, the second month of the rainy season according to the Jaina calendar, and runs over a period of about ten days which is the period of Parjuṣaṇā. The festivities include *tapasyā* which means fasts, sometimes as long as a month or beyond, *svādhyāya* or reading of texts, sitting in *sāmāyika* or equanimity, visiting temples or monks as often as possible, and so on. The Jaina year starts with the month of Agrahāyaṇa which is the first month of the Jaina calendar synchronising with November-December, and this along with three following months forms the first third of the year which is winter or fall. The Jain word for this season is Hemanta. The second third of the Jaina year, again consisting of four months, is summer which ends with Āṣāḍha. The remaining third consisting of four months with which the year ends constitutes the rainy season. Parjuṣaṇā at the latest must start at the expiry of one month and 20 days of the rainy season, but never later than that, though it may start earlier and continue for any length. Under exceptional circumstances or under conditions created by a natural calamity, it may start even in Āṣāḍha and continue till the end of Agrahāyaṇa. Where the aim is the enrichment of the spirit, the longer the period, the better. By universal practice, however, it is restricted to about ten days for the Śvetāmbaras, called Parjuṣaṇā followed by another ten called Daśalakkhani for the Digambaras. Parjuṣaṇā is also a Sāṁvatsarika or annual festivity, though as it has come down to us, it is the name given to the last day of Prajuṣaṇā of the Śvetāmbaras, the pitch of spiritual activity, which is followed by the usual *kṣamāpaṇā* or forgiving-and-begging-to-be-forgiven. Even Sāmvatsarika does not fall on the same day for all Śvetāmbaras, some observing it a day earlier, or to put it differently, others observing it a day later.

As to Bhadrabāhu, the celebrated author of the *Kalpa Sūtra*, our information is very scanty except the innumerable works which are attributed to his authorship. We know nothing about the date and place of his birth, his family and parents, except that he belonged to a line called Prācīna or 'ancient', beyond which the implication of the word is anybody's guess. Even the list of church leaders in the *Kalpa Sūtra* makes a scant mention of him. All we know about him is that Rājagṛha, once the capital of the Magadhan Empire, was his seat till he migrated to the south, and that before he did so, he might have on several occasions visited his dear disciple Candra Gupta Maurya, the founder of the Mauryan Empire at Pāṭaliputra which had then shot up into prominence as the capital city in place of Rājagṛha. Later, even Candra Gupta is said to have joined his spiritual master in the south and spent his last days there, throwing out his life in the prescribed Jaina way through a long fast. Bhadrabāhu has been called a Śrutakevalin, which means that though he was not a Kevalin nor the direct recipient of *Śruta* knowledge, he knew by heart the 12 *Aṅgas*, including the twelfth one, *Dṛṣṭivāda*, which is since lost. In anticipation of a great famine in the north, when food would be difficult to get for his monks, we have been told, the celebrated leader preferred to move to the safer south, with many monks following him thither. He settled at Śrāvaṇa Belgolā in the Mysore State and propounded the religion of the Jainas to a completely alien though receptive audience. It is remarkable that under Bhadrabāhu, Jainism became the religion of this region and remained so for about a thousand years after his death. In his absence, the leadership of the Jaina church in the north fell on one Sthūlabhadra who was responsible for convening the first Jaina Council at Pāṭaliputra where only eleven Jaina *Āgamas* could be collected and put to writing. The twelfth *Aṅga* is said to have contained much scientific material and was known only to Bhadrabāhu, and none else, and as Bhadrabāhu was not available, it could not be jotted down. Keeping in view the importance of this work, and the fact that Bhadrabāhu was still alive, which must have been known to the church leaders in the north, it would appear somewhat curious that when the texts were being written, no effort should or could have been made either to bring him to the north, or to hold the meeting in the south, or to associate him in some way with the deliberations and maintain touch with him, or at least to get the text of *Dṛṣṭivāda* from him by rushing an emissary to the south. The inability or reluctance of conveners of the Council to take anyone of these courses seems inexplicable at this date and the callousness with which they preferred to leave the gap unbridged is somewhat startling. It is not even known if Bhadrabāhu had any information about the Council and its deliberations, but it is pretty certain that even after the deliberations, no effort whatsoever was made to have his concurrence and have the texts checked by him. It appears that soon after his exodus to the south, Bhadrabāhu was no more than a name in the north, though in the south, this foreigner's memory is still preserved in the Kannaḍa literary tradition which holds him in the highest esteem. Connecting together the disconnected threads, the present writer cannot help saying that it was one more schism in the Jaina church of which the latest victim was Bhadrabāhu, like Indrabhūti Gautama earlier, and the story of the impending famine which was circulated might have been a convenient fabrication. This appears plausible in view of the Digambara dominance in the south, while the Jaina church in the north is dominantly Śvetāmbara. This may be a further reason for the continued Digambara belief that all the traditional texts became extinct with Bhagavān Mahāvīra. At least it is not very convincing to think that a man of Bhadrabāhu's stature was afraid of the famine and escaped to the south to save his own and a few other people's lives. Further research is, however, invited on this dubious item also. We have it on the authority of the medieval scholar Hemacandra that Bhadrabāhu passed away 170 years after the liberation of Bhagavān Mahâvīra. Quoted below is the relevant couplet:

वीरमोक्षाद् वर्षशते सप्तत्यग्रे गते सति ।
भद्रवाहुरपि स्वामी ययौ स्वर्गं समाधिना ॥

Sixth in the line downward from Bhagavān Mahâvīra, Bhadrabāhu has been attributed with the authorship of many works. At least three or four *Āgamas* are attributed directly to his pen, but his particular association is said to be with the *Cheda Sūtras*, of which at least three are due to him. Of the three *Kalpa* texts, he is said to have produced at least two, *Bṛhat Kalpa* and *Pañca Kalpa*. He was gifted with a superhuman memory which preserved the *Āgamic* texts after Bhagavān Mahāvīra and helped their recording and subsequent propagation, without which perhaps Jainism would have been lost after the medieval age. Dharmaghoṣa, the author of *Iśimaṇḍala*, attributes the following works to the authorship of Bhadrabāhu:

> दशवैकालिकस्याचारांगसूत्रकृतांगयोः ।
> व्यवहारार्षभाषितावश्यकानाम् इतः क्रमात् ।
> उत्तराध्ययन-सूर्यप्रज्ञप्त्योः कलकस्य च ॥
> दशाश्रुताख्यस्कन्धस्य निर्युक्तिर्दशसोऽन्नोत् ।
> तथाऽन्यां भगवांश्चक्रे संहिताम् भाद्रवाहवीम् ॥

The list is too long to go unchallenged and some of the works named therein, like *Uttarādhyayana* and *Daśavaikālika* must have handed down from the past. But in so far as Bhadrabāhu preserved them in his own memory, the claim is all right. All things said, however, it must be admitted that his was a superhuman intellect which produced many works and left inspiration for many more. The present generation of the Jainas owes not a little debt of gratitude to one who perserved the texts in his memory which has helped them to retain their identity, though in a very truncated form, for which Bhadrabāhu was not responsible in any way against the vast welter of Hinduism, which is by no means a small thing particularly when one recalls that Buddhism got lost in the land of its birth and Gautama Buddha has been given a position in the Hindu pantheon.

The date of the present translation is February 10, 1971-April 7, 1972. Its publication has, however, been delayed due to factors beyond control. It is at last going to the readers, and the writer hopes that they will find it useful.

For the illustrations, the writer is grateful to the Editor of the Jain Journal, Jain Bhavan, Calcutta, who made available the blocks and to the publishers who readily agreed to use all of them.

12 Duff Street,
Calcutta 6. K. C. LALWANI
29.3.1979.

Triśalā's Lucky Dreams

I

जिण-चरित्तम्

समणे भगवं महावीरे

Biographical sketches of the Jinas

Śramaṇa Bhagavān Mahāvīra

णमो अरिहंताणं[1]
णमो सिद्धाणं
णमो आयरियाणं[2]
णमो उवज्झायाणं[3]
णमो लोए सव्वसाहुणं

Obeisance to the Victors
Obeisance to the Liberated Souls
Obeisance to the Preceptors
Obeisance to the Teachers
Obeisance to the Monks
In all the worlds.

एसो पंच-णमोक्कारो सव्वपापप्पणासणो ।
मंगलाणं च सव्वेसिं पढमं हवइ मंगलं ॥

This five-fold obeisance ends all sins and bondages;
Among all forms of bliss, this is Number One.

[पंचहत्थुत्तरे]

तेणं कालेणं तेणं समएणं[4] समणो भगवं महावीरे पंच हत्थुत्तरे होत्था । तं जहा—हत्थुत्तराहिं चुए चइत्ता गब्भं वक्कंते । हत्थुत्तराहिं गब्भाओ गब्भं साहरिए । हत्थुत्तराहिं जाए । हत्थुत्तराहिं मुंडे भवित्ता अगाराओ अणगारियं पव्वइए । हत्थुत्तराहिं अणंते अणुत्तरे निव्वाघाए निरावरणे कसिणे पडिपुण्णे केवल-वर-णाण-दंसणे[5] समुप्पण्णे । साइण परिणिव्वुए[6] भयवं ॥ १

[five Uttara-phālgunīs in the life of Mahāvīra]

At that time, in that period, Śramaṇa Bhagavān Mahāvīra had, when the moon was in conjunction with the asterism Uttara-phālgunī, five auspicious events, which were
at the Uttara-phālgunī, he descended, and having descended, he entered into the womb;
at the Uttara-phālgunī, he was transferred from one womb to another;

at the Uttara-phālgunī, he was born;
at the Uttara-phālgunī, he was tonsured, and having given up home, he courted the life of the homeless (monk);
at the Uttara-phālgunī (again), he became the master of infinite, supreme, unobstructed, unimpeded, absolute and perfect *kevala* knowledge and faith.
(But) at the Svāti, he entered into liberation. 1

[देवाणंदाए माहणीए कुच्छिंसि]

तेणं कालेणं तेणं समएणं समणे भगवं महावीरे जे से गिम्हाणं चउत्थे मासे
अट्ठमे अट्ठमे पक्खे आसाढ-सुद्धे[7] । तस्स णं आसाढ-सुद्धस्स छट्ठी-पक्खेणं
महाविजय-पुप्फुत्तर-पवर-पुंडरीयाओ महाविमाणाओ[8] वीसंसागरोवमट्ठि-
तीयाओ (आउक्खएणं भवक्खएणं ठिइक्खएणं) अणंतरं चयं चयित्ता इहेव
जम्बुद्दीवे दीवे भारहे वासे इमीसे ओसप्पिणीए[9] सुसमसुसमाए समाए विइक्कं-
ताए सुसमाए समाए विइक्कंताए सुसमदुस्समाए समाए विइक्कंताए दुस्सम-
सुसमाए समाए बहुविइक्कंताए (सागरोपम-कोडाकोडीए बायालीसाए
वाससहस्सेहिं ऊणियाए) पंचहत्तरीए वासेहिं अद्धनवमेहि[10] यमासेहिं सेसेहिं
एक्कवीसाए तित्थयरेहिं इक्खाग-कुल-समुप्पन्नेहिं कासव-गोत्तेहिं दोहि य
हरिवंस-कुल-समुप्पण्णेहिं गोयम-सगोत्तेहिं तेवीसाए तित्थयरेहिं विइक्कं-
तेहिं समणे भगवं महावीरे चरिमे तित्थयरे पुव्वतित्थयरनिद्दिट्ठे माहण-
कुंडगामे नयरे उसभदत्तस्स माहणस्स कोडालसगोत्तस्स भारियाए देवाणंदाए
माहणीए जालंधर-सगोत्ताए पुव्व-रत्तावरत्त-काल-समयंसि हत्थुत्तराहिं
णक्खत्तेणं जोगमुवागएणं आहार-वक्कंतीए भव-वक्कंतीए सरीर-वक्कंतीए
कुच्छिसि गब्भत्ताए वक्कंते । २

[*in the womb of brahmin lady Devānandā*]

At that time, in that period, in the fourth month of summer, in the eighth fortnight, on the sixth day of the bright-half of the month of Āṣāḍha, having completed his life for 20 *sāgaropamas*, in the great *vimāna* named Mahāvijaya-puṣpottara, which is the best among all the lotus-like *vimānas*, (on the exhaustion of life-span, existence and stay), Śramaṇa Bhagavān Mahāvīra descended,

and having descended in the land named Bhārata-varṣa in the isle (= continent) of Jambūdvīpa, when had ended all the years of the all-bracing part of the descension phase of the time-cycle,[9] all the years of the bracing part, all the years of the bracing-unbracing part, and many years of the unbracing-bracing part, (on the expiry of crores of *sāgaropamas*, less 42,000 years), when there still remained 75 years 8½ months of this part;

after the liberation of 21 *tīrthaṅkaras* who were born in the race of Ikṣvāku in the line of Kāśyapa, and of two others born in the race of Hari in the line of Gautama, 23 tīrthaṅkaras (in all), and

after the exhaustion of his title to the intake, life-span and physical frame (in the aforesaid *vimāna*),

at a time when the moon was in conjunction with the asterism Uttara-phālgunī, at the confluence of the two halves of the night, as directed by the preceding *tīrthaṅkaras*, Śramaṇa Bhagavān Mahāvīra entered as an embryo in the womb of the brahmin-lady Devānandā of the line of Jālandhara, the consort of a brahmin named Ṛṣabhadatta of the line of Kodāla. in the brahminical city of Kundagrāma. 2

[तिण्णाणोवगए]

समणे भगवं महावीरे तिण्णाणोवगए आवि होत्था। चइस्सामि त्ति जाणइ। चयमाणे ण जाणइ। चुएमि त्ति जाणइ। जं रयणिं च णं समणे भगवं महावीरे देवाणंदाए माहणिए जालंधरसगोत्ताए कुच्छिंसि गब्भत्ताए वक्कंते तं रयणिं च णं सा देवाणंदा माहणी सयणिज्जंसि सुत्तजागरा ओहीरमाणी ओहीरमाणी इमे एयारूवे उराले कल्लाणे सिवे धण्णे मंगल्ले सस्सिरीए चोद्द महासुमिणे पासित्ता णं पडिबुद्धा ॥ ३

[*master of three types of knowledge*]

Śramaṇa Bhagavān Mahāvīra was the master of three types of knowledge. Knew he—'I shall descend'. Knew he not—'I am descending'. Knew he—'I have descended'.

The night during which Śramaṇa Bhagavān Mahāvīra entered as an embryo in the womb of the brahmin-lady Devānandā of the line of Jālandhara, during that night, the brahmin-lady Devānandā lying on her couch, half asleep and half awake, dreamt these noble, beautiful, blissful, blessed, auspicious and fortunate 14 great dreams and woke up. 3

[चोद्दस महासुमिणे]

तं जहा—

गय वसह सीह अभिसेय
दाम ससि दिणयरं झयं कुम्भं ।
पउमसर सागर विमाण
भवण रयणुच्चय सिहिं च ॥ ४

[*fourteen great dreams*]

They are:

an elephant, an ox, a lion, anointment,
a garland, the moon, the sun, an ensign, a jar,
a lotus lake, a sea, celestial abode (*vimāna-bhavana*),
a heap of gems and a burning flame. 4

[पडिबुद्धा उसभदत्तं माहणं एवं वयासी]

तएणं सा देवाणंदा माहणी (ते सुमिणे पासत्ति ते सुमिणे) पासित्ता णं पडि-
बुद्धा समाणी हट्ठ-तुट्ठ-चित्त-माणंदिया पीइमणा परमसोमणसिया हरिस-
वस-विसप्पमाण-हियया धारा-हय-कयंवुयं पिव समुस्ससिय-रोम-कूवा
सुमिणोग्गहं करेइ । करित्ता सयणिज्जाओ अब्भुट्ठेइ । अब्भुट्ठित्ता अतुरियं
अचवलं (अविलंबियाए) रायहंससरिसीए गईए[11] जेणेव उसभदत्ते माहणे ।
तेणेव उवागच्छइ । उवागच्छित्ता उसभदत्तं माहणं जएणं विजएणं बद्धावेइ ।
बद्धावित्ता भद्दासणवरगया आसथ्या वीसथ्या सुहासणवरगया करयल-परि-
ग्गहियं सिरसावत्तं दसणहं मथ्थए अंजलिं कट्टु[12] एवं वयासी ॥ ५

[*having awaken, said as follows to brahmin Ṛsabhadatta*]

Thereafter (i.e., after having seen the dreams,) brahmin-lady Devānandā, having awaken, was happy, pleased, joyous, delighted, exceedingly enraptured, with her heart throbbing with glee, with her pore-hairs thrilled like the pollens of the *kadamba* flower when hurt by rain-drops; (and she)

firmly fixed (welcomed) the dreams (in her mind);

then having come out of her bed, at unhasty, unfaltering, (short), and swan-like pace, came she where lay brahmin Ṛsabhadatta;

and having come, she adored (and addressed) him saying,

"Glory be to thee! Victory be to thee!"

Then being calm and composed, she sat in a comfortable posture on a cushion, and having touched her head with the ten finger-tips on her folded palms, she made the following observation. 5

एवं खलु अहं देवाणुप्पिया । अज्ज सयणिज्जंसि सुत्तजागरा ओहीरमाणी ओहीरमाणी इमे एयारूवे ओराले जाव···सस्सिरीए चोद्दस महासुमिण्णे पासित्ता णं पडिबुद्धा । तं जहा गय जाव···सिहिं च ॥ ६

एएसि णं देवाणुप्पिया । ओरालाणं जाव···चोद्दसण्हं महासुमिणाणं के मण्णे कल्लाणे फलवित्तिविसेसे भविस्सइ ॥ ७

"O beloved of the gods! This night, while in bed, half-asleep and half-awake, I got up on seeing (the following) noble, till fortunate, 14 great dreams, which are an elephant, etc., till a burning flame. 6

"O beloved of the gods! What blissful outcome do these noble, till fortunate, 14 great dreams indicate?" 7

[तेसिं सुविणाणं अथ्थोग्गहं करेइ]

तए णं से उसभदत्ते माहणे देवाणंदाए माहणीए अंतिए एयम् अट्ठं[13] सोच्चा निसम्म हट्ठ-तुट्ठ जाव. . .हियए धारा-हय-कलम्बुयं पिव समूसुसिय-रोम-कूवे सुमिणोग्गहं करेइ । करित्ता ईहं अणुपविसइ । अणुपविसित्ता अप्पणो साभाविएणं मइपुव्वएणं बुद्धिविण्णाणेणं तेसिं सुमिणाणं अथ्थोग्गहं करेइ । करित्ता देवाणंदं माहणिं एवं वयासी ॥

[*accepts the meaning of the dreams*]

Then, brahmin Ṛṣabhadatta, having heard from the brahmin-lady Devānandā, became happy and pleased, till with his pore-hairs thrilled with glee like the pollens of the *kadamba* flower when hurt by rain-drops, and welcomed the dreams. Immersed was he in thinking, and, by his inherent intellect and insight, he determined the meaning of the dreams, and quoth as follows to the lady. 8

ओराला णं तुमे देवाणुप्पिये सुमिणा दिट्ठा । कल्लाणा णं सिवा धण्णा मंगल्ला सस्सिरीया आरोग्ग-तुट्ठि-दीहाउ-कल्लाण-मंगल्ल-कारगा णं तुमे देवाणुप्पिये सुमिणा दिट्ठा । तं जह—अथ्थलाभो देवाणुप्पिए । भोगलाभो

सुक्खलाभो देवाणुप्पिए । पुत्तलाभो एवं खलु तुमं देवाणुप्पिए । नवण्हं
मासाणं बहुपडिपुण्णाणं अद्धट्ठमाणं राइंदियाणं विइक्कंताणं सुकुमाल-पाणि-
पायं अहीण-पडिपुण्णपंचिंदिय-सरीरं लक्खण-वंजण-गुणोववेयं माणुम्माण-
प्पमाण-पडिपुण्ण-सुजाय-सव्वंग-सुंदरंगं ससिसोमाकारं कंतं पियदंसणं सुरूवं
दारयं पयाहिसि ॥ ९

"O beloved of the gods! You have dreamt very noble dreams. Surely are these dreams of yours, of beloved, etc., noble, blissful, auspicious, graceful, healing, pleasing, givers of long life and givers of non-ending fortune. O beloved, etc.! (signify they) the acquisition of wealth, of happiness, of friends, of progeny. O beloved, etc. ! From to-day, on the full completion of 9 months and 7½ day-nights, you will give birth to a son, with charming hands and feet (limbs), with the five organs of senses flawless and sharp, with a well-built frame, graceful like the moon, tender, pleasing and beautiful. He will bear auspicious signs and auspicious marks, with high traịts, fully developed in size, stature and weight, well-born, and with features graceful. 9

सेवियणं दारए उम्मुक्कवालभावे विण्णाय-परिणय-मित्ते जोव्वणगं अणुप्पत्ते
रिउव्वेय-जउव्वेय-सामवेय-अथव्वणवेय इतिहास-पंचमाणं निग्घण्टुछट्ठाणं
संगोवंगाणं सरहस्साणं चउण्हं वेयाणं सारए पारए धारए सडंगवी सट्ठितंत-
विसारए संखाणे (सिक्खाणे) सिक्खा कप्पे वागरणे छंदे निरुत्ते जोइसाम्
अयंणे अण्णेसु य बहूसु बंभण्णएसु (परिव्वायएसु) णएसु सुपरिणिट्ठिए आवि
भविस्सइ ॥ १०

तं ओराला णं तुमे देवाणुप्पिए जाव...आरोग्ग-तुट्ठि-दीहाउ-अमंगल्ल-कल्लाण-
कारगा एां तुमे सुविणा दिट्ठुत्ति कट्टु भुज्जो भुज्जो अणुवूहइ ॥ ११

[*the boy will acquire great knowledge*]

"Then the new-born, having lived well through his childhood, will step into his youth, mature with knowledge and development; and then he will learn the fundamentals of, first, the Ṛg-Veda, second, the Yajur-veda, third, the Sāma-veda, fourth, the Atharva-veda, fifth, Chronology, and sixth, Terminology; different disciplines, sub-disciplines and mysteries (philosophies) thereunder, and become expert in them, and upholder of them; he will also learn the *ṣaṣṭhi-tantra* (of Kapila), the Science of

Numbers (Education), the hexology consisting of phonetics-metre-grammar-rhetoric-etymology-astronomy, and many others in the brahminical (ecclesiastical) erudition, and become expert in them. 10

"So do I say, O beloved, etc., the dreams dreamt by you are noble, etc., till healing, pleasing and givers of long life, bliss and welfare."

(Thus he) repeatedly expressed his great satisfaction. 11

[देवाणंदा माहणी ते सुमिणे पडिच्छइ]

तए णं सा देवाणंदा माहणी उसभदत्तस्स माहणस्स अंतिए एयम् अट्ठं सोच्चा
निसम्म हट्ठ-तुट्ठ जाव···हियया करयल-परिग्गहियं दसणहं सिरसावत्तं मथ्थए
अंजलिं कट्टु उसभदत्तं माहणं एवं वयासी ॥ १२
एवमेयं देवाणुप्पिया । तहमेयं देवाणुप्पिया । अवितहमेयं देवाणुप्पिया ।
असंदिद्धमेयं देवाणुप्पिया । इच्छियम् एयं देवाणुप्पिया । पडिच्छियम्
एयं देवाणुप्पिया । सच्चेणं एसम् अट्ठे जहेयं तुब्भे वयह त्ति कट्टु ते सुमिणे
सम्मं पडिच्छइ । ते सुमिणे सम्मं पडिच्छित्ता उसभदत्तेणं माहणेणं सद्धि
ओरालाइं माणुस्सगाइं भोगभोगाइं भुंजमाणी विहरइ ॥ १३

[*brāhmaṇī Devānandā welcomes the dreams*]

Having heard this account from brahmin Ṛṣabhadatta, brahmin-lady Devānandā was pleased, happy, etc., till her heart throbbed with glee, and (she) touched her head with the ten nail-tips of her palms, and addressed unto him the following words. 12

"It is right, O beloved of gods! It is so. It is true, O beloved of gods! There's no doubt (in what you say), O beloved of gods! That is what I desire, O beloved of gods! That is what I accept, O beloved of gods! What has been stated by you is the true meaning (of them)."

So saying she welcomed the dreams. Having welcomed the dreams, she enjoyed many noble pleasures worthy of human beings in the company of brahmin Ṛṣabhadatta. 13

[सक्के देविंदे]

तेणं कालेणं तेणं समएणं सक्के देविंदे देवराया वज्जपाणी पुरंदरे सतक्कतू सहस्सक्खे मघवं पाकसासणो दाहिणड्ढ-लोगाहि वई बत्तीस-विमाण-सय-सहस्साहिवई एरावणवाहणो सुरिंदे अरयंबरवथ्थधरे आलइय-माल-मउडे णव-

हेम-चारु-चित्त-चंचल-कुंडल-विलिहिज्ज-माणागंडे (महड्ढिए महज्जुइए
महब्बले महायसे महाणुभावे महासुक्खे) भासुर-बोंदी-पलंबमाण-वणमाले
सोहम्मे कप्पे सोहम्म-वडिंसगे विमाणे सुहम्माए सभाए सक्कंसि सीहासणंसि
से णं तथ्थ बत्तीसाए विमाण-वास-सय-साहस्सीणं चउरासीए सामाणिय-
साहस्सीणं तायत्तीसाए तायत्तीसगाणं चउण्हं लोगपालाणं अट्ठण्हं अग्गमाहि-
सीणं सपरिवाराणं तिण्हं परिसाणं सत्तण्हं अणियाणं सत्तण्हं अणियाहिवईणं
चउण्हं चउरासीतीए आय-रक्ख-देव-साहस्सीणं अण्णेसिं च बहूणं सोहम्म-
कप्पवासीणं वेमाणियाणं देवाणं देवीणं य आहेवच्चं पोरेवच्चं सामित्तं
भट्टित्तं महत्तरगत्तं आणा-ईसर-सेणावच्चं कारेमाणे पालेमाणे महया
हयणट्ट-गीय-वाइय-तंती-तलताल-तुडिय-घण-मुइंग-पडु-पडह-वाइय-खेणं दिव्वाइं
भोग-भोगाइं भुंजमाणे विहरइ ॥ १४

[*Śakra, the king of gods*]

At that time, in that period, Śakra, the highest among gods, the king of gods, the wielder of the thunderbolt, the destroyer of towns, the performer of a hundred sacrifices, with a thousand eyes, Maghavān, the punisher of (the demon) Pāka, the master of the southern half of *loka* (sphere), the lord of 32,00,000 *vimānas*, the bestrider of the elephant Airāvata, the chief of the *suras*; with spotless-clean and sky-like robes, with his crown decorated with garlands, with ear-rings made of pure gold and highly attractive, dangling on his cheeks; (the most fortunate, the most brilliant, the most mighty, the most glorious, the most powerful, the most happy), with a splendid body, wearing a down-reaching garland of forest-flowers; (such one) was seated on the throne of the Śakras, in the council-hall named Sudharmā in the *vimāna* named Saudharmāvataṁsa, in the (heaven called) Saudharma-kalpa;

(such one) exercised and maintained supreme command, administration, management, guidance, direction, sovereign power and generalship over 32,00,000 dwellers of *vimānas*, 84,000 dwellers of *vimānas* of similar rank and life-span (with himself), 33 chief gods, 4 guardians of the spheres, 8 principal consorts with their retinue, 3 courts, 7 regiments, 7 commanders of regiments, celestial body-guards/*aides-de-camp* 84,000 strong, and an innumerable number of gods and goddesses residing in the Saudharma-kalpa;

(such one) was spending his time enjoying many pleasures permitted to divine beings, under the great din of incessant storytelling, stage play, music, and playing on instruments like *vīṇā*, *karatāla*, *tūrya*, big drums, *paṭu*, *paṭaha*, and many others. 14

[समणं भगवं महावीरं देवाणंदाए माहणीए कुच्छिसि पासेइ]

इमं च णं केवलकप्पं जंबुद्दीवं दीवं विउलेणं ओहिणा आभोएमाणे आभोएमाणे विहरइ। तत्थ णं समणं भगवं महावीरं जंबुद्दीवे दीवे भारहे वासे दाहिणड्ढभारहे माहण-कुंडग्गामे नयरे उसभदत्तस्स माहणस्स कोडाल-सगोत्तस्स भारियाए देवाणंदाए माहणीए जालंधरसगोत्ताए कुच्छिसि गब्भत्ताए वक्कंतं पासइ। पासित्ता हट्ठ-तुट्ठ-चित्तमाणंदिए णंदिए पीइमणे परमसोमणस्सिए हरिसवस-विसप्पमाण-हियए धारा-हय-णीव-सुरभि-कुसुम-चंचुमालइय-ऊसविय-रोम-कूवे विकसिय-वर-कमल-णयण-वयणे पयलिय-वर-कडग-तुडिय-केऊर-मउड-कुंडल-हार-विरायंते-वच्छे पालबं-पलबंमाण-घोलंत-भूसण-धरे ससंभमं तुरियं चवलं सुरिंदे सीहासणाओ अब्भुट्ठेइ। अब्भुट्ठित्ता पाय-पीढाओ पच्चोरुहइ। पच्चोरुहित्ता वेरुलिय-वरिट्ठ-रिट्ठ-अंजण-निउणोविय-मिसिमिसिंत-मणि-रयण-मंडियाओ पाउयाओ ओमुयइ। ओमुइत्ता एग-साडियं उत्तरासंगं करेइ। करित्ता अंजलि-मउलिय-ग्गहत्थे तित्थयराभिमुहे सत्तट्ठ पयाइं अणुगच्छइ। अणुगच्छित्ता वामं जाणुं अंचेइ। अंचित्ता दाहिणं जाणुं धरणितलंसि साहट्टु तिक्खुत्तो मुद्धाणं धरणितलंसि निवेसेइ। निवेसित्ता ईसिं पच्चुण्णमइ। पच्चुण्णमित्ता कडग-तुडिय-थंभियाओ भुयाओ साहरइ। साहरित्ता करयल-परिग्गहियं सिरसावत्तं दसणहं मत्थए अंजलिं कट्टु एवं वयासी॥ १५

[*saw Śramaṇa Bhagavān Mahāvīra in the womb of brāhmaṇī Devānandā*]

At that time, (Śakra) was on an observation tour of the isle of Jambūdvīpa Kevala-kalpa by dint of his profound *avadhi* knowledge. There he saw, in the isle of Jambūdvīpa, in the southern half of Bhārata-varṣa, in the brahmin city of Kundagrāma, Śramaṇa Bhagavān Mahāvīra, lodged in the form of an embryo in the womb of brāhmaṇī Devānandā of the line of Jālandhara, wife of brahmin Ṛsabhadatta of the line of Kodāla.

Having seen (him), he was happy and glad in his mind, overwhelmed with joy, delighted and highly enraptured, with his heart expanded with joy, with his pore-hairs thrilled and standing erect like the fragrant flowers of *nīpa* beaten by rain-drops, his face and eyes wearing happiness like the best lotus-petals in full bloom.

He had beautiful bracelets on his hands, bangles and *keyūra* dangling, crown on his head, rings on the ears, and necklace decorating his breast, with pendants of ornaments hanging and swinging. Astounded and in confusion and haste, the king of the gods rose from his throne, descended to the foot-stool, and took off his slippers, polished with expertise with the best cream of the *vaidūrya* colour, deep and shining, and beset with glittering gems and stones.

Then he placed a portion of the seamless robe on his shoulders in the shape of *uttarīya.* Then with the fingers on his palms arranged and folded in the shape of a flower bud, he advanced seven or eight steps towards the (would-be) *tīrthaṅkara.* Then bending his left knee, and supporting (himself) with his right knee on the floor, he placed his head thrice on the ground. Then slightly raising his head, he composed his arms decorated with bracelets and bangles, touched his head with the extended ten fingers of his folded palms and prayed thus. 15

[नमोक्कारं करेइ]

नमो त्थु णं अरहंताणं भगवंताणं आदिगराणं तित्थगराणं सयं-संबुद्धाणं
पुरिसोत्तमाणं पुरिस-सीहाणं पुरिसवर-पुंडरीयाणं पुरिसवर-गंधहत्थीणं
लोगुत्तमाणं लोगनाहाणं लोगहियाणं लोगपईवाणं लोग-पज्जोयगराणं अभय-
दयाणं चक्खुदयाणं मग्गदयाणं सरणदयाणं जीवदयाणं बोहिदयाणं धम्म-
दयाणं धम्मदेसयाणं धम्मनायगाणं धम्मसारहीणं धम्मवर-चाउरंत[14] चक्क-
वट्टीणं दीवा ताणं सरणं गई पइट्ठा अप्पडिहय-वर-शाण-दंसण-धराणं वियट्ट-
छउमाणं जिणाणं जावयाणं तिण्णाणं तारयाणं बुद्धाणं बोहयाणं मुत्ताणं मोय-
गाणं सव्वूण्णुणं सव्वदरिसीणं सिवं अयलम् अरुयम् अणंतम् अक्खयं अव्वाबाहम्
अपुणरावत्ति-सिद्धि-गइ-नामधेयं ठाणं संपत्ताणं णमो जिणाणं जिय-भयाणं णमो
त्थु णं समणस्स भगवओ महावीरस्स आदिगरस्स चरम-तित्थगरस्स पुव्वंतित्थ-
यर-निद्दिट्ठस्स । वंदामि णं भगवंतं तत्थगयं इहगए। पासउ मे भगवं तत्थगए
इहगयं ति कट्टु समणं भगवं महावीरं वंदइ नमंसइ। नमंसित्ता सीहा-
सण-वरंसि पुरत्थाभिमुहे सन्निसन्ने । तए णं तस्स सक्कस्स देविंदस्स देवरन्नो

अयम् एयारूवे अज्झत्थिये (अब्भत्थिये) चिंतिए पत्थिए मणोगये संकप्पे समुप्पाज्जित्था ॥ १६

[*obeisance by Śakra*]

"Obeisance to the *arhats* and *bhagavats*;

obeisance to the *ādikaras*, the *tīrthaṅkaras* and the self-enlightened ones;

obeisance to the best among men, the lions among men, the best lotus among men, the elephants of the *gandhana* species among men;

obeisance to the best in the world, the guides of the world, the benefactors of the world, the beacon-lights of the world, the enlighteners of the world;

obeisance to the liberators from fear, the givers of vision, the givers of the path, the givers of refuge, the givers of life and the givers of enlightenment;

obeisance to the givers of law, the preachers of law, the masters of law, the leaders of law and the world-monarchs of law, who are the best in all the four directions;

obeisance to those who are liberated from (the bondage of) wrong knowledge, who are the holders of unrestricted and best knowledge and faith, who (in this world) are the light, the liberators, the refuge, the movers and the givers of rest;

obeisance to those who are the victors and the givers of victory, the saviours and the saved, the givers of enlightenment and the enlightened, the givers of liberation and the liberated;

obeisance to the all-knowing, all-seeing Jinas, who have conquered fear, and who have attained the happy, stable, formless, infinite, imperishable, unobstructed and never-to-yield perfection, status and existence;

obeisance to the Śramaṇa Bhagavān Mahāvīra, the *ādikara*, the last *tīrthaṅkara*, whose advent was determined by the preceding *tīrthaṅkaras*.

From this station, do I pay homage and obeisance to the Lord who is there, and may the Revered Lord from there cast his gracious glances at me here."

So saying, he (again) paid homage and obeisance to the Śramaṇa Bhagavān Mahāvīra, and sat on his excellent throne facing the east. At this time, this coveted (commendable) and reflective idea took shape in the mind of Śakra, the king of gods and the highest of gods. 16

[न भूयं न भविस्सं एयं]

न एयं भूयं । न एयं भव्वं । न एयं भविस्सं । जं णं अरहंता वा चक्कवट्टी वा बलदेवा वा वासुदेवा वा अंतकुलेसु वा पंतकुलेसु वा तुच्छकुलेसु वा दरिद्द-कुलेसु वा किविणकुलेसु वा भिक्खागकुलेसु वा माहणकुलेसु वा आयाइंसु वा आयाइंति वा आयाइस्संति वा ॥ १७

एवं खलु अरहंता वा चक्कवट्टी वा बलदेवा वा वासुदेवा वा उग्गकुलेसु वा भोगकुलेसु वा राइण्ण कुलेसु वा इक्खागकुलेसु वा खत्तियकुलेसु वा हरिवंश-कुलेसु वा अण्णयरेसु वा तहप्पगारेसु वा विसुद्ध-जाइ-कुल-वंसेसु वा आयाइंसु वा आयाइंति वा आयाइस्संति वा ॥ १८

[...*has never been, nor will ever be*...]

"It has never been, nor is, nor will ever be, that either an *arhat* or a *cakravarti*, or a *baladeva* or a *vāsudeva*, has ever come, comes or will ever come in low families, mean families, degraded families, poor families, miserly families, beggar families (or) brāhmin families. 17

"Indeed, an *arhat*, a *cakravarti*, a *baladeva* or a *vāsudeva* has come, comes or will come in high families, noble families, royal families, families in the race of Ikṣvāku, kṣatriya families, families in the race of Hari, or similar other families of pure descent and pure race. 18

[एसे वि भावे लोगच्छेरयभूए समुप्पज्जइ . . . . .
णो चेव जोणि-जम्मण निक्खमणेणं निक्खमंति]

अत्थि पुण एसे वि भावे लोगच्छेरयभूए अणंताहिं ओसप्पिणी-उस्सप्पिणीहिं विइक्कंताहिं समुप्पज्जइ णामगोत्तस्स व कम्मस्स अक्खिणस्स अवेइयस्स अणिज्जिण्णस्स उदएणं जं णं अरहंता वा चक्कवट्टी वा बलदेवा वा वासुदेवा वा अंतकुलेसु वा पंतकुलेसु वा तुच्छ-दरिद्द-भिक्खाग-किविण-(माहण) कुलेसु वा आयाइंसु वा आयाइंति वा आयाइस्संति वा कुच्छिसि गब्भत्ताए वक्कमिंसु वा वक्कमंति वा वक्कमिस्संति वा । णो चेव णं जोणि-जम्मण-णिक्खमणेणं णिक्खमिंसु वा णिक्खमंति वा णिक्खमिस्संति वा ॥ १९

अयं च णं समणे भगवं महावीरे जंबुद्दीवे दीवे भारहे वासे माहण-कुंडगामे णयरे

उसभदत्तस्स माहणस्स कोडाल-सगोत्तस्स भारियाए देवाणंदाए माहणीए
जालंधर-सगोत्ताए कुच्छिसि गब्भत्ताए वक्कंते ।। २०

[...or, is this unusual event possible...
never born from a lowly womb]

"Or, is it possible that such an unusual event may even take place in the time-flow of ascensions and descensions? Maybe, for reasons unknown, for not being able to exhaust or win over the bondage of name, race and *karma*, some *arhat*, *cakravarti*, *baladeva* or *vāsudeva* has, does or will come, and has been, is or will be lodged as an embryo in a womb in a low family, mean family, degraded family, poor family, beggar family, miserly [brahmin] family;

but certain it is that such one has never been, nor is, nor will
ever be brought forth by birth from such a (lowly) womb. 19

"This Śramaṇa Bhagavān Mahāvīra is (at this time) staying lodged as an embryo in the womb of brāhmaṇī Devānandā of the line of Jālandhara, wife of brahmin Ṛṣabhadatta of the line
of Kodāla, in Bhārata-varṣa in the isle of Jambūdvīpa. 20

[तं जीयं समणं देवाणंदाए कुच्छीओ तिसलाए
कुच्छिसि साहराविहत्तए. . .हरिणेगमेसिं एवं वयासी]

तं जीयम् एयं तीय-पच्चुप्पण्ण-मणागयाणं सक्काणं देविंदाणं देव-राईणं अरहंते भगवंते तहप्पगारेहिंतो अंतकुलेहिंतो पंतकुलेहिंतो तुच्छ-दरिद्द-भिक्खाग-किविण-कुलेहिंतो तहप्पगारेसु वा उग्गकुलेसु वा भोगकुलेसु वा राइण्ण कुलेसु वा णाय-खत्तिय-हरिवंस-कुलेसु वा अण्णरयेसु वा तहप्पगारेसु विसुद्ध जाइ-कुल-वंसेसु वा (रज्ज-सिरिं कारमाणेसु पालमाणेसु) साहरा-वित्तए। तं सेयं खलु मम वि समणं भगवं महावीरं चरम-तित्थयरं पुव्व-तित्थयर-निद्दिट्ठं माहण-कुण्डगामाओ णयराओ उसभदत्तस्स माहणस्स कोडाल-सगोत्तस्स भारियाए देवाणंदाए माहणीए जालधंर-सगोत्ताए कुच्छीओ खत्तिय-कुण्डगामे णयरे णायाणं खत्तियाणं सिद्धथ्थस्स खत्तियस्स कासव-गोत्तस्स भारियाए तिसलाए खत्तियाणीए वासिट्ठ-सगोत्ताए कुच्छिसि गब्भत्ताए साहरावित्तए। जे वि य णं से तिसलाए खत्तियाणीए गब्भे तं पि य णं देवाणं-दाए माहणीए जालंधर-सगोत्ताए कुच्छिसि गब्भत्ताए साहरावित्तए त्ति कट्टु एवं संपेहेइ। एवं संपेहित्ता हरिणेगमेसिं पायत्ताणियाहिवइं देवं सद्दावेइ।
हरिणेगमेसिं देवं सद्दावित्ता एवं वयासी ।। २१

[...*eternal practice to transfer from Devānandā's to Triśalā's womb*..*to Harinegameśi, said thus*]

"In such a situation, it has been the eternal practice of the Śakra, the king of gods and the highest of gods, in all (the three) periods, past, present and future, to have the *arhats* or the *bhagavats* transferred from such low families, mean families, poor families, beggar families or miserly families to high families, noble families, royal families, Jñātṛ-kṣatriya families, families in the race of Hari, or any other of pure breed and pure descent (who are in enjoyment of a kingdom and are ruling over it). So, now, it is my bounden duty that I transfer the embryo of Śramaṇa Bhagavān Mahāvīra, the last of the *tīrthaṅkaras*, whose advent had been determined by the *tīrthaṅkaras* preceding him, from the womb of brāhmaṇī Devānandā of the line of Jālandhara, wife of brahmin Ṛṣabhadatta of the Kodāla line in the brahmin city of Kuṇḍagrāma, and lodge the embryo in the womb of the kṣatriya-lady Triśalā of the line of Vasiṣṭha, wife of kṣatriya Siddhārtha, in the clan of the Jñātṛ-kṣatriyas, in the line of Kāśyapa, in the kṣatriya city of Kuṇḍapura. And also do I transfer the embryo from the womb of kṣatriyāṇī Triśalā, and lodge it in the womb of brāhmaṇī Devānandā of the Jālandhara line."

Thus decided he, and then looked around and called the *deva* Harinegameśi, the commander of the divine infantry. Having called *deva* Harinegameśi, said he thus. 21

एवं खलु देवाणुप्पिया । ण एयं भूयं । ण एयं भव्वं । ण एयं भविस्सं जं णं अरहंता व चक्कवट्टी वा बलदेवा वा वासुदेव वा अंत-पंत-किविण-दरिद्द-तुच्छ-भिक्खाग-माहण-कुलेसु वा आयाइंसु वा आयाइंति वा आयाइस्संति वा । एवं खलु अरहंता वा चक्क-बल-वासुदेवा वा उग्गकुलेसु वा भोग-राइन्न-खत्तिय-इक्खाग-हरिवंस-कुलेसु वा अण्णयरेसु वा तहप्पगारेसु विसुद्ध-जाइ-कुल-वंसेसु आयाइंसु वा आयाइंति वा आयाइस्संति ॥ २२

अत्थि पुण एसे भावे लोगच्छेरयभूए अणंताहिं उस्सप्पिणी-ओसप्पिणीहिं विइक्कंताहिं समुप्पज्जइ णामगोत्तस्स कम्मस्स अक्खीणस्स अवेइयस्स अणिज्जिण्णस्स उदएणं जं णं अरहंता वा चक्कवट्टी वा बलदेवा वा वासुदेवा वा अंतकुलेसु वा पंतकुलेसु वा तुच्छ-दरिद्द-किविण-भिक्खाग-कुलेसु वा

आयाइंसु वा आयाइंति वा आयाइस्संति वा । णो चेव णं जोणि-जम्मण-
णिक्खमणेणं णिक्खमिंसु वा णिक्खमंति वा णिक्खमिस्संति वा ॥ २३
अयं च णं समणे भगवं महावीरे जंबुद्दीवे दीवे भारहे वासे माहण-कुण्डगामे
णयरे उसभदत्तस्स माहणस्स कोडाल-सगोत्तस्स भारियाए देवाणंदाए
माहणीए जालंधर-सगोत्ताए कुच्छिसि गब्भत्ताए वक्कंते ॥ २४
तं जीयं एयं तीय-पच्चुप्पन्नम् अणागयाणं सक्काणं देविंदाणं देवराईणम् अर-
हंते भगवंते तहप्पगारेहिंतो अंतकुलेहिंतो पंतकुलेहिंतो तुच्छ-किविण-दरिद्द-
भिक्खाग-माहण-कुलेहिंतो तहप्पगारेसु उग्ग-कुलेसु वा भोग-राइन्न (नाय)
खत्तिय-इक्खाग-हरिवंस-कुलेसु वा अन्नयरेसु वा तहप्पगारेसु विसुद्ध-जाइ-
कुल-वंसेसु वा साहराविंत्तए ॥ २५

"Indeed, O beloved of the gods! It has never been, nor is, nor will ever be, that either an *arhat* or a *cakravarti*, or a *baladeva* or a *vāsudeva*, has ever come, comes or will ever come in low families, mean families, degraded families, poor families miserly families, beggar families or brahmin families. Indeed, an *arhat* a *cakravarti*, a *valadeva* or a *vāsudeva*, has come, comes or will come in high families, noble families, royal families, families in the race of Ikṣvâku or Hari, or any other of pure descent and pure blood. 22

"Or, may it be so that such an unusual event has taken place in the time-flow of ascensions and descensions. Maybe, for reasons unknown, for not being able to exhaust or win over the bondage of name, race and *karma*, some *arhat*, *cakravarti*, *baladeva* or *vāsudeva* has, does or will come, and has been, is or will be lodged as an embryo in a womb in a low family, mean family, degraded family, poor family, beggar family, or miserly family; but certain it is that such one has never been, nor is, nor will ever be brought forth by birth from such (lowly) womb. 23

"This Śramaṇa Bhagavân Mahâvîra is (at this time) staying lodged as an embryo in the womb of brâhmaṇī Devânandâ of the line of Jālandhara, wife of brahmin Rṣabhadatta of the Kodāla line, in Bhārata-varṣa in the isle of Jambūdvīpa. 24

"In such a situation, it has been the eternal practice of the Śakra, the king of gods and the highest of gods, in all periods, past, present and future, to have the *arhats* or the *bhagavats* transferred from such low families, mean families, poor families, beggar families, or miserly families to high families, noble families, royal families, (Jñātṛ) kṣatriya families, families in the race of Ikṣvāku or Hari, or any other of pure blood and descent. 25

[देवाणंदाए कुच्छीग्रो तिसलाए कुच्छिसि साहराहि]

तं गच्छ णं तुमं समणं भगवं महावीरं माहण-कुण्डग्गामाग्रो णयराग्रो उसभ-दत्तस्स कोडालसगोत्तस्स भारियाए देवाणंदाए माहणीए जालंधर-सगोत्ताए कुच्छीग्रो खत्तिय-कुण्डग्गामे णयरे णायाणं खत्तियाणं सिद्धथ्थस्स खत्तियस्स कासवगोत्तस्स भारियाए तिसलाए खत्तियाणीए वासिट्ठ-सगोत्ताए कुच्छिसि गब्भत्ताए साहराहि । जे वि य णं से तिसलाए खत्तियाणीए गब्भे तं पि य णं देवाणंदाए माहणीए जालंधर-सगोत्ताए कुच्छिसि गब्भत्ताए साहराहि । साहरित्ता मम एयं ग्राणत्तियं खिप्पमेव पच्चाप्पिणाहि ॥ २६

[...so transfer from Devānandā's to Triśalā's womb]

So go ye to the brahmin city of Kuṇḍagrāma, and transfer the embryo of Śramaṇa Bhagavān Mahāvīra from the womb of brāhmaṇī Devāṇandā of the Jālandhara line, wife of brahmin Ṛṣabhadatta of the Kodāla line, to the womb of kṣatriyāṇī Triśalā of the Vasiṣṭha line, wife of Siddhārtha, a Jñātṛ-kṣatriya of the line of Kāśyapa, in the kṣatriya city of Kuṇḍa-grāma; and the embryo in the womb of kṣatriyāṇī Triśalā, transfer and lodge it in the womb of brāhmaṇī Devānandā of the Jālandhara line;
and having done so, report at once the fulfilment of the commission." 26

तए णं से हरिणेगमेसी पायत्ताणियाहिवई देवे सक्केणं देविंदेणं देवरण्णा एवं वुत्ते समाणे हट्ठतुट्ठे ग्राणंदिए जाव ··हियये करयल जाव···त्ति कट्टु एवं जं देवो ग्राणवेइ त्ति ग्राणाए विणएणं वयणं पडिसुणेइ । एवं पडिसुणित्ता सक्कस्स देविंदस्स देवरण्णो ग्रंतिग्राग्रो परिणिक्खमइ उत्तरपुरत्थिमं दिसीभागम् ग्रवक्कमइ । ग्रवक्कमित्ता वेउव्वियसमुग्धाएणं समोहणइ । समोहणित्ता संखिज्जाइं जोयणाइं दंडं निस्सरइ। तं जहा रयणाणं वयराणं वेरुलियाणं लोहि-यक्खाणं मसारगल्लाणं हंसगब्भाणं पुलयाणं सोगंधियाणं जोइरसाणं (जोइ-सराणं) ग्रंजणाणं ग्रंजण-पुलयाणं (रयणाणं) जायरूवाणं ग्रंकाणं फलिहाणं रिट्ठाणम् ग्रहावायरे पोग्गले[15] परिसाडेइ । परिसाडित्ता ग्रहासुहुमे पोग्गले परियादियति ॥ २७

Being thus commissioned by Śakra, the king of gods and the highest among gods, Deva-Harinegameśi, the commander of the divine infantry, became elated and happy. His heart was expanded in great joy. He touched his head with fingers arranged on his folded palms and received the order with due humility saying, "As Your Majesty pleases." After this, having left the presence of Śakra, he descended in the north-east direction. Having descended, he spread, by dint of his magical powers, snares of hypnotism. (Soon,) distance became reduced like sticks and started moving out fast. Then he threw out the gross particles of jewels, such as *vajra*, *vaidūrya*, *lohitākṣa*, *masāragalla* *haṁsa-garva*, *pulaka*, *saugandhika*, *jyotirasa*, (*jytisvara*), *añjana* *añjana-pulaka*, (*rayaṇa*) *jātarūpa*, *subhaga*, *aṅka*, *sphaṭika* and *ariṣṭa*, like (insignificant) berries, retaining (only) subtle substance (of them). 27

परियादिइत्ता दुच्चंपि वेउव्विय-समुग्घायेणं समोहणइ । समोहणित्ता उत्तर-वेउव्वियं रूवं विउव्वइ । विउव्वित्ता ताए उक्किट्ठाए तुरियाए चवलाए छेश्राए चंडाए जयणाए उद्धुयाए सिग्धाए दिव्वाए देवगईए वीतीवयमाणे तिरियम् श्रसंखेज्जाणं दीवसमुद्दाणं मज्झमज्झेणं जेणे व जंबुद्दीवे दीवे जेणेव भारहे वासे जेणेव माहण-कुण्डग्गामे णयरे जेणेव उसभदत्तस्स माहणस्स गिहे जेणेव देवाणंदा माहणी तेणेव उवागच्छइ । उवागच्छित्ता श्रालोए समणस्स भगवश्रो महावीरस्स पणामं करेइ । करित्ता देवाणंदाए माहणीए सपरिजणाए श्रोसोवणिं दलइ । दलित्ता श्रसुभे पोग्गले श्रवहरइ सुभे पोग्गले पक्खिवइ । पक्खिवित्ता श्रणुजाणउ मे भगवं त्ति कट्टु समणं भगवं महावीरं श्रव्वाबाहम् श्रव्वाबाहेणं करयलसं पुडेणं गिण्हइ । गिण्हित्ता जेणेव खत्तिय कुंडगामे णयरे जेणेव सिद्धथ्थस्स खत्तियस्स गिहे जेणेव तिसला खत्तियाणी तेणेव उवागच्छइ । उवागच्छित्ता तिसलाए खतियाणीए सपरिजणाए श्रोसोवणिं दलइ । दलित्ता श्रसुभे पोग्गले श्रवहरइ । श्रवहरिता सुभे पोग्गले पक्खिवइ । पक्खिवित्ता समणं भगवं महावीरं श्रव्वावाहम् श्रव्वाबाहेणं तिसलाए खत्तियाणीए कुच्छिसि गब्वत्ताए साहरइ । जे वि य णं से तिसलाए खत्तियाणीए गब्भेतं पि य णं देवाणंदाए माहणीए जालंधर-सगोत्ताए कुच्छिसि गब्भत्ताए साहरइ । साहरित्ता जम् एव दिसिं पाउभूए तम् एव दिसिं पडिगए ॥ २८

Then for the second time, he spread his magical powers, and having done so, he transformed himself into a definitive form.

Thereafter, he passed obliquely at paces excellent, quick, active, sure, tremendous, victorious, exalted, rapid, divine and befitting a god, through innumerable isles and oceans, and arrived in Bhārata-varṣa in the isle of Jambū-dvīpa, to the brahmin city of Kuṇḍagrāma, at the residence of brahmin Ṛṣabhadatta, to brāhmaṇī Devānandā. Then he paid homage and obeisance to the presence of Śramaṇa Bhagavān Mahāvīra. After this, he cast brāhmaṇī Devānandā, with her retinue, into a deep slumber, withdrew inauspicious matter and spread auspicious ones. Then saying, "May the Venerable one graciously permit me", and without causing any disturbance, he took (the embryo of) Śramaṇa Bhagavān Mahāvīra on his palms. With this, he rushed to the kṣatriya city of Kuṇḍagrāma, to kṣatriyāṇī Triśalā, at the residence of kṣatriya Siddhārtha. There he cast kṣatriyāṇī Triśalā, with her retinue, under a spell of deep slumber, withdrew inauspicious matter and scattered auspicious ones. Then he placed Śramaṇa Bhagavān Mahāvīra, in embryo, and without causing any disturbance, in the womb of kṣatriyāṇī Triśalā; and, the one that was lodged in the womb of kṣatriyāṇī Triśalā, he placed in the womb of brāhmaṇī Devānandā of the Jālandhara line, and disappeared in the direction from whence he came. 28

ताए उक्किट्ठाए तुरियाए चवलाए चंडाए छेआए जयणाए उद्धयाए सिग्घाए दिव्वाए देव-गईए तिरियम् असंखेज्जाणं दीव-समुद्दाणं मज्झं मज्झेणं जोयण-साहस्सीएहिं विग्गहेहिं उप्पयमाणे उप्पयमाणे जेणामेव सोहम्मे कप्पे सोहम्म-वडिंसए विमाणे सक्कंसि सीहासणंसि सक्के देविंदे देवराया तेणमेव उवागच्छइ। उवागच्छित्ता सक्कस्स देविंदस्स देवरन्नो एयम् आणत्तियं खिप्पं एव पच्च-प्पिणइ। (तेणं कालेणं तेणं समएणं समणे भगवं महावीरे तिण्णाणोवगए यावि होत्था। साहरिज्जिस्सामि त्ति जाणइ साहरिज्जमाणे णो जाणइ साहरिएमि त्ति जाणइ) ॥ २९

With his body extended over a thousand *yojanas*, and at paces excellent, quick, active, sure, tremendous, victorious, exalted, rapid, divine and befitting a god, he flew across innumerable isles and oceans, and arrived at the Saudharma-kalpa, to the *vimāna* named Saudharmāvataṁsa where, on the throne, was seated Śakra, the king of gods and the highest among gods, and quickly reported the execution of his order to Śakra, the king of gods and the highest among gods.

(At that time, in that period, Śramaṇa Bhagavān Mahāvīra was in possession of three types of knowledge; knew he, 'I shall be removed'; knew he not, 'I am being removed'; knew he, 'I have been removed.'] 29

[आसोय-बहुलस्स तेरसीपक्खेणं हत्थुत्तराहिं णक्खत्तेणं सहारिए]

तेणं कालेणं तेणं समएणं समणे भगवं महावीरे जे से वासाणं तच्चे मासे पंचमे पक्खे आसोय-बहुले । तस्स णं आसोय-बहुलस्स तेरसी-पक्खेणं बासीइं राइंदिएहिं विइक्कंतेहिं तेसीइमस्स राइंदियस्स अंतरा वट्टमाणे हियाणुकंपएणं देवेणं हरिणेगमेसिणा सक्क-वयण-संदिट्ठेणं माहण-कुण्डग्गामाओ णयराओ उसभदत्तस्स माहणस्स कोडाल-सगोत्तस्स भारियाए देवाणंदाए माहणीए जालंधर-सगोत्ताए कुच्छीओ खत्तिय-कुंडग्गामे णयरे सिद्धथ्थस्स खत्तियस्स कासव-गोत्तस्स भारियाए तिसलाए खत्तियाणीए वासिट्ठ-सगोत्ताए पुव्व-रत्तावरत्त-कालसमयंसि हत्थुत्तराहिं णक्खत्तेणं जोगमुवागएणं अव्वाबाहं अव्वाबाहेणं कुच्छिंसि गब्भत्ताए साहरिए । ३०

[...was transferred at the Uttara-phālgunī on the thirteenth day of dark half of Āśvina]

At that time, in that period, (the embryo of) Śramaṇa Bhagavān Mahāvīra was in the third month, in the fifth fortnight, on the thirteenth day of the dark half of the month of Āśvina, having completed 82 day-nights (in the womb), 83rd day-night running. By the order of Śakra, the well-wishing and sympathetic Deva Harinegameśi removed at midnight, when the moon was in conjunction with the asterism Uttara-phālgunī, the embryo of Mahāvīra, in tact, from the womb of brāhmaṇī Devānandā of the Jālandhara line, wife of brahmin Ṛṣabhadatta of the Kodāla line, to the womb of kṣatriyāṇī Triśalā of the Vasiṣṭha line, wife of kṣatriya Siddhārtha in the line of Kāśyapa. 30

[देवाणंदाए चोद्दस महासुमिणे तिसलाए हडे]

जं रयणिं च णं समणे भगवं महावीरे देवाणंदाए माहणीए जालंधर-सगोत्ताए कुच्छीओ तिसलाए खत्तियाणीए वासिट्ठ-सगोत्ताए कुच्छिंसि गब्भत्ताए साहरिए तं रयणिं च णं सा देवाणंदा माहणी सयणिज्जंसि सुत्तजागरा ओही-

रमाणी इमे एयारूवे ओराले कल्लाणे सिवे धण्णे सस्सिरीए चोद्दस महासुमिणे तिसलाए खत्तियाणीए हडे पासित्ता णं पडिबुद्धा ।
(तं जहा – गय उसभ) ॥ ३१

[fourteen great dreams of Devānandā stolen by Triśalā]

The night during which (the embryo of) Śramaṇa Bhagavân Mahâvīra was removed from the womb of brāhmaṇī Devānandā of the Jâlandhara line to the womb of kṣatriyāṇī Triśalâ of the Vasiṣṭha line, during that night, brāhmaṇī Devânandā, half-asleep and half-awake in her bed, saw that her fourteen great dreams, noble, till fortunate, were being stolen away by kṣatriyāṇi Triśalā. Having seen thus she woke up. 31

[तिसला चोद्दस महासुमिणे पासित्ता पडिबुद्धा]

जं रयणिं च णं समणे भगवं महावीरे देवाणंदाए माहणीए जालंधर-सगोत्ताए कुच्छीओ तिसलाए खत्तियाणीए वासिट्ठ-सगोत्ताए कुच्छिसि गब्भत्ताए साहरिए तं रयणिं च णं सा तिसला खत्तियाणी तंसि तारिसगंसि वासघरंसि अब्भितरओ सचित्त-कम्मे बाहिरओ दूमिय-घट्ठ-मट्ठे विचित्त-उल्लोय-चित्तय-तले मणि-रयण-पणासिय-अंधयारे बहु-सम-सुविभत्त-भूमि-भागे पंच-वण्ण-सरस-सुरभि-मुक्क-पुप्फ-पुंजोवयार-कलिए कालागुरु-पवर-कुण्डुरुक्क-तुरुक्क-दज्झंत-धूव-मघमघंत-गंधुद्धयाभिरामे सुगंध-वर-गंधिए गंध-वट्टि-भूए तंसि तारिसगंसि सयणिज्जंसि सालिंगण-वट्टिए उभओ विव्वयणे[16] उभओ उण्णए मज्झेणं गंभीरे गंगा-पुलिण-वालुअ-उद्दाल-सालिसए ओयविय-खोमिय-दुगुल्ल-पट्ट-पडिच्छण्णे सुविरइय-रय-त्ताणे रत्तंसुय-संबुए सुरम्मे आइणग-रूय-बूर-नवणीय-तूल-फासे सुगंधवर-कुसुम-चुन्न-सयणोवयार-कलिए पुव्व-रत्तावरत्त-काल-समयंसि सुत्तजागरा ओहीरमाणी इमे एयारूवे उराले कल्लाणे सिवे धण्णे मंगल्ले सस्सिरीए चोद्दस महासुमिणे पासित्ता णं पडिबुद्धा । तं जहा—

गय-वसह-सीह अभिसेय
दाम ससि दिणयरं झयं-कुंभं ।
पउमसर सागर विमाण
भवण रयणुच्चय सिहिं च ॥ ३२

[Triśala woke up on seeing fourteen great dreams]

During the night when Śramaṇa Bhagavân Mahâvira was removed from the womb of brāhmaṇī Devānandā of the Jâlandhara line to the womb of kṣatriyāṇī Triśalā of the line of Vasiṣṭha, during that night, the chamber in which kṣatriyāṇī Triśalā lay was, in its interiors, decorated with frescoes; in the exteriors, (it was) white-washed, clean and shining; with the centre of the brilliant ceiling depicted with fine paintings; the floor perfectly level and well-marked (with *svastika* and other auspicious marks); the darkness dispelled by jewels and precious stones; (the chamber) decorated with heaps of pleasant, fragrant and fresh flowers of multifarious colours and delighted by the curling, scented fumes of burning and fine *kundurukka* and *turuṣka*, as if (the chamber had been turned into) a pot of scented incense;

with a couch having a mattress of a full length, with pillows at head and foot, elevated at the two ends, with hollow in the middle, soft (for a walk) like sand on the bank of the Gaṅgā, covered with a sheet of ornamented linen, with a well-worked towel to wrap, covered with red mosquito curtains, delightful to the touch like fur, cotton or butter, besprinkled with fine and scented flowers and powder. On such a couch lay she, half-asleep and half-awake, and at the confluence of the prior and posterior halves of the night, she dreamt the following noble, till fortunate, 14 great dreams and woke up. They are

an elephant, an ox, a lion, anointment,
a garland, the moon, the sun, an ensign, a jar,
a lotus lake, a sea, celestial abodes (*vimāna-bhavana*)
a heap of gems and a burning flame. 32

[चोद्दस सुमिणे पासेइ]

तए णं सा तिसला खत्तियाणी तप्पढमयाए तम्रोय-चउद्दंतं ऊसिय-गलिय-विपुल-जलहर-हार-निकर-खीर-सागर-ससंक-किरण - दग - रय-रयय - महासेल-पंडुरतरं समागय-महुयर-सुगंध-दाण-वासिय-कपोलमूलं देवराय-कुंजर-वर-प्पमाणं पिच्छइ सजल-घण-विपुल-जलहर-गज्जिय-गंभीर-चारु-घोसं इभं सुभं सव्व-लक्खण-कयंबियं वरोरुं ॥ ३३

[*saw fourteen dreams*]

1. Then kṣatriyāṇī Triśalā saw in her first dream an auspicious elephant, possessing good marks, very powerful, with beautiful thighs and four tusks, whiter than a vast water-less cloud,

or a heap of pearls, or an ocean of milk, or the beams of the moon, or the foam of waves or the silvery mountain; with its temples perfumed with scented fluid attracting bees; equalling in its physical dimensions the great Airāvata of the king of gods; trumpeting deep and fine like the thunder of a large rain-cloud. 33

२. तम्रो पुणो धवल-कमल-पत्त-पयराइरेग-रुव-प्पभं पहासमुदग्रोवहारेहिं सव्वग्रो चेव दिवयंतं ग्रइसिरिभर-पिल्लणा-विसप्पंत-कंत-सोहंत-चारु-ककुहं तणु-सुद्ध-सुकुमाल-लोमनिद्धच्छविं थिर-सुबद्ध-मंसलोवचिय-लट्ठ-सुविभत्त-सुंदरंगं पिच्छइ घण-वट्ठ-लट्ठ-उक्किट्ठ-तुप्पग्ग-तिक्खसिंगं दंतं सिवं समाण-सोहंत-सुद्ध-दंतं वसहं ग्रमियगुण-मंगल-मुहं ॥ ३४

2. Then (she saw) a tame, lucky bull, with complexion whiter than a heap of white lotus petals; illuminating all around by the diffusion of a glory of light; with a lovely, resplendent, beautiful hump displaying in all its grace; with a frame looking delightful and covered with fine, clean and tender hairs; with beauty emanating from well-set and well-formed muscles; with body proportioned and fine; with two beautiful horns, thick, round, gracious and fine; pointed at the tip and greased; with teeth equal, white and bright; with face indicating innumerable good qualities and auspicious marks. 34

३. तम्रो पुणो हार-निकर-खीर-सागर-ससंक-किरण-दग-रय-रयय-महासेल-पंडुरंगं रमणिज्ज-पिच्छनिज्जं थिरलट्ठ-पउट्ठ-वट्ट-पीवर-सुसिलिट्ठ-तिक्ख-दाढा-विडंबिय-मुहं परिकम्मिय-जच्च-कमल-कोमल-पमाण-सोहंत-लट्ठ-उट्ठं-रत्तुप्पल-पत्त-मउय-सुकुमाल-तालु-निल्लालियग्ग-जीहं मूसायय-पवर-कणग-ताविय-ग्रावत्तंत-वट्ट-तडि-विमल-सरिस-णयणं विसाल-पीवर-वरोरुं पडिपुन्न-विमल-खंधं मिउ-विसय - सुहुम - लक्खण-पसत्थ-वित्थिन्न - केसराडोव-सोहियं ऊसिय-सुनिम्मिय-सुजाय-ग्रप्फोडिय-लंगूलं सोमं सोमाकारं लीलायंतं नहय-लाग्रो उवयमाणं नियग-वयणं ग्रइवयंतं पिच्छइ सा गाढ-तिक्खग्ग-नहं सीहं णयण-सिरी-पल्लव-पत्त-चारु-जीहं । ३५

3. And then (she saw) a good-looking, delightful, moon-like and jovial lion jumping from the sky towards her face; with his body-complexion whiter than a heap of pearls, an ocean of milk, the beams of the moon, the foam of waves or the silvery

mountain; with mouth adorned with sharp teeth, well-set, thick and strong, and fixed lustre; with fine lips, soft like a noble lotus, well-proportioned and brilliant; with the tip of the tongue protruding; with palate mild and tender, like the petals of red lotus; with eyes round, thunder-like and gentle, revolving in the socket, like red-hot excellent gold just poured; with thighs beautiful and large; with developed and excellent shoulders; with a mane soft, white, fine, auspicious, broad and extended; with tail well-shaped and well-grown, erect and flapping; with claws deep and sharp; and with a beautiful tongue adorning the mouth-pit like newly sprouted shoots. 35

४. तओ पुणो पुण्ण-चंद-वयणा उच्चागय-ठाण-लट्ठ-संठियं पसत्थ-रूवं सुपइ-
ट्ठिय-कणगमय-कुम्भ-सरिसोवमाण-चलणं अच्चुण्णय-पीण-रइय-मंसल-उण्णय-
तणु-तंब-णिद्ध-णहं कमल-पलास-सुकोमल-कर-चरण-कोमल-वरंगुलिं कुरु-
विंदावत्त-वट्टाणुपुव्व-जंघं णिगूढ-जाणुं गय-वर-कर-सरिस-पीवरोरुं चामीकर-
रइय-मेहला-जुत्त-कंत-वित्थिन्न-सोणि-चक्कं जच्चंजण - भमर - जलय - पयर-
उज्जुय-सम-संहिय-तनुय-आइज्ज-लडह[17]-सुकुमाल-मउय-रमणिज्ज-रोम-राइं
नाभी-मंडल-सुंदर-विसाल-पसत्थ-जघणं करयल-माइय-पसत्थ-तिवलियमज्झं
णाणा-मणि-कणग-रयण-विमल-महातवणिज्जाभरण - भूसण-विराइय - मंगुवंगिं
हार-विरायंत-कुंदमाल- परिणद्ध- जलजलित- थण-जुयल-विमल-कलसं आइअ-
पत्तिय-विभूसियेण सुभग-जालुज्जलेण मुत्ता-कलावेण उरत्थ-दीणार-मालय-
विरइएण कंठ-मणि-सुत्तएण य कुंडल-जुयलुल्लसंत-अंसोवसत्त-सोभंत-सप्पभेणं
सोभा-गुण-समुदएणं आणण-कुडुंबिएणं कमलामल-विसाल-रमणिज्ज-लोयणं
कमल-पज्जलंत-कर-गहिय-मुक्कतोयं लीला-वाय-कय-पक्खएणं सुविसद-
कसिण-घण-सण्ह-लंबंत-केस-हत्थं पउम-द्दह-कमल-वासिणिं सिरिं भगवइं
पिच्छइ हिमवंत-सेल-सिहरे दिसा-गइंदोरु-पीवर-कराभि सिच्चमाणिं ॥ ३६

4. And then (she saw) Goddess Śrī, with her face like full moon, seated at the top of the Himavat mountain on a lotus in a lotus lake, highly auspicious, on a lofty throne at a beautiful elevation: with a firmly-placed golden tortoise as her befitting vehicle; with copper-tinged, delightful, fine and well-set on swelling, thick and dyed muscles; with lotus-*palāśa*-like tender fingers set on her dainty hands and feet; with round and well-formed legs adorned with an ornament called kuruvindāvarta; with two knees deep; with fleshy thighs resembling the

proboscis of an excellent elephant; with lovely and broad hips encircled by a golden zone; with a combination of a beautiful belly and a circular navel, containing a lovely array of hairs black as collyrium, black drone or cloud, straight, even, continuous, thin, long, admirable, handsome and soft; her waist having three wide folds encompassable in a palm; with ornaments and trinkets made of gold and set with many jewels and precious stones, with pure radiance, shining on her various limbs and body parts; with a pair of pure, cup-like, sparkling breasts, swollen, decorated with *kunda* flowers, bearing on them a necklace, with strings of pearls made by diligent and expert craftsmen, shining with wonderful strings, necklace of jewels, with a string of *dīnāras*, and a dangling pair of ear-rings touching her shoulders and diffusing brilliance; her face gracious, *kuṭumba*-like, shining with the combination of high traits; her beautiful eyes, lotus-like, pure and large; with her brilliant, lotus-like hands sprinkling water, which in gentle breeze served like a fan; her glossy, dark, thick, smooth hair hanging downward; such goddess Śrī on the top of the Himavat mountain was being anointed with water from the strong and large trunks of the guardian elephants. 36

५. तश्रो पुणो सरस-कुसुम-मंदार-दाम-रमणिज-भूयं चंपगासोग-पुण्णाग-णाग-पियंगु-सिरीस-मुग्गरग-मल्लिया-जाइ-जुहियंकोल्ल-कोज्ज-कोरिंट-पत्त-दमणय-णवमालिय-वउल-तिलय-वासंतिय-पउमुप्पल-पाडल-कुंदाइमुत्त-सहकार-सुरभि-गंधि श्रणुवम-मणोहरेणं गंधेणं दस दिसाश्रो वि वासयंतं सव्वोउय-सुरभि-कुसुम-मल्ल-धवल-विलसंत-कंत-बहु-वण्ण-भत्ति-चित्तं छप्पय-महुयरि-भमर-गण-गुम-गुमायंत-निलित-गुंजंत-देस-भागं दामं पिच्छइ णभंगण-तलाश्रो उवयंतं ॥ ३७

5. And then (she saw) floating down from the firmament a garland, looking as graceful as a bunch of *mandāra* flowers because of the combination of fresh blossoms, emitting delicious smell of *campaka*, *aśoka*, *punnāga*, *nāga*, *priyaṅgu*, *śiriṣa*, *mudgaraka*, *mallikā*, *jāti*, *juthi*, *ankolla*, *kejja*, *korinṭapatra*, *damanaka* *nava-mallikā*, *vakula*, *tilaka*, *vasantikā*, *padma*, *utpala*, *pāṭala*, *kunda*, *atimukta*, and *sahakāra* perfuming with fine and unexcelled fragrance ten sectors of the universe; with charming whiteness

of fragrant flowers of all seasons; splendid with the embellishment of multifarious colours in between, with the six-footers, bees and black drones swarming around, darkening, and filling with their noise, the entire neighbourhood. 37

६. ससिं च । गोखीर-फेण-दग-रय-रयय-कलस-पंडुरं सुभं हियय-मयण-कंतं पडिपुण्णं तिमिर-णिकर-घण-गुहिर-वितिमिर-करं पमाण-पक्खंत-राय-लेहं कुमुय-वण-णिबोहगं णिसा-सोभगं सुपरिमट्ठ-दप्पण-तलोवमं हंस-पडुवण्णं-जोइसा-मुह-मंडगं तमरिपुं मयण-सरापूरं समुद्द-दग-पूरगं दुम्मणं जणं दइय-वज्जियं पाय-ऐंहि सोसयंतं पुणे । सोम-चारु-रूवं पिच्छइ सा गगण-मंडल-विसाल-सोम-चंकम्म-माणतिलगं रोहिणि-मण-हियय-वल्लहं देवीपुण्ण-चंदं समुल्लसंतं ॥ ३८

6. And the moon,—white as cow's milk, or foam, or a silver cup, full of white hue in all parts, auspicious; dispeller of thick darkness of deep and swarthy caves; with its silvery crescent shining at the end of the two halves of the month; delight of the blossoms of lotus group, adorning the night, pure as the surface of the well-polished mirror, with bright hue like a swan, decoration of the firmament, enemy of darkness, like the arrow-quiver of Cupid, the god of Love, sweller of the water of oceans, exploiter of the disconsolate, separated from the sweet-heart, placid and beautiful; shining like the head-mark of the vast lunar disc (*soma-cakra*) in the sky; full moon, the delight of the heart and mind of Rohiṇī, dazzling in brilliance. 38

७. तओ पुणो तम-पडल-परिप्फुडं चेव तेयसा पज्जलंत-रूवं रत्तासोग-पगास-किंसुय-सुय-मूह-गुंजद्ध-राय-सरिसं कमल-वणालंकणं अंकणं जोइसस्स अंबर-तल-पईवं हिम-पडल-गलग्गहं गह-गणोरु-णायगं रत्ति-विणासं उदयत्थमणेसु मुहुत्त-सुह-दंसणं दुण्णिरिक्ख-रूवं रत्ति-मुद्धंत-दुप्पयारप्पमद्दणं सीय-वेग-महणं पिच्छइ मेरु-गिरि-सयय-परियट्टयं विसालं सूरं रस्सि-सहस्स-पयलिय-दित्त-सोहं ॥ ३९

7. And then the sun, the dispeller of the mass of darkness, burning radiant in its own self, like the red *aśoka*, or the blossomed *kiṁśuka*, or the bill of a parrot, or the (red) half of *guñja*; the ornament of lotus groups; the measure mark of

astronomical locations, the lamp of the firmament, the melter of snow-heaps, the illustrious leader of planets, the destroyer of nights, pleasant for a momentary vision at the rising and setting time, exceedingly hard to vision (for the rest of the day), the punisher of night-faring miscreants, the subduer of chill, with its luminous glory set forth by a thousandrays. 39

८. तम्रो पूणो जच्च-कणग-लट्ठि-पइट्ठियं समूह-णील-रत्त-पीय-सुक्किल-सुकुमालुल्लसिय-मोरपिच्छ-कय-मुद्धयं धयं म्रहियस्ससिरीयं फालीय-संख-ककुद-दग-रय-रयय-कलस-पंडुरेण मत्थयत्थेण सीहेण रायमाणेण रायमाणं भित्तुं गगण-तल-मंडलं चेव ववसिएणं पिच्छइ सिव-मउय-मारुय-लयाहय-कंपमाणं म्रइप्पमाणं जण-पिच्छणिज्ज-रूवं ॥ ४०

8. Then an ensign, fastened to a staff of pure gold, an attractive sight for the people, unusually large in size, with its crest made of tender and delightful peacock feather, deep blue, red, yellow and white, exceedingly gracious; as if a lion, white like crystal, or conch-shell, or *aṅka*-stone, or *kunda* flower, or foam of water, or a silver cup, was floating to and fro in the firmament, (as if) to deprive a king of his dignity by the dignity of another king. Beaten by gentle stroke of pure breeze, the brilliant ensign was fluttering. 40

९. तम्रो पुणो जच्च-कंचणुज्जलंत-रूवं णिम्मल-जल-पुण्णम् उत्तमं दिप्पमाण-सोहं कमल-कलाव-परिरायमाणं पडिपुण्णय-सव्वमंगल-भेय-समागमं पवर-रयण-परायंत-कमलट्ठियं णयण-भूसण-करं पभासमाणं सव्वम्रो चेव दीवयंतं सोम-लच्छी-णिभेलणं सव्व-पाव-परिवज्जियं सुभं भासुरं सिरि-वरं सव्वोउय-सुरभि-कुसुम-म्रासत्त-मल्ल-दामं पिच्छइ सा रयय-पुण्ण-कलसं ॥ ४१

9. Then (saw) a full jar of precious (silvery?) metal, resplendent with fine gold, full of pure water, super-excellent and shining in beauty, surrounded and decorated with boquets of water lilies, marked all over by prosperity and happiness, placed on a lotus excelling even a jewel, like the peaceful abode of the goddess of Wealth, delight of the eye, free from all sins, splendid, shining and exquisitely beautiful; casting its brilliance in all directions, and decorated with garlands made of fragrant flowers of all seasons. 41

१०. तओ पुण रवि-किरण-तरुण-बोहिय-सहस्सपत्तसुरभितर-पिंजर-जलं जलचर-पहकर-परिहत्थग-मच्छ-परिभुज्जमाण-जल-संचयं महंत जलतं इव कमल-कुबलय-उप्पल-तामरस-पुंडरीओरु-सप्पमाण-सिरि-समुदएणं रमणिज्ज-रूव-सोहं पमुइयंत-भमर-गण-मत्त-महुयरि-गणुक्करोलिज्झमाण-कमलं कायं-बग-बलाहय-चक्क-कलहंस-सारस-गव्विय-सउण-गण-मिहुण-सेविज्जमाण-सलिलं पउमिणि-पत्तोवलग्ग-जल-विंदु-णिचय-चित्तं पिच्छइ सा हियय-णयण-कंतं पउमसरं णाम सरं सरुहाभिरामं ॥ ४२

10. Then a lake named lotus lake, delight of the eye and of the heart, with beautiful sight; with water (looking) yellow and perfumed by one-thousand-petalled lotuses just blossomed in the rays of the sun; abounding with swarms of aquatics dwelling in water, and fish moving inside; very large and brilliant; with *kamala*, *kuvalaya*, *utpala*, *tāmarasa* and *puṇḍarīka* dangling with glee; the lake itself looking splendid and delightful because of the brilliant blossoms of multifarious flowers; with black drones and infatuated bees swarming in thousands and licking honey from lotus to lotus; with proudly mating and moving pairs of swans, cranes, *cakravākas*, Indian cranes, ducks and many others living on water; with water drops splendidly sparkling on lotus leaves. 42

११. तओ पुणो चंद-किरण-रासि-सरिस-सिरि-वच्छ-सोहं चउगमण-पवड्ढ-माण-जल-संचयं चवल-चंचलुच्चाय-पमाण-कल्लोल-लोलंत-तोयं पडु-पवणाहय-चलिय-चवल-पागड-तरंग-रंगंत-भंग-खोखुब्भमाण-सोभंत-णिम्मल-उक्कड-उम्मि-सह-संबंध-धावमाणो णियत्त-भासुरतराभिरामं महा-मगर-मच्छ-तिमि-तिमिंगिल-णिरुद्ध-तिलितिलियाभिधाय-कप्पूर-फेण-पसरं 'महाणई-तुरिय-वेगमागय-भम-गंगावत्त-गुप्पमाणुच्चलंत-पच्चो-नियत्त - भममाण-लोल-सलिलं पिच्छइ खीरोय-सायरं सरय-रयणिकर-सोम-वयणा ॥ ४३

11. Then she, whose face was splendid like the moon in autumn, saw a milk-sea, its surface glittering like the moon beams; its milks welling and rushing in four (all) directions, restless and mobile, with excessively high waves; with its distinct billows, driven by sharp wind and playful, dashing against the shore and breaking into an endless brilliance; the sea itself

looking bright and pleasant because of the rolling and re-rolling of sharp and distinct waves; with camphor-like white foam coming up from the lashing (tails) of the great tortoises, fish, whales, *timiṅgila*, *niruddha* and *tilitilika* and spreading far; with big rivers rushing into the sea and creating whirlpools called *gaṅgāvarta*, wherein water is incessantly restless and moving round. 43

१२ तश्रो पुणो तरुण-सूर-मंडल-समप्पभं दिप्पमाण-सोहं उत्तम-कंचण-महा-मणि-समूह-पवर-तेय-श्रट्ठ-सहस्स-दिप्पंत-णह-प्पईवं कणग-पयर-लंबमाण-मुत्ता-समुज्जलं जलंत-दिव्व-दामं ईहामिग-उसभ-तुरग-णर-मगर-विहग-बालग-किण्णर-रुरु-सरभ-चमर-संसत्त-कुंजर-वणलय-पउमलय-भत्ति-चित्तं गंधव्वोपव-ज्जमाण-संपुण्ण-घोसं णिच्चं सजल-घण-विउल-जलहर-गज्जिय-सद्दाणुनाइणा देव-दुंदुहि-महारवेणं सयलम् श्रवि जीवलोयं पूरयंतं कालागुरु-पवर-कुंदुरुक्क-तुरुक्क-डज्झंत-धूव वासंग-उत्तम-मघमघंत-गंधुद्धयाभिरामं णिच्चालोयं सेयं सेयप्पभं सुखराभिरामं पिच्छइ सा साश्रोवभोगं वर-विमाण-पुंडरीयं ॥ ४४

12. Then (she saw) a celestial abode, the very best among the *vimānas*, abode of perpetual joy and happiness, ever lit and lotus-like; with brilliance like the disc of the morning sun; its one thousand and eight excellent columns made of fine gold, inlaid with great gems, looking like a brilliant light in the sky; with pearls fastened to its glittering curtain; decorated with frescoes depicting wolves, bulls, horses, men, dolphins, birds, snakes, *kinnaras*, *rurus*, *sarabhas*, *camaras*, *saṁsaktakas* (a beast of prey), elephants, wild creepers and lotus creepers. There was audible all the time music arising from the concerts played by the *gandharvas*. The surrounding was all the time sounded by the rumblings of thick and rain clouds. The great din of the drums of the gods even penetrated the world of living beings. All the time, beautiful fragrance was emanating from the burning incense, the best of black aloe, *kundarukka* and *turukka*, and the whole place was filled up by the scented fumes. It (*vimāna*) shed continuous light, was white and of excellent lustre, delight for the highest of gods, and affording joy and pleasure. 44

१३. तश्रो पुण पुलग-वेरिंदणील-सासग-कक्केयण-लोहियक्ख-मरगय-पवाल-सोगंधिय-फलिह-हंसगब्भ-श्रंजण-चंदप्पह-वर-रयणेहिं महियल-पइट्ठियं गगण-मंडलंतं पभासयंतं तुंगं मेरु-गिरि-सण्णिकासं पिच्छइ सा रयण-णिकर-रासिं ॥४५

13. Then again, (she saw) a heap of jewels, as high as Mount Meru, and containing (in the heap) *pulaka*, *vajra*, *indranīla*, *sasyaka*, *karketana*, *lohitākṣa*, *marakata*, *pravāla*, *saugandhika*, *sphāṭika*, *haṁsa-garva*, *añjana*, *candrakānta* and many others. Though placed on the ground, the light emanating from that heap shone till the farther end of the sky. 45

१४. सिहिं च । सा विउलुज्जल-पिंगल-महु-घय-परिसिच्चमाण-णिद्धूम-धगधगाइय-जलंत-जालुज्जलाभिरामं तरतम-जोग-जुत्तेहिं जाले-पयरेहिं अण्णुमण्णम् इव अणुपइण्णं पिच्छइ जालुज्जलणग अंबरं व कत्थइ पयंतं अइवेग-चंचलं सिहिं ॥ ४६

इमे एयारिसे सुभे सोमे पिय-दंसणे सुरूवे सुविणे दट्ठूण-सयण-मज्झे पडिबुद्धा अरविंद-लोयणा-हरिस-पुलइयंगी ।

एए चउदस सुविणे
सव्वा पासेइ तित्थयरमाया ।
जं रयणि वक्कमई
कुच्छिसि महायसो अरिहा ॥ ४६अ

14. And a burning flame. She saw a flame, trembling and in vehement motion, exceedingly bright, poured with honey-like yellow *ghee* (clarified butter), smokeless, bright because of the burning glow, and extremely beautiful. Its intertwined flames were jumbled up like limbs, piled one on the other, and their blaze brightened the firmament at many places. 46

On seeing these auspicious dreams, graceful, pleasant and lovely, (she), the lotus-eyed one, woke up in her bed, with her body bristling with joy.

These fourteen dreams
Are seen by mother of a *tīrthaṅkara*
During the night when enters
In her womb the great-famed *arhat*. 46A

[तिसला सिद्धत्थं पडिबोहेइ]

तए णं सा तिसला खत्तियाणी इमे एयारूवे ओराले चोद्दस महासुमिणे पासित्ता णं पडिबुद्धा समाणी हट्ठ-तुट्ठचित्तं जाव...विसप्पमाण-हियया धाराहय-कलंबु-(-पुप्फ) यं पिव समूस्सिय-रोम-कूवा सुमिणोग्गहं करेइ । करित्ता सयणिज्जाओ अब्भुट्ठेइ । अब्भुट्ठित्ता पाय-पीढाओ पच्चोरुहइ । पच्चोरुहित्ता

अतुरियं अचवलं असंभंताए अविलंबियाए राय-हंस-सरिसीए गईए जेणेव सयणिज्जे जेणेव सिद्धत्थे खत्तिए तेणेव उवागच्छइ। उवागच्छित्ता सिद्धत्थं खत्तियं ताहिं इट्ठाहिं कंताहिं मणुण्णाहिं मणामाहिं ओरालाहिं कल्लाणाहिं सिवाहिं धण्णाहिं मंगल्लाहिं सस्सिरीयाहिं हिययगमणिज्जाहिं हियय-पल्हायणि-ज्जाहिं मिय-महुर-मंजुलाहिं गिराहिं संलवमाणी संलवमाणी पडिबोहेइ ॥४७

[*Triśalā wakes up Siddhārtha*]

Then, she, kṣatriyâṇī Triśalā, having seen these fourteen great and noble dreams, woke up, became happy, glad, pleased, joyful, very much delighted, with her heart expanded, with her pore-holes thrilling like the *kadamba* flower struck by rain drops, and welcomed the dreams. Then she came out of her bed, and descended from the foot-stool. Then she moved at slow, steady, unoverwhelmed, even, swan-like pace, the direction of the couch where lay kṣatriya Siddhârtha and awakened him by addressing him with kind, pleasing amiable tender, noble, blissful, auspicious, blessed, helpful fortune-giving, heart-moving, heart-delighting, measured, sweet and soft words. 47

तए णं सा तिसला खत्तियाणी सिद्धत्थेणं रण्णा अब्भणुण्णाया समाणी-णाणा-मणि-रयण-भत्ति-चित्तंसि भद्दासणंसि णिसियइ। णिसियित्ता आसत्था वीसत्था सुहासण-वर-गया सिद्धत्थं खत्तियं ताहिं इट्ठाहिं जाव...संलवमाणी संलवमाणी एवं वयासी ॥ ४८

Then kṣatriyâṇī Triśalā, with the permission of king Siddhârtha, sat down on a noble seat, inlaid with various gems, and decorated with sundry miniatures; then being composed and calm in her comfortable seat, she addressed him with kind, till soft, words and said thus. 48

एवं खलु अहं सामी अज्ज तंसि तारिसगंसि सयणिज्जंसि सालिंगण-वट्टिए उभओ विब्बोयणे उभओ उण्णए मज्झेणं गंभीरे गंगा-पुलिण-वालुअ-उद्दाल-सालिसए-ओयविय-खोमिय-दुगुल्लपट्ट-पडिच्छण्णे सुविरइय-रयत्ताणे रत्तंसुय-संबुए सुरम्मे आईणग-रूयबूर-नवणीय-तूल-फासे सुगंध-वर-कुसुम-चुण्णसय-णोवयार-कलिए पुव्व-रत्तावरत्त-काल-समयंसि-सुत्तजागरा ओहीरमाणी ओहीरमाणी इमेयारूवे ओराले कल्लाणे सिवे धण्णे मंगल्ले सस्सिरीए चोद्दस महासुमिणे पासित्ता णं पडिबुद्धा। तं जहा –

गय उसभ सीह अभिसेय दाम ससि दिणयरं झयं कुम्भं ।
पउम-सर सागर विमाण-भवण रयणुच्चय सिंहि च ॥
तं एएसिं सामी ओरालाणं चोद्द-सण्हं महा-सुमिणाणं के मण्णे कल्लाणे फल-
वित्ति-विसेसे भविस्सइ । ४९

"My dear ! To-day, I, while lying on the bed, that had a side-pillow of full human length, with two pillows at two ends, with the two ends raised (a little), and hollow in the centre, soft to lie on like the sand on the bank of the Gaṅgā, covered with a beautiful linen, decorated with a well-wrought towel, covered with red curtains, soft like fur, cotton or butter, and sprayed with the best and most fragrant flower-powder, I, half-asleep and half-awake, at the confluence of the two halves of the night, woke up on seeing these noble dreams. They are:

an elephant, an ox, a lion, anointment, a garland, the moon, the sun, an ensign, a jar, a lotus lake, a sea, a celestial abode, a heap of gems and a burning flame.

"Oh my dear : Tell me what blissful outcome is portended by these fourteen noble and great dreams." 49

तए णं से सिद्धथ्थे राया तिसलाए खत्तियाणीए अंतिए एयमट्ठं सोच्चा णिसम्म
हट्ठ-तुट्ठ-चित्ते आणंदिए पीइ-मणे परम-सोमणस्सिए हरिस-वस-विसप्पमाण-
हियए धारा-हय-णीव-सुरहि-कुसुम-चंचुमालइय-रोंम-कूवे ते सुमिणे ओगिण्हइ ।
ओगिण्हित्ता ईहं पविसइ । पविसित्ता अप्पणो साहाविएणं मइ-पुव्वएणं
बुद्धिविन्नाणेणं तेसिं सुमिणाणं अथ्थोग्गहं करेइ । करित्ता तिसलं खत्तियाणिं
ताहिं इट्ठाहिं जाव. . . मंगल्लाहिं मिय-महुर-सस्सिरीयाहिं वग्गूहिं संलवमाणे
संलवमाणे एवं वयासी । ५०

Then, on hearing these words of kṣatriyāṇī Triśalā, and understanding them, king Siddhārtha became happy and pleased, very much delighted, his heart expanded with glee and his poreholes became thrilled like the petals of the delightful *nīpa* blossoms when hurt by rain drops, and welcomed/received the dreams. Having received them, he was immersed in his thought. Then he determined the significance of the dreams by his natural talent and analytical faculty, whereon addressing kṣatriyāṇī Triśalā with kind ... till measured, sweet and soft words, said he thus. 50

ओराला णं तुमे देवाणुप्पिए सुमिणा दिट्ठा। कल्लाणा णं तुमे देवाणुप्पिए सुमिणा दिट्ठा । एवं सिवा धण्णा मंगल्ला सस्सिरीया आरोग्ग-तुट्ठि-दीहाऊ-कल्लाण-मंगल्ल-कारगा णं तुमे देवाणुप्पिए सुमिणा दिट्ठा । अत्थलाभो देवाणुप्पिए । भोगलाभो देवाणुप्पिए । पुत्तलाभो देवाणुप्पिए । सोक्खलाभो देवाणुप्पिए । रज्जलाभो देवाणुप्पिए । एवं खलु तुमं देवाणुप्पिए णवण्हं मासाणं बहुपडिपुण्णाणं अद्धट्ठमाणं राइंदियाणं विइक्कंताणं अम्हं कुलकेउं अम्हं कुलदीवं कुल-पव्वयं कुलवडिंसयं कुलतिलयं कुल-कित्ति-करं कुल-दिणकरं कुल-आधारं कुल-णंदि-करं कुल-जस-करं कुल-पायवं कुल-विवद्धण-करं सुकुमाल-पाणि-पायं अहीण-संपुण्णं-पंचिंदिय-सरीरं लक्खण-वंजणगुणोववेयं माणुम्माण-प्पमाण-पडिपुण्ण-सुजाय-सव्वंग-सुंदरंगं ससि-सोमाकारं कंतं पिय-दंसणं सुरूवं दारयं पयाहिसि । ५१

"Oh beloved of the gods! Surely very noble are these dreams seen by you. Oh beloved of the gods! Surely blissful are these dreams seen by you. Surely are they auspicious, blest, helpful, fortunate, givers of healing, happiness and long life and non-ending weal and bliss. Oh beloved of the gods! They portend the acquisition of wealth, of happiness, of progeny, of friends, and of kingdom; in consequence of which, on completion of full 9 months and 7½ day-nights, you will give birth to a boy, who will be the ensign of our line, the lamp of our line, the crown of our line, the head-mark of our line, the giver of glory to our line, the sun of our line, the support of our line, the joy of our line, the giver of fame to our line, the tree of our line, the exalter of our line;

with tender hands and feet, free from any deficiency or depression in the organs of senses and in the body, with gracious marks and auspicious traits, well-proportioned in length, height and weight, with a frame beautiful all over, calm like the moon, pleasing, pleasant and beautiful. 51

से वि य णं दारए उम्मुक्क-बाल-भावे विण्णाय-परिणय-मित्ते जोव्वण-गमणुप्पत्ते सूरे वीरे विक्कंते वित्थिण्ण-विउल-बल-वाहणे रज्ज-वई राया भविस्सइ । ५२

"Then passing through his childhood, the boy will attain the knowledge and development due to youth and step into his youth; then at youth, he will be brave, gallant and valorous, and become the master and king of a vast kingdom, with a large army, and extensive wagons. 52

तं ओराला णं तुमे जाव ..दिट्ठत्ति कट्टु दोच्चं पि तच्चं पि अणुबूहइ । तए णं सा तिसला खत्तियाणी सिद्धत्थस्स रण्णो अंतिए एयमट्ठं सोच्चा णिसम्म हट्ठ-तुट्ठ-चित्त-माणंदिया जाव हियया कर-यल-परिग्गहियं दसणहं मत्थए अंजलिं कट्टु एवं वयासी । ५३

"So, oh beloved of the gods, surely very noble are these dreams of yours."

And he repeated these twice or thrice. Kṣatriyāṇī Triśalā too, on hearing these from king Siddhārtha, and understanding them, became highly pleased, delighted and happy, with her mind full of joy, with her heart throbbing in glee, and with her poreholes expanded like the *kadamba* flower struck by rain-drops, (whereon) touching her head with her ten fingers set on her folded palms, she said thus. 53

एवमेयं सामी । अवितहमेयं सामी । असंदिद्धमेयं सामी । इच्छियमेयं सामी । पडिच्छियमेयं सामी । इच्छिय-पडिच्छियमेयं सामी । सच्चेणं एसमट्ठे से जहेतं तुब्भे वदह त्ति कट्टु ते सुमिणे सम्मं पडिच्छइ । पडिच्छित्ता सिद्धत्थेणं रण्णा अब्भणुण्णाया समाणी णाणा मणि-रयण-भत्ति-चित्ताओ भद्दासरणाओ अब्भुट्ठेइ । अब्भुट्ठित्ता अतुरियं अचवलं असंभंताए अविलंबियाए रायहंस-सरिसीए गईए जेणेव सए सयणिज्जे तेणेव उवागच्छइ । उवागच्छित्ता एवं वयासी । ५४

"What you say is right, my lord! It is just, my lord! It is true, my lord! There's no doubt in it, my lord! It is desired, my lord! It is expected, my lord! What you say is the correct significance of the dreams, my lord!"

So saying, she (again) rightly welcomed the significance of the dreams. Having welcomed them, she, with the permission of king Siddhārtha, rose from her seat inlaid with various gems and depicted with sundry miniatures. Then at paces slow, steady, unoverwhelmed, even and swan-like, she went to the place where stood her bed, and said thus (unto herself). 54

मा मै ते उत्तमा पहाणा मंगल्ला सुमिणा अण्णेहिं पाव-सुमिणेहिं पडिहम्मिस्संति त्ति कट्टु देवय-गुरुजण-संबद्धाहिं पसत्थाहिं मंगल्लाहिं धम्मियाहिं लट्ठाहिं कहाहिं सुमिण-जागरियं पडिजागरमाणी पडिजागरमाणी विहरइ । ५५

"Lest other evil dreams counteract these best, most excellent and blissful dreams (if I sleep again). . .", with this apprehension, she submitted herself to the practice of 'post-dream awakening', and spent her time awake by listening to discourses regarding gods and spiritual guides, bracing, blissful, pious and agreeable. 55

तए णं सिद्धत्थे खत्तिए पच्चूस-काल-समयंसि कोडुंबियपुरिसे सद्दावेइ । सद्दावित्ता एवं वयासी । ५६

खिप्पमेव भो देवाणुप्पिया । अज्ज सविसेसं वाहिरियं उवट्ठाणसालं गंधोदय-सित्तं सुइय-संमज्जिओवलित्तं सुगंधवर-पंच-वण्ण-पुप्फोवयार-कलियं कालागुरु-पवर-कुंदुरुक्क-तुरुक्क-उज्झंत-धूव-मघमघंत-गंधुद्धयाभिरामं सुगंध-वर-गंधियं गंधवट्टिभूयं करेह कारावेह । करित्ता य कारयित्ता य सीहासणं रयावेह । रयावित्ता ममेयं आणत्तियं खिप्पमेव पच्चप्पिणह । ५७

Then at day-break, kṣatriya Siddhārtha sent for the keepers of the royal household and, having called them, said thus: 56
"Oh beloved of the gods! Urgently to-day and with special haste, make ready and have made ready the exterior hall of audience, duly cleaned with the brooms, duly besprinkled with fragrant water, and duly besmeared; decorate and have decorated the place with scented flowers of five (sundry) colours; delight the hall with curling and scented fumes of burning black aloe, *kundurukka* and *turukka*; fill it with fragrance of the sweet essence of flowers, etc., so that the hall may turn into a vessel of fragrance. Having done these, erect a throne. And, on due completion of (my) order, report it to me at once. 57

तए णं ते कोडुंबिय-पुरिसा सिद्धत्थेणं रण्णा एवं वुत्ता समाणा हट्ठ-तुट्ठ जाव... हियया कर-यल जाव कट्टु 'एवं सामि' त्ति आणाए विणएणं वयणं पडिसुणंति । पडिसुणित्ता सिद्धत्थस्स खत्तियस्स अंतिआओ पडिणिक्खमंति । पडिणिक्खमित्ता जेणेव बाहिरिया उवट्ठाणसाला तेणेव उवागच्छंति । उवागच्छित्ता खिप्पमेव सविसेसं बाहिरियं उवट्ठाणसालं गंधोदय-सित्तं

सुइय-जाव...सीहासणं रयावित्ति । रयावित्ता जेणेव सिद्धथ्ये खत्तिए तेणेव उवागच्छंति । उवागच्छित्ता कर-यल-परिग्गहियं दसणहं सिरसा वत्तं अंजलिं कट्टु सिद्धथ्थस्स खत्तियस्स तं आणत्तियं-पच्चप्पिणंति । ५८

On being ordered thus by king Siddhārtha, the keepers of the royal household pleased, happy and joyful, with their heart throbbing in great delight, with their pore-holes expanded like the *kadamba* flower hurt by rain-drops, touched their head with their ten fingers on their folded palms, and accepted the royal order saying, "As Your Majesty commands!"

Having accepted (the royal order), they moved out from the presence of kṣatriya Siddhārtha, and hurried to the external hall of audience. Then they themselves made ready and got it done, duly broomed it, duly besprinkled it with scented water, duly had it besmeared; decorated it with scented flowers of five (sundry) colours; made it delightful with curling and scented fumes of burning black aloe, *kundurukka* and *turukka*; filled it with the fragrance of sweet flower essence, etc., so that the hall turned into a fragrant vessel. Having finished these, they erected the throne in the hall, and then they came back to kṣatriya Siddhārtha, touched their head with ten fingers on their folded palms, and reported to him the execution of the order. 58

तए णं सिद्धथ्ये खत्तिए कल्लं पाउ-प्पभायाए रयणीए फुल्लुप्पल-कमल-कोमलुम्मिल्लियंमि अहपंडुरे पभाए रत्तासोग-प्पगास-किसुय-सुय-मुह-गुंजद्ध-राग-सरिसे (बंधुजीवग-पारावण-चलण-णयण-परहुय-सुरत्त-लोयण-जासुयण-कुसुम-रासि-हिंगुलय-णियराइरेय-रेहंत-सरिसे) कमलायर-संड-बोहए उद्वियंमि सूरे सहस्स-रस्सिमि दिणयरे तेयसा जलंते (अहक्कमेण उइए दिवायरे तस्स य कर-पहरापरद्धंमि अंधयारे बालायव-कुंकुमेणं खचिय व्व जीवलोए) सयणिज्जाओ अब्भुट्ठेइ । ५९

Next day, the night having ended, at dawn, when blossomed the soft lotuses and nymphaeas; when rose the sun, red like the *aśoka*, the *kiṁśuka*, the bill of the parrot, the (red) half of *guñja* fruit; [like the feet and eyes of the dove, the scarlet eyes of the cuckoo, a heap of *jabā* flowers, and more red than vermillion]; the delight of lotuses, and burning in its own thousand rays; when the sun rose at the right time, [when darkness was lashed out by its rays, and when the world of living beings was enlivened with its light], kṣatriya Siddhārtha came out of his bed. 59

अब्भुट्ठित्ता पायपीढाओ पच्चोरुहइ। पच्चोरुहित्ता जेणेव अट्टणसाला तेणेव उवागच्छइ। उवागच्छित्ता अट्टणसालं अणुपविसइ। अणुपविसित्ता अणेग-वायाम-जोग्ग-वग्गण-वामद्दण-मल्ल-जुद्ध-करणेहिं संते परिस्संते सय-पाग-सहस्स-पागेहिं सुगंध-तिल्लमाइएहिं पीणणिज्जेहिं दीवणिज्जेहिं मयणिज्जेहिं विहणिज्जेहिं दप्पणिज्जेहिं सव्विदिय-गाय-पल्हायणिज्जेहिं अब्भंगिए तिल्लचम्मंसि णिउणेहिं पडिपुण्णपाणि-पाय-सुकुमाल-कोमल-तलेहिं पुरिसेहिं अब्भंगण-परिमद्दणुव्वलण-करण-गुण-णिम्माएहिं छेएहिं दक्खेहिं पट्ठेहिं कुसलेहिं मेहावीहिं जिय-परिस्समेहिं अट्ठिसुहाए- मंस-सुहाए, रोम-सुहाए, चउव्विहाए सुह-परिकम्मणाए संवाहणाए संवाहिए समाणे अवगय-परिस्समे अट्टणसालाओ पडिणिक्खमइ। ६०

Having got up, he descended from the foot-stool, and went to the hall of gymnastic exercises. There, he applied himself to many wholesome exercises, like jumping, muscular exercise, and wrestling, and on being tired and exhausted, he got his body massaged with pleasant, stimulating, envigorating, exhilarating, strength-giving, nourishing-the-sense-organs-and-the-limbs, and in-pouring oils boiled a hundred and a thousand times by masseurs, who were experts, trained in their profession, skilled, excellent, intelligent and untiring. The hand-palms and feet-soles of these masseurs were soft, and they had their body-frames with well-developed limbs. They were experts in rubbing (oil), in massaging, in stimulating strength, and were experienced in the outcome of these. Having seated (him) on the oily leather, they started massaging and anointing him giving his limbs pleasure in four senses, viz., pleasure to the bones, pleasure to the flesh, pleasure to the skin and pleasure to the poreholes. His fatigue and exhaustion having (thus) been removed, he moved out from the gymnasium. 60

पडिणिक्खमित्ता जेणेव मज्जणघरे तेणेव उवागच्छइ। उवागच्छित्ता मज्जण-घरं अणुपविसइ। अणुपविसित्ता समुत्त-जालाकुलाभिरामे विचित्त-मणि-रयण-कोट्टिम-तले रमणिज्जे ण्हाणमंडवंसि णाणा-मणि-रयण-भत्ति-चित्तंसि

ण्हाणपीढंसि सुहणिसण्णे पुप्फोदएहि य गंधोदएहि य उसिणोदएहि य सुद्धोदएहि य कल्लाण-करण-पवर-मज्जण-विहीए मज्जिए । तथ्थ कोउय[18]—सएहिं बहुविहेहिं कल्लाणग-पवर-मज्जणावसाणे पम्हल-सुकुमाल-गंध-कासाइय-लूहियंगे अहय-सुमहग्घ-दूस-रयण सुसंवुडे सरस-सुरभि-गोसीस-चंदणाणुलित्त-गत्ते सुइ-माला-वण्णग-विलेवणे आविद्ध-मणि-सुवण्णे कप्पिय-हारद्धहार-तिसरय-पालंब-पलंबमाणे कडि-सुत्तय-कय-सोभे पिणिद्ध-गेविज्जे अंगुलिज्जग-ललिय-कयाभरणे वर-कडग-तुडिय-थंभिय-भुए अहिय-रूव-सस्सिरीए कुंडल-उज्जो वियाणणे मउड-दित्त-सिरए हारोत्थय-सुकय-रइय-वच्छे मुद्दिया-पिंगलंगुलिए पालंब-पलंबमाण-सुकय-पड-उत्तरिज्जे णाणा-मणि-कणग-रयण-विमल-महरिह-णिउणोविय-मिसिमिसिंत-विरइय-सुसिलिट्ठ-विसिट्ठ - णद्ध-आ - विद्ध-वीर-वलए किं वहुणा कप्प-रुक्खए चेव अलंकिय-विभूसिए णरिंदे सकोरिंट-मल्ल-दामेणं छत्तेणं धरिज्जमाणेणं सेय-वर-चामराहिं उद्धूव्वमाणीहिं मंगल-जय-सद्द-कयालोए अणेग-गणणायग-दंडणायग-राइसर-तलवर-माडंबिय-कोडुं-बिय-मंति-महामंति-गणग-दोवारिय-अमच्च-चेड - पीढमद्द-णगर - णिगम-सिट्ठि - सेणावइ-सत्थवाह-दय-संधिपाल सद्धिं संपरिवुडे धवल-महा-मेह-णिग्गए इव गेह-गण-दिप्पंतरिक्ख-तारा-गणाणमज्झे ससि'व्व पियदंसणे णरवई णरिंदे णर-वसहे णर-सीहे अब्भहिय-राय-तेय-लच्छीए दिप्पमाणे मज्जणघराओ पडिणिक्खमइ । ६१

Having come out from the gymnasium, he went in the direction of the bath-room. Then he entered into the bath-room. Having entered that room, which gave a pleasant sight, decorated as it was with an intricate net-work of pearls; and its floor inlaid with sundry gems and precious stones, and exceedingly beautiful he sat comfortably on the bathing stool containing many gems and precious stones, and having many miniature paintings on, and took bath in the usual, excellent and pleasant form, combined with healthy exercises, with water scented with flowers and with essences, with tepid water and pure water.

When this healthy and excellent bath under many hundred-fold pleasures was over, he dried his body with a soft, scented, red-coloured turkish towel; (then he) dressed himself in precious and best of robes;

he had his body rubbed with soft and scented *gośīrṣa* and sandal pastes; after this were celebrated and performed hundreds of after-bath, pleasant, blissful and blest ceremonies;

then were placed on him a wreath of flowers purified by the spray of sandal paste and a gold necklace set with pearls; a three-fold necklace of pearls*, with a pearl pendant dangling therefrom;

a golden zone at the waist; a collar round his neck; rings on his tender fingers; bangles and bracelets adorning the arms; ear-rings brightening the face;

and a shining crown—all these imparting extra grace to his charming person; the out-stretched bunches of necklace adorning the breast; yellow rings imparting a golden tinge to his fingers; a pearl border hanging down from the silken shoulder-cloth; and a pair of armlets, a very symbol of his valour and gallantry, inlaid with gems and precious stones, and made from fine gold, finely inlaid and set, joints duly fixed, brightened, polished and prepared by expert hands;

to be precise, well-dressed and well-decorated, (looked he) like the *kalpa* tree, the leader of men; with an umbrella decorated with wreaths and garlands of *koriṇṭa* flowers held above him; with the finest of white *cāmara* fanning; greeted (was he) at his appearance with auspicious shouts of victory;

and attended, followed by innumerable chieftains, satraps, kings, princes, knights, sheriffs, heads of families, ministers, chief ministers, astrologers, counsellors, valets, dance-masters, citizens, traders, merchants, guild-leaders, generals, caravan-chiefs, messengers, and frontier-guards, he, the monarch, leader of men, bull among men, lion among men, came out from the room of showers, like the pleasant-looking moon in the company of stars, planets and other heavenly bodies glittering, as if emerging out of a great, white cloud, (the king) shining with enormous royal authority and fortune. 61

णिक्खमित्ता जेणेव बाहिरिया उवट्ठाणसाला तेणेव उवागच्छइ। उवागच्छित्ता सीहासणंसि पुरत्थाभिमुहे णिसीयति। ६२

णिसीयित्ता अप्पणो उत्तरपूरत्थिमे दिसीभाए अट्ठ भद्दासणाइं सेय-वत्थ-पच्चुत्थुयाइं सिद्धत्थय-कय-मंगलोवयाराइं रयावेति। रयावित्ता अप्पणो अदूरसामंते णाणा-मणि-रयण-मंडियं अहिय-पेच्छणिज्जं महग्घर-पट्टणुग्गयं सण्ह[19]-पट्ट-भत्ति-सय-चित्त-ताणं ईहामिय-उसभ-तुरय-णर-मगर-विहग-वालग-किणर-रुरु-सरभ-चमर-कुंजर-वणलय-पउमलय-भत्ति-चित्तं अब्भितरियं जव-

* A necklace of 18, 9 and 3 strings of pearls, according to Jacobi.

णियं अंछावेइ[20] । अंछावित्ता णाणा-मणि-रयण-भत्ति-चित्तं अथ्थरय-मिउ-
मसूरगोथ्थयं सेय-वथ्थ-पच्चुत्थुयं सुमउय अंग-सुह-फरिसगं विसिट्ठं
तिसलाए खत्तियाणीए भद्दासणं रयावेइ । रयावित्ता कोडुंबिय-पुरिसे
सद्दावेइ । सद्दाविंत्ता एवं वयासी । ६३

Having come out, he moved in the direction of the external hall of audience, and having gone there, he sat down on the throne with his face turned towards the east. 62

Having taken his seat, he got erected in the north-eastern side of him, eight chairs of state, covered with white cloth, and sanctified with mustard. Having got them erected, neither very near nor very far from him, in (another) corner, he got placed an interior screen, decorated with sundry jewels and precious stones, extremely worth-seeing, very costly due to the use of the finest silk, adorned with innumerable pieces of fine needle-work made with fine threads and depicting miniatures of wolves, bulls, horses, men, dolphins, birds, snakes, *kinnaras*, *rurus*, *śarabhas*, *camaras*, elephants, wild creepers and lotus creepers. Then he got erected a special chair of state for kṣatriyāṇī Triśalā, bedecked with sundry gems and precious stones, covered with white cloth, very soft, comfortable to touch, and out-fitted with a coverlet and a soft pillow. Having got it done, he sent for the keepers of the royal household, and these having arrived, he said thus. 63

खिप्पमेव भो देवाणुप्पिया । अट्ठंग-महा-णिमित्त-सुत्तथ्थ-धारए विविह-सत्थ-
कुसले सुविण-लक्खण-पाढए सद्दावेह । तए णं ते कोडुंबिय-पुरिसा सिद्धथ्थेणं
रण्णा एवं वुत्ता समाणा हट्ठ-तुट्ठ जाव...हियया करयलं जाव...पडिसुणंति । ६४

"Oh beloved of the gods! Hurry up and bring forth (hither) the interpreters of the significance of dreams, who well knoweth the science of prognostics with its eight branches, and are well-versed in other sciences too."

Having been ordered thus by king Siddhārtha, the keepers of the royal household, happy, pleased, highly delighted in mind, with their heart thrilled with joy, and with their pore-holes expanded like *kadamba* flower hurt by rain-drops, touched their head with

ten fingers on their folded palms and received the order with due submission by saying:
"As Your Majesty commands!" 64

पडिसुणित्ता सिद्धथ्थस्स खत्तियस्स अंतिआओ पडिणिक्खमंति । पडिणिक्खमित्ता कुंडपुरं णगरं मज्झंमज्झेणं जेणेव सुविण-लक्खण-पाढगाणं गेहाइं तेणेव उवागच्छंति । उवागच्छित्ता सुविण-लक्खण-पाढए सद्दाविंति । ६५

तए णं ते सुविण-लक्खण-पाढगा सिद्धथ्थस्स खत्तियस्स कोडुंबिय-पुरिसेहिं सद्दाविया समाणा हट्ठ-तुट्ठ जाव···हियया ण्हायाकय -वलि-कम्मा कय-कोउय-मंगल-पायच्छित्ता सुद्धप्पवेसाइं मंगलाइं वथ्थाइं पवराइं परिहिया अप्प-महग्घाभरणालंकिय-सरीरा सिद्धथ्थय-हरियालिया-कय-मंगल-मुद्धाणा सएहिं सएहिं गेहेहिंतो निग्गच्छंति । णिग्गच्छित्ता खत्तिय-कुंडग्गामं णगरं मज्झंमज्झेणं जेणेव सिद्धथ्थस्स रण्णो भवण-वर-वडिंसग-पडिदुवारे तेणेव उवागच्छंति ।

Having received the order, and assuring compliance thereof, (they) moved out from the presence of kṣatriya Siddhārtha. Having moved out, they turned their steps, wending through the city of Kundapura, towards that district wherein resided the interpreters of the significance of dreams. Having reached there, they called them out. 65

Then the interpreters of the significance of dreams, being called by the house-keepers of kṣatriya Siddhārtha, became highly pleased, happy and delighted, their hearts throbbing with joy, and their pore-holes expanding like the *kadamba* flower hurt by rain-drops. These then having taken their bath, finishing their offerings, performing auspicious righs like wearing head-marks, and also expiatory acts, (having touched their feet in order to avoid wicked eyes, according to commentators), wearing clean and lucky garments and shoulder silk to match, suitable for admittance to the royal court, adorning their bodies with costly ornaments, and putting for the sake of good omen mustard and *dūrvā* (grass) sprouts on their (respective) heads, they started from their homes. Then having moved through the kṣatriya city of Kuṇḍapura, they reached the main portal of king Siddhārtha's excellent palace, a jewel among palaces. 66

उवागच्छित्ता भवण-वर-वडिंसग-पडिदुवारे एगओ मिलंति जेणेव बाहिरिया

उवट्ठाणसाला जेणेव सिद्धथ्थे खत्तिए तेणेव उवागच्छंति । करयल-परिग्गहियं
जाव···कट्टु सिद्धथ्थं खत्तियं जएणं विजएणं वद्धावेंति । ६७

Having reached there, they all assembled together, and then moved inside the exterior hall of audience wherein was (seated) kṣatriya Siddhârtha. Then having touched their head with the ten fingers on their folded palms, they greeted kṣatriya Siddhârtha by wishing him glory and victory. 67

तए णं ते सुमिण-लक्खण-पाढगा सिद्धथ्थेणं रण्णा वंदिय-पूइय-सक्कारिय-सम्मा-
णिय समाणा पत्तेयं पत्तेयं पुव्वण्णथ्थेसु भद्दासणेसु णिसीयंति । ६८

तए णं सिद्धथ्थे खत्तिए तिसलं खत्तियाणि जवणियंतरियं ठवेइ । ठवित्ता
पुप्फ-फल-परिपुण्ण-हथ्थे परेणं विणएणं ते सुमिण-लक्खण-पाढए एवं
वयासी । ६९

Then having been duly honoured and duly received by king Siddhârtha, who paid them obeisance and homage, and made them suitable offerings, one by one, the interpreters of the significance of dreams resumed their seats which had been erected earlier. 68

Then king Siddhârtha made kṣatriyāṇī Triśalâ sit behind a screen. Thereafter, taking fruits and flowers in his hands, with great humility, he said thus to the interpreters of the significance of dreams. 69

एवं खलु देवाणुप्पिया ! अज्ज तिसला खत्तियाणी तंसि तारिसगंसि । जाव ...
सुत्तजागरा ओहिरमाणी ओहिरमाणी इमे एयारूवे ओराले चोद्दस महासुमिणे
पासित्ता णं पडिबुद्धा । ७०

तं जहा । गय उसभ गाहा । ७१

तं तेसिं चोद्दसण्हं महासुमिणाणं देवासुप्पिया । ओरालाणं के मण्णे कल्लाणे फल-
वित्तिविसेसे भविस्सइ । तए णं ते सुमिण-लक्खण-पाढगा सिद्धथ्थस्स खत्ति-
यस्स एयमट्ठं सोच्चा णिसम्म हट्ठ-तुट्ठ जाय-हियया ते सुमिणे ओगिण्हंति ।
ओगिण्हित्ता ईहं अणुपविसंति । अणुपविसित्ता अण्णमण्णेणं सद्धिं संलावेंति । ७२

"Oh beloved of the gods! Last night, kṣatriyâṇī Triśalâ, lying on a bed, which had a long pillow of the body's length, etc., as aforesaid, half asleep and half awake, at the confluence

of the two halves of the night, saw the following noble,... till fortunate fourteen great dreams and woke up. 70
"They are: an elephant, an ox and so on. 71
"Oh beloved of the gods! Now it behoves thee to divulge to what blest outcome do these fourteen great dreams portend." On hearing these words of kṣatriya Siddhârtha and understanding them, those interpreters of the significance of dreams were delighted at heart, pleased and joyful, and so on, and they fixed the dreams in their mind. Having fixed them in their mind, they entered upon considering them, and discussed them (threadbare) among themselves. 72

संलावित्ता तेसिं सुमिणाणं लद्धट्ठा गहियट्ठा पुच्छियट्ठा विणिच्छियट्ठा अभिगयट्ठा सिद्धथ्थस्स रण्णो पुरओ सुमिण-सथ्थाइं उच्चारेमाणा उच्चारेमाणा सिद्धथ्थं खत्तियं एवं वयासी । ७३

Having discussed them, they sought to determine correctly the apparent meaning of the dreams, to consider divergent meanings as they cropped up from the discussion, to arrive at a consensus and therefrom to a final meaning (that had the concurrence of all), and thereafter they said thus to kṣatriya Siddhârtha (supporting their interpretation) by reading from the dream books. 73

एवं खलु देवाणुप्पिया। अम्हं सुमिण-सथ्थे वायालीसं सुमिणा। तीसं महासुमिणा। बावत्तारिं सव्वसुमिणा दिट्ठा। तथ्थ णं देवाणुप्पिया ! अरहंत-मायरो वा चक्कवट्टि-मायरो वा अरहंतंसि वा चक्कहरंसि वा गब्भंबक्कममाणंसि एएंसि तीसाए महासुमिणाणं इमे चउद्दस महासुमिणे पासित्ता णं पडिबुज्झंति। ७४
तं जहा । गय० गाहा ।७५। ७५
वासुदेवमायरो वा वासुदेवंसिगब्भंवक्कममाणंसि एएसिं चउद्दसण्हं महासुमिणाणं अण्णयरे सत्त महासुमिणे पासित्ताणं पडिबुज्झंति । ७६
बलदेव-मायरो वा बलदेवंसि गब्भं वक्कममाणंसि एएसिं चोद्दसण्हं महासुमिणाणं अण्णयरे चत्तारि महासुमिणे पासित्ता णं पडिबुज्झंति । ७७
मंडलिय-मायरो वा मंडलियंसि गब्भं वक्कंते समाणे एएसिं चउद्दसण्हं महासुमिणाणं अण्णयरं महासुमिणं एगं पासित्ता णं पडिबुज्झंति । ७८

"Oh beloved of the gods! Recorded in our dream books are 42 dreams and 30 great dreams, total of all dreams being 72.

Oh beloved of the gods! When the embryo of an *arhat* or a *cakravarti* enters into the womb, then the mothers of the *arhats* and *cakravartis* wake up on seeing 14 out of these 30 great dreams. 74

"They are: an elephant, etc. 75

"When the embryo of a *vāsudeva* enters into the womb, (they) wake up on seeing any 7 out of these 14 great dreams. 76

"When the embryo of a *baladeva* enters into the womb, the mothers of the *baladevas* wake up on seeing any 4 of these 14 great dreams. 77

"When the embryo of a *māṇḍalika* enters into the womb, the mothers of the *māṇḍalikas* wake up on seeing any one of these 14 great dreams. 78

इमेयाणि देवाणुप्पिया। तिसलाए खत्तियाणीए चउद्दस महासुमिणा दिट्ठा। तं ओराला णं देवाणुप्पिया। तिसलाए खत्तियाणीए सुमिणा दिट्ठा। जाव मंगलकारगा णं देवाणुप्पिया। तिसलाए खत्तियाणीए सुमिणा दिट्ठा। तं जहा। अत्थलाभो देवाणुप्पिया। भोगलाभो देवाणुप्पिया। पुत्तलाभो देवाणुप्पिया। सुक्खलाभो देवाणुप्पिया। रज्जलाभो देवाणुप्पिया। एवं खलु देवाणुप्पिया। तिसला खत्तियाणी नवण्हं मासाणं बहुपडिपुण्णाणं अद्धट्ठमाणं राइंदियाणं विइक्कंताणं तुम्हं कुलकेउं कुलदीवं कुलपव्वयं कुलवडिंसगं कुलतिलयं कुलकित्तिकरं कुलदिणयरं कुल-आधारं कुलणंदिकरं कुलजसकरं कुलपायवं कुलविवद्धणकरं सुकुमाल-पाणिपायं अहीण-पडिपुण्ण-पंचिंदिय-सरीरं लक्खणवंजण गुणोवेयं माणुम्माणप्पमाण-पडिपुण्ण-सुजाय-सव्वंगसुंदरंगं ससिसोमाकारं कंतं पियदंसणं सुरूवं दारयं पयाहिति। ७९

"Oh beloved of the gods! Out of these, kṣatriyāṇī Triśalā has seen (all the) 14 great dreams. So, oh beloved of the gods, the dreams dreamt by kṣatriyāṇī Triśalā are surely noble. Oh beloved of the gods! The dreams or kṣatriyāṇī Triśalā are extremely useful. They are surely blissful, auspicious, blest, fortunate, givers of health, happiness and long life; and they signify non-ending bliss and excellence.

Oh beloved of the gods! (They) indicate the acquisition of wealth, of comforts, of progeny, of friends, of kingdom. So do we say, oh beloved of the gods, on the completion of full nine months and 7 day-nights, kṣatriyāṇī Triśalā will give birth to a

son; who will be the ensign of the line, the lamp of the line, the crown of the line, the head-mark of the line, the giver of glory to the line, the sun of the line, the support of the line, the joy of the line, the giver of fame to the line, the tree of the line, the exalter of the line;
with tender hands and feet, free from any deficiency or depression in the organs of senses and in the body, with gracious marks and auspicious traits, well-proportioned in length, height and weight, with a frame beautiful all over, calm like the moon, pleasing, pleasant and beautiful. 79

से वि य णं दारए विण्णाय-परिणय-मित्ते उम्मुक्कबालभावे जोव्वणगमणुप्पत्ते सूरे वीरे विक्कंते विथ्थिण्ण-बल-वाहणे चाउरंत-चक्कवट्टी रज्जवती राया भविस्सइ । जिणे वा तेलोक्क-णायगे धम्म-चक्कवट्टी । ८०

तं ओराला णं देवाणुप्पिया तिसलाए खत्तियाणीए सुमिणा दिट्ठा । जाव··· आरोग्ग-तुट्ठि-दीहाउ-कल्लाण-मंगल्लकारगा णं देवाणुप्पिया । तिसलाए खत्तियाणीए सुमिणा दिट्ठा ।

"Then on completion of his childhood, he will attain knowledge and development due to youth, and step into his youth; and in his youth, he will be brave, gallant and valorous, and become the master and king of a vast territory, with a large army, and extensive wagons, or (in the alternative), he will be the spiritual leader of the three worlds, the leading-most in religion, the spiritual world-monarch, the victor *Jina*. 80
"So do we say, oh beloved of the gods! These dreams of kṣatriyāṇī Triśalā are very noble indeed. Surely, oh beloved of the gods! do these dreams, as seen by kṣatriyāṇī Triśalā, portend to auspicious omens. Surely, oh beloved of the gods, are these dreams, as seen by kṣatriyāṇī Triśalā, blissful, auspicious and blest, givers of health, happiness and long life, and harbingers of non-ending bliss and excellence." 81

तते से सिद्धथ्थे राया तेसिं सुमिण-लक्खण-पाढगाणं एयमट्ठं सोच्चा निसम्म हट्ठ-तुट्ठ जाव ··· हियए करयल जाव ··· कट्टु ते सुमिण-लक्खण-पाढगे एवं वयासी ।

On hearing and receiving these words from the interpreters of the dreams, king Siddhārtha was happy, delighted and pleased;

his heart was throbbing with great joy, and his pore-holes expanded like the *kadamba* flower beaten by rain-drops. He touched his head with the ten fingers on his folded palms, and said thus unto the interpreters of the significance of the dreams: 82

एवमेयं देवाणुप्पिया । इच्छियमेयं पडिच्छियमेयं इच्छिय-पडिच्छिययेयं देवाणुप्पिया । सच्चे णं एसमट्ठे से जहेयं तुब्भे वयहंत्ति कट्टु ते सुमिणे सम्मं पडिच्छइ । पडिच्छित्ता ते सुमिण-लक्खण-पाढए विउलेणं असणेणं पुप्फ-वध्थ-गंधमल्लालंकारेणं सक्कारेति सम्माणेति सक्कारित्ता सम्माणित्ता विउलं जीवियारिहं पीइदाणं दलयति । दलयिता पडिविसज्जेइ । ८३

"Oh beloved of the gods! It is correct (as you say). Oh beloved of the gods! It is just. Oh beloved of the gods! It is true. Oh beloved of the gods! There's no doubt in it. Oh beloved of the gods! It is desired. Oh beloved of the gods! It is expected. Oh beloved of the gods! The meaning you have given is wholly correct."
So saying, he duly welcomed the dreams. Having done so, he gave unto the interpreters of the significance of the dreams much food articles, flowers, clothes, perfumes, wreaths and ornaments, and duly adored and honoured them; and having bestowed on them enormous gifts out of joy, which were enough to support them through life, he took leave of them. 83

तए णं सिद्धथ्थे खत्तिए सीहासणाओ अब्भुट्ठेइ । अब्भुट्ठित्ता जेणेव तिसला खत्तियाणी जवणियंतरिया तेणेव उवागच्छइ । उवागच्छित्ता तिसलं खत्तियाणि एवं वयासी । ८४

Then kṣatriya Siddhārtha got up from the throne, and went behind the screen where was seated kṣatriyāṇī Triśalā and said thus unto her; 84

एवं खलु देवाणुप्पिए । सुमिण-सथ्थंसि बायालीसं सुमिणा जाव··· एगं महासुमिणाणं पासित्ता णं पडिबुज्झंति । ८५

इमेयाणि तुमे देवाणुप्पिए । चोद्दस महासुमिणा दिट्ठा । तं ओराला णं तुमे जाव·· जिणे वा तेल्लोक्क-नायगे धम्म-वर-चक्कवट्टी । ८६

"Oh beloved of the gods! The dream books record 42 dreams, ... till wake up on seeing only one great dream. 85
"Of these, oh beloved of the gods, 14 great dreams have been seen by you. Noble indeed are these dreams seen by you,... till (you will give birth to) a victor *Jina*, the spiritual leader of the three worlds, the spiritual world monarch. 86

तए णं सा खत्तियाणी एयमट्ठं सोच्चा निसम्म हट्ठ-तुट्ठ जाव . . . हियया करयल
जाव कट्टु ते सुमिणे सम्मं पडिच्छइ । ८७
पडिच्छित्ता सिद्धत्थेणं रण्णा अब्भणुण्णाया समाणी णाणा-मणि-रयण-भत्ति-
चित्ताओ भद्दासणाओ अब्भुट्ठेइ । अब्भुट्ठित्ता अतुरियं अचवलं असंभंताए
अविलंबियाए राय-हंस—सरिसीए गईए जेणेव सए भवणे तेणेव उवागच्छइ ।
उवागच्छित्ता सयं भवणं अणुपविट्ठा । ८८

Then kṣatriyāṇī Triśalā, on hearing and understanding these, became joyous in mind, happy and pleased..till she touched her head with her ten fingers on her folded palms, and in a befitting manner, she welcomed the dreams. 87
Having welcomed the dreams, she, with the permission of king Siddhārtha, got up from her seat of state decorated with many gems and adorned with many miniatures, and at paces, neither hasty, nor uncertain, nor uneven or long, swan-like, repaired to her own palace. Having reached there, she entered into her own chamber. 88

जप्पभिइं च णं समणे भगवं महावीरे तं णाय-कुलं साहरि एतप्पभिइं च णं
बहवे वेसमण-कुंडो-धारिणो[21] तिरिय-जंभया[22] देवा सक्क-वयणेणं से जाइं/
इमाइं पुरा-पोराणाइं महा-णिहाणाइं भवंति । तं जहा पहीण-सामियाइं
पहीण-सेउयाइं पहीण-गोत्तागाराइं उच्छिन्न-सामियाइं उच्छिन्न-सेउयाइं
उच्छिन्न-गोत्तागाराइं गामागर-णगर-खेड-कब्बड-मंडब-दोणमुह-पट्टणासम-
संबाहा-सण्णिवेसेसु सिंघाडएसु वा तिएसु वा चउक्केसु वा चच्चरेसु वा चउ-
मुहेसु वा महापहेसु वा गामट्ठाणेसु वा णगरट्ठाणेसु वा गाम-णिद्धमणेसु वा णगर-
णिद्धमणेसु वा आवणेसु वा देवकुलेसु वा सभासु वा पवासु वा आरामेसु वा
उज्जाणेसु वा वणेसुवा वणसंडेसु वा सुसाण-सुण्णागार-कंदर-संति-संधि सेलो-
वट्ठाण-भवण-गिहेसु वा संणिक्खित्ताइं चिट्ठति-ताइं सिद्धत्थ-राय-भवणंसि
सोहरंति । ८९

Ever since Śramaṇa Bhagavân Mahâvīra was brought into the family of the Jñâtṛs, many *devas* of the animal world, and the *jṛmbhaka** world the order-bearers of Vaiśravaṇa (Kuvera, the god of wealth), at the command of Śakra, brought to the palace of kṣatriya Siddhârtha, great treasures of diverse kind, ancient and old, such as, treasures that had no owner, no user, no family protector, or treasures whose owners, users and family protectors had been dead, or treasures which had been stored or hidden in the villages, cluster of villages, towns, towns surrounded with mud low walls, bad (isolated) towns, towns surrounded within a mile and a half by villages, towns accessible by land and/or water, natural strongholds, granaries, halting places for caravans, inns, triangular places, quadrangular places, courtyards, squares, highways, ruins of an extinct village, ruins of an extinct town, village water outlets, town water outlets, (occasional) markets, temples, assembly halls, water-falls, parks, gardens, woods, groves, cremation grounds, vacant houses, mountain crevices, caves, waiting rooms, secret rooms, houses on an elevation, halls of audience or palaces. 89

जं रयणि च णं समणे भगवं महावीरे णाय-कुलंसि साहरिए तं रयणि च णं णायकुलं हिरण्णेणं वड्ढित्था सुवण्णेणं वड्ढित्था धणेणं धण्णेणं रज्जेणं रट्ठेणं वड्ढित्था बलेणं वाहणेणं कोसेणं कोट्ठागारेणं पुरेणं अंतेउरेणं जणवएणं जस-वएणं वड्ढित्था विपुल-धण-कणग-रयण-मणि-मोत्तिय-संखसिलप्पवाल-रत्त-रयणमाइएणं संत-सार-सावइज्जेणं अईव पीइ-सक्कार-समुदयेणं अभिवड्ढित्था । तए णं समणस्स अम्मा-पिऊणं अयमेयारूवे अज्झत्थिए चिंतिए पत्थिए मणोगए संकप्पे समुप्पज्जित्था । ९०

During the night, in which Śramaṇa Bhagavân Mahâvīra entered into the family of the Jñâtṛs, during that night, in the house of the Jñâtṛs, increased silver and gold, increased wealth and grains, kingdom and territory, transport, treasures and storehouses, palaces and *seraglios*, subjects and fame; also increased their vast treasure in gold, gems, jewels, pearls, conches, stones, corals, rubies and many others, all genuine, real, valuable, the cream of treasures.

*A species of Vyantaras of subhuman (animal) species.

Thereafter, in the minds of the parents of Śramaṇa Bhagavān Mahāvīra, took shape an ardent resolve: 90

जप्पभिइं च णं अम्हं एस दारए कुच्छिसि गब्भत्ताए वक्कंते तप्पभिइं च णं अम्हे हिरण्णेणं वड्ढामो सुवण्णेणं वड्ढामो धणेणं धण्णेणं रज्जेणं रट्ठेणं बलेणं वाहणेणं कोसेणं कोट्ठागारेणं पुरेणं अंतउयेणं जणवएणं वड्ढामो विपुल धण-कणग-रयण-मणि-मोत्तिय-संख-सिल-प्पवाल-रत्तरयणमाइएणं संत-सार- सावएज्जेणं पीइ-सक्कारेणं अईव अभिवड्ढामो तं जया णं अम्हं एस दारए जाए भविस्सइ तया णं अम्हे एथस्स दारगस्स एयाणुरूवं गोण्णं गुण-निप्फण्णं णामधिज्जं करिस्सामो 'वद्धमाणो' त्ति । ९१

"Ever since this our boy has been begotten, our silver has increased and so our gold, our wealth and grains, kingdom and territory, army and transport, treasures and stores, palaces and *seraglios*, subjects and fame; also have increased our vast treasures in gold, gems, jewels, pearls, conches, stones, corals, rubies and many others, all genuine, real, valuable, the cream of treasures; and we have also grown much in popularity, liberality and other good deeds:

"so when this boy will be born, shall we, in conformity with his high qualities, name this boy, all meritorious and endowed with all high traits, as 'Vardhamāna'." 91

तए णं समणे भगवं महावीरे माउ-अणुकंपणट्ठाए णिच्चले णिप्फंदे णिरेयणे अल्लीण-पल्लीण-गुत्ते यावि होथ्था । तएणं तीसे तिसलाए खत्तियाणीए अयमेयारूवे जाव समुप्पज्जिथ्था । हडे मे से गब्भे मडे मे से गब्भे चुए मे से गब्भे गलिए मे से गब्भे । एस मे गब्भे पुव्विं एयइ इयाणिं णो एथइ त्ति कट्टु ओहयमण-संकप्पा चिंता-सोग-सागरं पविट्ठा करयल-पल्हथ्थ-मुही अट्टज्झाणोवगया भूमि-गय-दिट्ठिया झियाइ । तं पि य सिद्धथ्थ-राय-भवणं उवरय-मुइंग-तंती-तलताल-णाडइज्ज-जणं अणुज्जं दीण-विमणं विहरइ । ९२

Now, Śramaṇa Bhagavān Mahāvīra, out of compassion for his mother, did not move, nor stir, nor quiver, but remained contracted and motionless. At this, in the mind of kṣatriyāṇī Triśalā took shape, in deep anxiety, an idea:

"That my progeny-in-womb is stolen, that my progeny is dead, that my progeny has fallen, that my progeny is lost.

Formerly, this progeny in the womb used to move, but now it does not."

So saying, and thinking that 'all my heart's desire has fallen astray', she was plunged into a deep sea of sorrow and misery; and reposing her head on her hand, overcome by painful reflections, and casting her eyes on the ground, she was immersed in anxious thoughts. And in the palace of king Siddhārtha too, the concert of drums and instruments, the clapping of hands, dramatical performances, and merry-making by the people,—all came to a stop, and they felt dejected, deprived and restless. 92

तए णं समणे भगवं महावीरे माउए एयमेयारूवं अज्झत्थियं पत्थियं मणोगयं संकप्पं समुप्पण्णं विजाणित्ता एग-देसेणं एयइ। ९३

तए णं सा तिसला खत्तियाणी तं गब्भं एयमाणं वेवमाणं चलमाणं फंदमाणं जाणित्ता हट्ठ-तुट्ठ जाव...हियया एवं वयासी: णो खलु मे गब्भे हडे जाव...णो गलिए एस मे गब्भे पुव्वि णो एयइ एयाणि एयइ त्ति कट्टु हट्ठ-तुट्ठ जाव... हियया एवं वा विहरइ। तए णं समणे भगवं महावीरे गब्भमत्थे इमेयारूवं अभिग्गहं अभिगिण्हइ। णो खलु मे कप्पइ अम्मा-पिईहिं जीवंतेहिं मुंडे भवित्ता अगार-वासाओ अणोगारियं पव्वइत्तए। ९४

Then Śramaṇa Bhagavân Mahāvīra, having known about the anxious reflections in the mind of the mother, moved a little on the side. 93

Feeling her child in the womb quivering, trembling, moving and stirring, kṣatriyāṇī Triśalā became happy, pleased, and joyful, highly delighted in her mind, her heart was throbbing with glee. Quoth she:

"Nay, forsooth, my progeny-in-womb is not stolen, my progeny is not dead, my progeny is not fallen, nor is he lost. Formerly it moved not, but now it moves."

So saying, she became pleased, happy and joyful, highly delighted in her mind, her heart throbbing with glee, and in this state she passed her days.

Then Śramaṇa Bhagavân Mahāvīra, lodged in the womb, made the following resolve:

"It will not be worthwhile on my part to court the life of a homeless monk by giving up the life of a householder, and by undergoing a tonsure, so long as my parents are alive." 94

तए णं सा तिसला खत्तियाणी ण्हाया कय-बलि-कम्मा कय-कोउल-पायच्छित्ता सव्वालंकार-विभूसिया णाइ-सीएहिं णाइ-उण्हेहिं णाइ-तित्तेहिं णाइ-कडुएहिं णाइ-कसाएहिं णाइ-अबिलेहिं णाइ-महुरेहिं णाइ-णिद्धेहिं णाइ-लुक्खेहिं णाइ उल्लेहिं णाइ-सुक्खेहिं सव्वत्तु-भयमाण-सुहेहिं भोयण-च्छायण-गंधमल्लेहिं ववगय-रोग-सोग-मोह-भय-परिस्समा सा जं तस्स गब्भस्स हियं मियं पच्छं गब्भपोसणं तं देसे य काले य आहारमाहारेमाणी विवित्त-मउएहिं सयणासणेहिं पइरिक्क-सुहाए मणाणुकूलाए विहारभूमीए पसत्थ-दोहला संपुण्ण दोहला संमाणिय-दोहला अविमाणिय-दोहला वोच्छिण्ण-दोहला विवणीय-दोहला सुहं सुहेणं आसयइ सयइ चिट्ठइ णिसीयइ तुयट्टइसुहं सुहेणं तं गब्भं परिवहइ । ९५

From that time on, kṣatriyāṇī Triśalā took bath, made offerings, performed auspicious rites and expiatory acts; adorned her body with all ornaments; took neither very cold nor very hot, nor very bitter, pungent, astringent, sour or sweet, nor very rough, wet or dry, but pleasant for different seasons, food, wear, perfumes and flowers, because of which were kept aside sickness, sorrow, faint, fear and fatigue; ate only such food as was helpful for the progeny-in-womb, adequate, nourishing, able to support the embryo, consistent with time (season) and place; lay on a soft and comfortable couch and sat on a soft and comfortable seat, untouched by others:
strolled on places agreeable and delightful to the mind, with all her desires honoured and fulfilled in details, and with meticulous care, none of her desires being overlooked, and all her desires being separately fulfilled one by one;
enjoying joy in sleep, joy in living, joy in sitting, joy in reposing, joy in decorating her skin, in brief, being the mistress of all joys, she carried the weight of the embryo. 95

तेणं कालेणं तेणं समएणं समणे भगवं महावीरे जे से गिम्हाणं पढमे मासे दोच्चे पक्खे चित्त-सुद्धे तस्स णं चित्त-सुद्धस्स तेरसी-दिवसेणं णवण्हं मासाणं बहु-पडिपुण्णाणं अद्धट्ठमाणं राइंदियाणं विइक्कंताणं (उच्चट्ठाण-गएसु गहेसु पढमे चंद-जोगे सोमासु दिसासु वितिमिरासु विसुद्धासु जइएसु सव्व-सउणेसु पयाहिणाणु-कूलंसि भूमि-सप्पिसि-मारुयंसि पवायंसि णिप्फण्ण-मेयणीयंसि कालंसि पमुइय-पक्किलिएसु सव्व-जणवएसु) पुव्व-रत्तावरत्त-काल-समयंसि हत्थुत्तराहिं णक्खत्तेणं जोगमुवागएणं आरोग्गारोग्गं दारयं पयाया । ९६

At that time, in that period, in the second fortnight of the first month of the summer season, on the thirteenth day of the bright half of *caitra*, on the completion of 9 months and 7 day-nights, [when the planets were high up in their exaltations, when all the directions were clear, bright and pure, by the touch of the moon in its principal conjunction, when all the omens were auspicious, when the favourable southerly wind kissed the ground, when the earth was full of corn, and when all the human beings were delighted and at play, then,] at the confluence of the first half and the second half of the night, at the conjunction of the moon with the asterism Uttara-phâlgunī, Śramaṇa Bhagavān Mahâvīra was born in a healthy body as son (to Triśalâ) who was also in perfect health. 96

(जं रयणि च णं समणे भगवं महावीरे जाए तं रयणि च णं बहुहिं देवेहिं देवीहिं य उययंतेहि य उप्पयंतेहि य उज्जोविया वि होथ्था ।)
जं रयणि च णं समणे भगवं महावीरे जाए तं रयणि च णं वहूहिं देवेहिं देवीहिं य उवयंतेहिं उप्पयंतेहिं (देवुज्जोए एगालोए लोए देव-सण्णिवाया) उप्पि-
जलभाण[23]-भूया कहकहग-भूया यावि होथ्था । ९७
जं रयणि च णं समणे भगवं महावीरे जाए तं रयणि च णं बहवे वेसमण-कुंड-धारी तिरिय-जंभगा देवा सिद्धथ्थ-राय-भवणंसि हिरण्णवासं च सुवण्णवासं च वइरवासं च वथ्थवासं च आभरणवासं च पत्तवासं च पुप्फवासं च फलवासं च बीयवासं च मल्लवासं च गंधवासं च वण्णवासं च चुण्णवासं च वसुहारवासं च वासिंसु । (पियट्ठयाए पियं णिवेएमो पियं ते भवउ मउडवज्जं जहा मालियं
उमोयं मथ्थए धोयइ ।) ९८

(During the night when Śramaṇa Bhagavān Mahāvīra was born, there was a divine lustre everywhere created by many descending and ascending gods and goddesses.)
During the night when Śramaṇa Bhagavān Mahāvīra was born, as many gods and goddesses descended and ascended, [there being a great conflux of gods, which gave a divine light to the world, the whole world was] struck by fear, and there was noise and confusion—'What's this ? 'Why this ?' 97
During the night when Śramaṇa Bhagavān Mahāvīra was born, many gods of the animal world and of the *jṛmbhaka* world, the order-bearers of Vaiśravaṇa, showered in the residence of King Siddhârtha silver, gold, jewels, garments, ornaments, leaves,

flowers, fruits, seeds, wreaths, perfumes, sandal, powder, and riches.

("Offer we these dear things for the use of our very dear one. May these be dear unto thee !"

So saying they took off their garlanded head-covers and washed their heads.) 98

तए णं सिद्धत्थे खत्तिए भवणवइ-वाणमंतर-जोइस-वेमाणिएहिं देवेहिं तित्थ-
यर-जम्मण-अभिसेय-महिमाए कयाए समाणीए पच्चुस-काल-समयंसि णगर-
गुत्तिए सद्दावेइ । सद्दावित्ता एवं वयासी । ९९

खिप्पमेव भो देवाणुप्पिया कुंडपुरे णगरे चारग-सोहणं करेह । करित्ता माणु-
म्माण-वद्धणं करेह । करित्ता कुंडपुरं णगरं सब्भिंतर-वाहिरियं आसिय-संम-
ज्जि-उवलेवियं संघाडग-तिय-चउक्क-चच्चर-चउम्मुह-महापह-पहेसु सित्त-
सूइ-संमट्ठ-रच्छंतरावण-वीहियं मंचाइ-मंच-कलियं णाणाविहराग-भूसिय- ज्झय-
पडाग-मंडियं ला-उल्लोइय[24]-महियं गोसीस-सरस-रत्त-चंदण-द्दर-दिण्ण-
पंचंगुली-तलं उवचिय-वंदण-कलसं- वंदण-घड-सुकय-तोरण-पडिदुवार-देवभागं
आसत्तोसत्त-विपुल-वट्ट-वग्घारिय-मल्ल-दाम-कलावं पंच-वण्ण-सरस-सुरभि-
मुक्क-पुप्फ-पुंजोवयार-कलियं-कालागुरु-पवर-कुंदुरुक्क-दुरुक्क-डज्झंत-धूव-मघ-
मघंत-गंधुद्धुयाभिरामं सुगंध-वर-गंधियं गंधवट्टिभूयं णड-णट्टग-जल्ल-मल्ल-
मुट्ठिय-वेलंबग-कहग-पाडग-लासग[25]—आरक्खग-लंख-मंख-तूणइल्ल-तुंबवीणिय-
अणेग-तालायराणुचरियं करेह या कारावेह य । करित्ता य कारवित्ता य जूय-
सहस्सं च मुसल-सहस्सं च उस्सवेह । उस्सवित्ता मम एयं आणत्तियं पच्च-
प्पिणह । १००

Then the *bhavanapatis*, the *vyantaras*, the *jyotiṣkas*, the *vaimānikas* and other celestial beings (*devas*) having performed the rites to celebrate the birth of a *tīrthaṅkara*, early in the morning, kṣatriya Sīddhārtha called the city guards and addressed them thus. 99

"Oh beloved of the gods ! Quickly open the prison-gates of Kuṇḍapura and set free the prisoners, and increase the weights and measures. Having done these, get besprinkled with water, broomed and smeared, and also do these yourselves, both inside and outside the city of Kuṇḍapura where four roads meet, where three roads meet, the squares, open spaces, four-door mansions, thoroughfares and all other places;

erect and get erected in the middle of roads and on approaches to the shopping centres innumerable platforms, high and low, and get these platforms decorated with multi-coloured flags and banners;

decorate and have decorated all places with coloured canopies, scatter fried rice, imprint at diverse places five fingers in open palm with *gośirṣa*, fresh red sandal, and *dardara* (sandal); place and have placed luck-foreboding pitchers (at various places) and beautify and have beautified the door part of each arch with homage vases;

decorate and have decorated all places with flower garlands tied loosely and tied tightly, thus making them very thick;

fill and have filled the whole town with fragrance by burning the best black aloe, *kundurukka* and *turukka* with incenses, and turn the whole city into a cup of fragrance by spraying perfumes;

engage and have engaged many players, dancers, rope-dancers, wrestlers, boxers, jesters, story-tellers, ballad-singers, actors, messengers, pole dancers, fruit-mongers, bag-pipers, lute players and *tālācaras* with these innumerable attendants;

and erect and have erected a thousand pillars and a thousand posts and start the festivities. Thus giving start to the festivities, report to me the execution of my orders." 100

तए णं ते कोडुंबिय-पुरिसा सिद्धथ्थेणं रण्णा एवं वुत्ता समाणा हट्ठ तुट्ठ जाव... हियया करयल-जाव...पडिसुणिता खिप्पमेव कुंडपुरे णगरे चारग-सोहणं जाव... उस्सवित्ता जेणेव सिद्धथ्थे राया तेणेव उवागच्छंति । उवागच्छित्ता करयल जाव. . . कट्टु सिद्धथ्थस्स रण्णो एयमाणत्तियं पच्चप्पिणंति । १०१

Thus having been ordercd by king Siddhârtha, the royal-household keepers (city-guards)/became glad at heart, happy, joyful and delighted, their hearts throbbing with glee. (They) touched their head with ten fingers as aforesaid, till hurried to Kuṇḍapura to open the prison gates, and so on,...till (again) started the festivities. Having started the festivities, they touched their head with their ten fingers, and reported to king Siddhârtha the execution of his orders. 101

तए णं सिद्धत्थे राया जेणेव अट्टणशाला तेणेव उवागच्छइ । उवागच्छित्ता सव्वोरोहेणं सव्व-पुप्फ-गंध-वथ्थ-मल्लालंकार-विभूसाए सव्व-तुडिय-सद्द-णिणाएणं महया इड्ढीए महया जुईए महया बलेणं महया वाहणेणं महया समुदएणं महयातुडिय-जमग-समग-प्पवाइएणं संख-पणव-भेरिझल्लरि-खर-मुहि-हुडुक्क-मुरज-मुइंग-दुंदुहि-णिग्घोस-णाइय-खेणं उस्सुक्कं उक्करं उक्किट्ठं अदिज्जं अमिज्जं अभड-प्पवेसं अदंड-कोदंडिमं अधरिमं गणिया-वर-णाडइज्ज-कलियं अणेग-तालायराणुचरियं अणुद्धय-मुइंगं अमिलाय-मल्लदामं पमुइय-पक्कीलिय-स-पुरजण-जाणवयं दस-दिवसं ठिइ-पडियं[26] करेइ । १०२

Then king Siddhārtha went in the direction of the gymnasium. (Description of exercises, bath etc., as before) Thereafter, with entire royal household, and (himself) adorned wilh flowers, perfumed robes, garlands and ornaments, king Siddhārtha held for ten days *sthiti-pratijya* ceremony under the din and sound of trumpets, with great state and grandeur, attended by a large train of soldiers, vehicles/and attendants, and with innumerable guests and visitors, with the city filled by the sound, din and noise of conches, cymbals, drums, castanets, horns, small drums, kettle drums, *murajas*, *mṛdaṅgas* and *dundubhis* ;

with the abolition of all excises, customs and agricultural taxes, with the cessation of purchase and sale, weighing and measuring at the shops, with the abolition of all disproportionate punishments and bad punishments, with the cancellation of debts, with prohibition imposed on collectors to enter the residence of subjects:

with dance by the best dancing girls continuing, followed suitably at every step by the sounds of *mṛdaṅga*, with garlands of fresh flowers never allowed to dry, and with the city dwellers and the dwellers of the entire realm deeply immersed in merry-making, festivities and play. 102

तए णं से सिद्धत्थे राया दसाहियाए ठिइ-पडियाए वट्टमाणीए सइए य साह-स्सिए य सय-साहस्सिए य जाए य दाए य भाए य दलमाणे य दवावेमाणे य सइए य साहस्सिए य सय-साहस्सिए य लंभे पडिच्छमाणे य पडिच्छमाणे य एवं विहरइ । १०३

In the course of this *sthiti-pratijyā* ceremony, which lasted for ten days, king Siddhārtha performed, and had performed, hundreds, thousands, hundred-thousands of sacrifices, offered and arranged the offer of hundreds, thousands, and hundred-thousands of presentations, and of hundreds, thousands and hundred-thousands of gifts of parcels of property; and also received and arranged to receive hundreds, thousands and hundred-thousands of offerings. 103

तए णं समणस्स भगवओ महावीरस्स अम्मा-पियरो पढमे दिवसे ठिइ-पडियं करेंति तइए दिवसे चंद-सूर-दंसणियं करेंति छट्ठे दिवसे धम्मजागरियं करेंति इक्कारसमे दिवसे विइक्कंते णिव्वत्तिए असुइ-जम्म-कम्म-करणे संपत्ते बारसाह-दिवसे विउलं असण-पाण-खाइम-साइमं उवक्खराविंति। उवक्खराविता मित्त-णाइ-णियग-सयण-संबंधि-परिजणं णायए य खत्तिए य आमंतित्ता तओ पच्छा ण्हाय कय-वलि-कम्मा कय-कोउय-मंगल-पायच्छित्ता मंगल्लाइं पवराइं वथ्थाइं परिहिया अप्प-महग्घाभरणालंकिय-सरीरा भोयण-वेलाए भोयण-मंडवंसि सुहासण-वर-गया तेणं मित्त-णाइ-णियग-संबंधि-परिजणेणं णायेहिं सद्धि तं विउलं असण-पाण-खाइम-साइमं आसाएमाणा विसाएमाणा परि-भाएमाणा परिभुंजेमाणा विहरंति। १०४

On the first day, the parents of Śramaṇa Bhagavān Mahāvīra performed the *sthiti-prātijyā* ceremony; on the third day, they showed the infant to the sun and the moon; on the sixth day, they observed the superstitious vigil; and on the eleventh day, they performed operations and ceremonies for the removal of impurities caused by child birth; and on the twelfth day, they prepared plenty of food, drinks, dainties and spiced dishes. Having prepared these, they invited their friends, relations, kinsmen, agnates cognates and followers, together with the Jñātṛ kṣatriyas, themselves took bath, made offerings, performed auspicious rights and expiatory acts, put on auspicious and best robes, and few but costly ornaments, and on the arrival of the dinner time, assembled in the dining hall, sat on the best of cushions, and together with their friends, relations, kinsmen, agnates, cognates, followers, and Jñātṛ kṣatriyas, they partook, ate, tasted and interchanged bits of a large collection of food, drinks, dainties and spiced dishes. 104

जिमिय-भुत्तुत्तरागया वि य णं समाणा आयंता चोक्खा परम-सुइ-भूया तं। मित्त-णाइ-णियग-सयण-संबंधि-परिजणं णायए य खत्तिए य विउलेणं पुप्फ-वत्थ-गंध-मल्लालंकारेणं सक्कारिति सम्माणिति। सक्कारित्ता सम्मा-णित्ता तस्सेव मित्त-णाइ-णियग-सयण-संबंधि-परिजणस्स णायाण य खत्तियाण य पुरओ एवं बासी। १०५

When the dinner was over, they cleaned their mouth and teeth and mouth again, became clean, and assembled all, and having honoured and adored friends, relations, kinsmen, agnates, cognates, followers and Jñātṛ kṣatriyas, with plenty of flowers, garments, perfumed wreaths and ornaments, the king said unto them. 105

पुव्विपि णं देवाणुप्पिया अम्हं एयंसि दारगंसि गब्भं वक्कंतंसि समाणंसि इमे एयारुवे अज्झत्थिए चिंतिए पत्थिए जाव...समुप्पजित्था। जप्पभिइं च णं अम्हं एस दारए कुच्छिसि गब्भत्ताए वक्कंते तप्पभिइं च णं अम्हे हिरण्णेणं वड्ढामो सुवण्णेणं वड्ढामो धणेणं धण्णेणं जाव...सावइज्जेणं पीइसक्कारेणं अईव अभिवड्ढामो। सामंत-रायाणो वसमागया। १०६

तं जया णं अम्हं एस दारए जाए भविस्सइ तयाणं एयस्स दारगस्स इमं एयाणु-रूवं गुण्णं गुणणिप्फण्णं णामधिज्जं करिस्सामो वद्धमाणो त्ति। ता अज्ज अम्हं मणोरह-संपत्ती जाया। तं होउ णं अम्हं कुमारे वद्धमाणे णामेणं। १०७

"Oh beloved of the gods! Formerly, when this our boy was lodged in the womb, in our mind, we formulated and held the following very ardent prayer:

"From the time that this our boy has been begotten, our silver has increased and so our gold, wealth, till all things of substance, and so also love and amity; and even our vassals have duly submitted to our suzerainty. 106

"So when this our boy will be born, we shall suitably name this worthy one, endowed with all high qualities, as 'Vardhamâna'. Now, to-day, all our wishes have reached their fruition, and so our boy may henceforth be known as 'Vardhamāna'. 107

समणे भगवं महावीरे कासवे गोत्तेणं। तस्स णं तओ णामधिज्जा एवम् आहि-ज्जंति। तं जहा—अम्मा-पिउ-संतिए वद्धमाणे सह-संमुइयाए समणे अयले भय-भेरवाणं परीसहो[27] वसग्गाणं खंति-खमे पडिमाणं पालगे धीमं अरइ-रइ-सहे-दविए वीरिय-संपण्णे देवेहिं से णामं कयं समणे भगवं महावीरे। १०८

Śramaṇa Bhagavān Mahavīra belonged to the Kâśyapa line. Three names were given to him. They were: Vardhamāna by his parents, Śramaṇa for his great equipoise against love as well as hatred, and Śramaṇa Bhagavān Mahāvīra by the celestial beings for his steadfastness in fears and dangers alike, for his ability to bear all hardships, like hunger, thirst, etc., for being a great forgiver when forgiveness was called for, for his adherence to the precise rules of penance, for his great wisdom, for his being alike in quiet and restlessness, for his being master of all controls, and for his gifts of vitality. 108

समणस्स भगवश्रो महावीरस्स पिया कासव गोत्तेणं । तस्स णं तश्रो णामधिज्जा एवम् श्राहिज्जंति । तं जहा—सिद्धथ्ये इ वा सिज्जंसे इव वा जसंसे इ वा । समणस्स णं भगवश्रो महावीरस्स माया वासिट्ठा गोत्तेणं । तीसे तश्रो नामधिज्जा एवम् श्राहिज्जंति । तं जहा—तिसला इ वा विदेहदिन्ना इ वा पियकारिणी इ वा । समणस्स णं भगवश्रो महावीरस्स पित्तिज्जे सुपासे जेट्ठे भाया नंदिवद्धणे भगिणी सुदंसणा । भारिया जसोया कोडिण्णा गोत्तेणं । समणस्स णं भगवश्रो महावीरस्स धूया कासवीगोत्तेणं । तीसे दो णामधिज्जा एवम् श्राहिज्जंति । तं जहा—श्रणोज्जा इ वा पियदंसणा इ वा । समणस्स णं भगवश्रो महावीरस्स नत्तुई कोसिया गोत्तेणं । तीसे णं दो नामधिज्जा एवम् श्राहिज्जंति । तं जहा—सेसवई वा जसवई वा । १०९

The father of Śramaṇa Bhagavān Mahâvīra belonged to the Kāśyapa line and he had three names (too) which were: Siddhārtha, Śreyasya and Yaśasya. The mother of Śramaṇa Bhagavān Mahāvīra belonged to the Vasiṣṭha line and she had three names which were Triśalā, Videhadattā and Priya-kāriṇī. The uncle of Śramaṇa Bhagavān Mahāvīra was Supārśva, his elder brother Nandi-vardhana, and his sister Sudarśanā: and wife Yaśodā was of the Kauṇḍinya line. The daughter of Śramaṇa Bhagavān Mahâvīra belonged to the Kāśyapa line and she was known by two names, which were Anavadyā and Priya-darśanā. Śramaṇa Bhagavān Mahāvīra's grand-daughter (from the side of his daughter) belonged to the line of Kauśika and she was known by two names, which were Śeṣavatī and Yaśovatī. 109

समणे भगवं महावीरे दक्खे दक्ख-पइण्णे पडिरूवे श्रालीणे भद्दए विणीए णाए णायपुत्ते णायकुलचंदे विदेहे विदेहदिण्णे विदेहजच्चे विदेह-सूमाले तीसं

वासाइं विदेहंसि कट्टु अम्मा-पिईहिं देवत्त-गएहिं गुरु-महत्तर-एहिं अब्भणुण्णाए
समत्त-पइण्णे । पुणरबि लोयंतिएहिं जीय-कप्पिएहिं देवेहिं ताहिं इट्ठाहिं
कंताहिं पियाहिं मणुण्णाहिं मणामाहिं श्रोरालाहिं कल्लाणाहिं सिवाहिं धण्णाहिं
मंगल्लाहिं मिय-महुर-सस्सिरीयाहिं हियय-गमणिज्जाहिं हियय-पल्हायणि-
ज्जाहिं गंभीराहिं अपुणरुत्ताहिं वग्गूहिं अणवरयं अभिणंदमाणा य अभिथ्थुण-
माणा य एवं वयासी । ११०

Intelligent, with aspirations of an intelligent man, the very perfection of beauty, with full controls, bearing auspicious marks, polite, well-known, himself a Jñātṛ kṣatriya, the son of a Jñātṛ kṣatriya, the moon of the Jñātṛ clan, Vaideha, the son of Videha-dattā, the best among the Vaidehas, the tender-most among the Vaidehas, Śramaṇa Bhagavān Mahāvīra, having spent 30 years in the country of Videha, fulfilled his promise, on the death of his parents and with the permission of the elders and superiors: and

on this occasion, following the established customs and practices, the *Lokāntika* gods incessantly praised and hymned him with these high, kind, dear, pleasant, pleasing, noble, helpful auspicious, fortunate, well-meaning, measured-sweet-decent, heart-appealing, heart-pleasing, grave and ever-fresh words. 110

जय जय णंदा । जय जय भद्दा/भद्दं ते खत्तिय-वर-वसभा । बुज्झाहि भगवं
लोग-णाहा सयल-जगज्-जीवहिग्रं पवत्तेहि धम्मतिथ्थं पर-हिय-सुह-णिस्सेयस-
करं सव्व-लोए सव्व-जीवाणं भविस्सइ ।
त्ति कट्टु जय-जय-सद्दं पउंजंति । १११

"Victory be to the joy of the world!
Victory be to one with auspicious marks!
Glory be to thee, oh bull among best kṣatriyas.
Awake, oh Lord, Master of the Universe,
Establish religion and order
For the well-being of all living beings.
These will bring supreme benefit,
The best of welfare and happiness,
To all beings in all the worlds."

So saying, they shouted 'victory' again and again. 111

पुव्विं पि णं समणस्सं भगवओ महावीरस्स माणुस्साओ गिहत्थ-धम्माओ
अणुत्तरे आभोइए अप्पडिवाई णाण-दंसणे होत्था । तए णं समणे भगवं
महावीरे तेणं अणुत्तरेणं आहोहिएणं णाण-दंसणेणं अप्पणो णिक्खमण-कालं-
आभोएइ। आभोएइत्ता चिच्चा हिरण्णं चिच्चा सुवण्णं चिच्चा धणं चिच्चा
धण्णं चिच्चा रज्जं चिच्चा रट्ठं एवं बलं वाहणं कोसं कोट्ठागारं चिच्चा पुरं
चिच्चा अंतेउरं चिच्चा जणवयं चिच्चा धण-कणग-रयण-मणि-मोत्तिय-संख-
सिल-प्पवाल-रत्त-रयणमाइयं संतसार-सावएज्जं विच्छड्डइत्ता विग्गोवइत्ता
दाणं दायारेहिं परिभाइत्ता दाणं दाइयाणं परिभाइत्ता । ११२

Even before Śramaṇa Bhagavān Mahāvīra courted the life of a house-holder, so coveted by the habits of men, he was in possession of unprecedented, unlimited and unimpeded knowledge and faith. So, with this unprecedented, unlimited and unimpeded *avadhi* knowledge and faith, Śramaṇa Bhagavān Mahāvīra perceived the time of his renunciation. On perceiving this, he gave up his silver, his gold, his wealth, his granaries, his majesty, his kingdom, his transport, his treasury, his store, his town, his *seraglio* and his subjects, and having given these up, and having discarded riches, gold, precious stones, jewels, pearls, conches, stones, corals, rubies and many other valuable objects, he had them distributed by donors (assistants) among indigent persons. 112

तेणं कालेणं तेणं समएणं जे से हेमंताणं पढमे मासे पढमे पक्खे मग्गसिर-बहुले
तस्स णं मग्गसिर-बहुलस्स दसमी-पक्खेणं पाईण-गामिणीए छायाए पोरिसीए
अभिणिव्वट्टाए पमाण-पत्ताए सुव्वएणं दिवसेणं विजएणं मुहुत्तेणं चंदप्पभाए
सीयाए स-देव-मणुयासुराए परिसाए समणुगम्ममाण-मग्गे संखिय-चक्किय-
मंगलिय-मुहमंगलिय-वद्धमाण-पूसमाण-घंटिय-गणेहिं ताहिं इट्ठाहिं कंताहिं
पियाहिं मणुण्णाहिं मणामाहिं ओरालाहिं कल्लाणाहिं सिवाहिं धण्णाहिं मंगल्लाहिं
मिय-महुर-सस्सिरीयाहिं (हियय-पल्हायणिज्जाहिं अट्ठ-सइयाहिं अपुण-
रुत्ताहिं) वग्गूहिं अभिणंदमाणा अभिसंथुणमाणा य एवं वयासी ।११३।

At that time, in that period, in the first month of winter, during the first fortnight, on the tenth day of the dark half of Mārgaśīrṣa, when the shadow turned eastward, and the first quarter was full and over, on the day named Subrata, at the hour (*muhūrta*) named Vijaya, seated on a chariot named Candraprabhā, he set out followed on the way by groups of gods, men, and *asuras*, and was surrounded by conch-blowers, bearers of arms, priests, courtiers, carrier-men, heralds, bards, bell-bearers and these showered on him praises and hymns with words high, kind, dear, pleasant, noble, healthful auspicious, fortunate, well-meaning, measured-sweet-decent, [heart-appealing, heart-pleasing, grave and ever-fresh]. 113

जय जय णंदा । जय जय भद्दा । भद्दं ते अभग्गेहिं णाणं-दंसण-चरित्तेहिं अजियाइं जिणाहि इंदियाइं जियं च पालेहि समण-धम्मं जिय-विग्घो वि य वसाहि तं देव । सिद्धि-मज्झे णिहणाहि राग-दोस-मल्ले तवेणं धिइ-धणिय-वद्ध-कच्छे मद्दाहि अट्ठ-कम्म-सत्तु झाणेणं उत्तमेणं सुक्केणं अप्पमत्तो हराहि आराहणा-पडागं च वीरा तेलक्क-रंग-मज्झे पाव य वितिमिरम् अणुत्तरं केवल-वर-णाणं गच्छ य मुक्खं परं पयं जिण-वरोवइट्ठेण मग्गेणं अकुडिलेणं हंता परीसह-चमूं । जय जय खत्तिय-वर वसभा । बहूइं दिवसाइं बहूइं पक्खाइं बहूइं मासाइं वहूइं उऊइं बहूइं अयणाइं बहूइं संवच्छराइं अभीए परीसहोवसग्गाणं खंति-खमे भय-भेखाणं धम्मे तेअविग्घं भवउ । त्ति कट्टु जय-जय-सद्दं पउंजंति ।

"Victory be to the joy of the world!
Victory to one with auspicious marks!
Glory be to thee.
Conquer thy unconquered senses
By unmutilated knowledge, faith and conduct,
Follow thee a *śramaṇa's* life, rightly acquired.
Oh Lord! Conquering all obstructions,
Live thee in perfection,
By penance, overpower attachment and hatred,—
The two mighty wrestlers.
Vigorously gird thy loin with steadfastness,
Crush the enemy, the eight *karmas*, by meditation—
Best and purest. Being uninfatuated,
Bear the banner of spiritual practices.
Or hero! In the arena of the three worlds.
Gain *kevala* knowledge and faith, supreme and best,
With no stain of obscurity.
Attain thee the highest state of liberation

By treading on the straight path,
As advised and chalked out by the best of *Jinas*.
Bravo! You have beaten the battalion of obstructions,
Victory to thee! A bull among the kṣatriyas.
By fearing not sundry omens and obstructions,
For many days, fortnights, months and seasons,
For many half-years and years full
Are thee capable of fortitude and rest
Even when in the midst of fear or danger.
May thy path be harm-free." 114

So saying, they shouted victory again and again.

तए णं समणे भगवं महावीरे णयण-माला-सहस्सेहिं पिच्छिज्जमाणे २ वयण-माला-सहस्सेहिं अभिथुव्वमाणे २ हिययमाला-सहस्सेहिं उण्णंदिज्जमाणे २ मणोरह-माला-सहस्सेहिं विच्छिप्पमाणे २ कंति-रूव-गुणेहिं पच्छिज्जमाणे २ अंगुलिमाला-सहस्सेहिं दाइज्जमाणे २ दाहिण-हत्थेणं बहूणं णर-णारी सहस्साणं अंजलि-माला-सहस्साइं पडिच्छमाणे २ भवण-पंति-सहस्साइं सम-इच्छमाणे २ तंती-तल-ताल-तुडिय-घण-मुइंग-गीय-वाइय-रवेणं महुरेण य मणहरेणं जय-सद्द-घोस-मीसिएणं मंजु-मंजुणा घोसेण य पडिबुज्झमाणे २ सव्विडढीए सव्व-जूईए सव्व-बलेणं सव्व-वाहणेणं सव्वसमुदाएणं सव्वाय-रेणं सव्व-विभूईए सव्व-विभूसाए सव्व-संभमेणं सव्व-संगमेणं सव्व-पगईएहिं सव्व-नाडएणं सव्व-तालायरेहिं सव्वोरोहेणं सव्व-पुप्फ-मल्लालंकार-विभू-साए सव्व-तुडिय-सद्द-संणिणाएणं महया इड्ढीए महया जुईए महया बलेणं महया वाहणेणं महया वर-तुडिय-जमग-समग-प्पवाइएणं संख-पणव-पडह-भेरि-भल्लरि-खरमुहि-दुंदुहि-णिग्घोष-णाइय-रवेणं कुंडपुरं णगरं मज्झंमज्झेणं णिगच्छइ । णिग्गच्छित्ता जेणेव णाय-संड-वणे उज्जाणे जेणेव असोग-वर-पायवे तेणेव उवागच्छइ ।

Then Śramaṇa Bhagavān Mahāvīra, gazed on by thousands of eyes, praised by thousands of mouths, extolled by thousands of hearts, being the object of thousands of wishes, coveted because of his splendour, beauty and virtues, pointed by thousands of fingers, responding with his right hand (to the greetings from) thousands of folded palms of several thousand men and women, moving on and on by leaving behind rows of thousands of dwellings;

greeted by sweet and delightful music of *vīnā*, cymbal, *tūrya* and great drum, with which were mixed sweet and bracing shouts of victory, and gentle and pleasant murmur of the people;
accompanied by all his pomp, all his splendour, all his army, all his train, all his retinue, all his munificence, all his grandeur, all his ornaments, all his majesty, all his men, all his subjects, all his actors, all his attendants, the entire *seraglio*, with all his flowers, wreaths, ornaments and robes on;
with the sound of all *tūryas*, with great pomp and great splendour, great army, great train, and the best of instruments, such as *turya*, *yamaka*, *samaka*, conch, *paṇava*, *paṭaha*, *bheri*, *jhallari*, *kharamukhi*, *dundubhi* and many others, (he) having passed through the city of Kuṇḍapura, reached the Jñāti-saṇḍa park, and arrived at the spot where stood the most excellent *aśoka* tree.115

उवागच्छित्ता असोग-वर-पायवस्स अहे सीयं ठावेइ । ठावित्ता सीयाओ पच्चोरुहइ । पच्चोरुहित्ता सयमेव आभरण-मल्लालंकारं ओमुयइ । ओमुइत्ता सयमेव पंचमुट्ठियं लोयं करेइ । करित्ता छट्ठेणं भत्तेणं अपाणएणं हत्थुत्तराहिं णक्खत्तेणं जोगमुवागएणं एगं देव-दूसम् आदाय एगे अबीए मुंडे भवित्ता अगाराओ अणगारियं पव्वइए । ११६

On reaching the most excellent *aśoka* tree, he ordered his palanquin to be placed beneath it. Then he came out of the palanquin. Thereafter, with his own hand, he took off his wreaths, fineries and ornaments. Having taken them off, he himself tonsured his head in five handfuls. Having done so, he courted the vow of taking food, devoid of water, only once after two full-meal days (missing six meals at a time), and during the day-time, till the time when the moon would be in conjunction with the asterism Uttara-phālgunī, at which, putting on a divine robe, and all alone, and without a second one (to attend), he tonsured his head and having given up the household order, he entered the order of the homeless monks. 116

समणे भगवं महावीरे संवच्छरं साहिय-मासं जाव...चीवरधारी होथ्था । तेण परं अचेले पाणि-पडिग्गहिए समणे भगवं महावीरे साइरेगाइं दुवालस वासाइं णिच्चं वोसट्ठ-काए चियत्त-देहे जे केइ उवसग्गा उप्पज्जंति । तं जहा—दिव्वा वा माणुसा वा तिरिक्ख-जोणिया वा अणुलोमा वा पडिलोमा वा—ते उप्पन्ने सम्मं सहइ खमइ तितिक्खइ अहियासेइ । ११७

Mahāvīra's Hardships

[facing p. 64

Śramaṇa Bhagavān Mahāvīra was with robes on for one full year and a month. Then he was devoid of cloth, and used the hollow of his palm as his begging bowl. For slightly more than twelve years, Śramaṇa Bhagavān Mahāvīra desisted from care of the body, and for times exposed it (to hardships). During this period, when any hardship came, he bore it in all respects, forgave it, overlooked it, believed it to be no hardship, howsoever severe, maybe due to divine wrath, or caused by men, animals or forces of nature, or by other adverse forces. 117

तए णं समणे भगवं महावीरे अणगारे जाए इरिया-समिए[28] भासा-समिए एसणा-समिए आयाण-भंड-मत्त-णिक्खेवणा-समिए उच्चार-पासवण-खेल सिंघाण-जल्ल-पारिट्ठावणिया-समिए मण-समिए वय-समिए काय-समिए मण-गुत्ते वय-गुत्ते काय-गुत्ते गुत्तिंदिए गुत्त-बंभह्यारी अकोहे अमाणे अमाए अलोहे संते पसंते उवसंते परिणिव्वुडे अणासवे[29] अममे अकिंचणे छिण्ण-गंठे णिरुवलेवे कंस-पाई[30] व मुक्क-तोए संखो इव णिरंजणे जीवे इव अप्पडिहय-गई गगणमिव णिरालंबणे वायु इव अप्पडिवद्धे सारय-सलिलं व सुद्ध-हियए पुक्खर-पत्तं-पिव णिरुवलेवे कुम्मो इव गुत्तिंदिए खग्गि-विसाणं व एग जाए विहग इव विप्पमुक्के भारुंड-पक्खी इव अप्पमत्ते कुंजर इव सोडीरे वसभो इव जायथामे सीहो इव दुद्धरिसे मंदरो इव अप्पकंपे सागरो इव गंभीरे चंदो इव सोम-लेसे[31] सूरो इव दित्ततेए जच्च-कणगं व जाय-रुवे वसुंधरा इव सव्व-फास-विसहे सुहय-हुयासणो इव तेयसा जलंते ।

[इमेसिं पयाणं दोण्णि संगहण-गाहाओ

कंसे संखे जीवे
गगणे वाऊ य सरय-सलिले य ।
पुक्खर-पत्ते कुम्मे
विहगे खग्गे या भारुंडे ॥
कुंजर वसभे सीहे
णगराया चेव सागरं अखोभे ।
चंदे सूरे कणगे
वसुंधरा चेव सुहय-हयवहे ॥]

णथ्थि णं तस्स भगवंतस्स कथ्थइ पडिबंधे । से य चउव्विहे पण्णत्ते । तं जहा—
दव्वओ खित्तओ कालओ भावओ ।

दव्वओ—सचित्ताचित्त-मीसएसु दव्वेसु । खित्तओ—गामे वा नगरे वा अरण्णे वा खित्ते वा खले वा अंगणे वा । कालओ—समए वा आवलियाए वा आणा-पाणुए वा थोवे वा खणे वा लवे वा पक्खे वा मुहुत्ते वा अहोरत्ते वा पक्खे वा

मासे वा उऊए वा अयणे वा संवच्छरे वा अण्णयरे वा दीह-काल-संजोए।
भावओ—कोहे वा माणे वा मायाए वा लोभे वा भए वा हासे वा पिज्जे वा
माया-दोसे वा कलहे वा अब्भक्खाणे वा पेसुण्णे वा पर-परिवाए वा अरइ-रई
वा मोसे वा जाव'''मिच्छा-दंसण-सल्ले वा तस्स णं भगवंतस्स णो एवं भवइ।
११८

Then Śramaṇa Bhagavān Mahāvīra became homeless; circumspect in movement, circumspect in words, circumspect in desires, circumspect in acceptance-accumulation-renunciation, circumspect in throwing out stool, urine, saliva and body dirt :

Restrained in mind, restrained in words, restrained in physical activities;

Guarding his thoughts, guarding his words, guarding his physical activities, guarding his organs of senses, guarding his chastity;

Without anger, without pride, without attachment, without greed, calm, grave, devoid of attachment, desisted from everything, freed from compulsion.

Without ego, without possession, with the tie (of worldly bondage) cut, free from any stain of worldliness:

Liberated by giving up suffering, like bell-metal unstained by water.

Sin-free like a conch taking no black dot, without obstruction like the course of life, without support like the firmament, without bound like the wind, pure at heart like water in autumn, without a smear like a lotus leaf, with organs of senses withdrawn like a tortoise, solitary like the rhino's horn, free like the birds, ever alert like the monstrous *bhāruṇḍa*, with a high status like an elephant, born strong like an ox, invincible like a lion, steadfast like Mount Mandara, deep like an ocean, mild like the moon, effulgent in prowess like the sun, pure like fine gold, bearing (with unconcern) all touches like the earth, like fire well-fed by offerings, shone he in his own splendour.

[Two precise verses for all these terms

(Like) bell-metal, conch and course of life,
(Like) firmament, wind and water in autumn,
(Like) lotus leaf, (like) tortoise
With organs withdrawn.
(Like) birds, a *bhāruṇḍa* and a rhino's horn.
(Like) an elephant, an ox and a lion,

Mount Mandara and the ocean deep.
(Like) the moon, the sun, and gold pure,
(Like) the earth, abode of treasures,
and well-fed fire.]

No more limitation was there for him, the Venerable One. Limitations have been stated to be four: limitation of objects, limitation of space, limitation of time and limitation of subjective senses.

Limitation of objects ; of animate objects, of inanimate objects, and of those in a mixed state;

Limitation of space ; of a village, a town, a forest, a farm, a house or a yard:

Limitation of time ; of a unit called *samaya*, of one called *āvalikā*, one called *ānāpānaka* or a deep-breath/respiration, one called a *stoka* (=7 respirations), one called a *kṣaṇa* (i.e., many respirations), one called a *lava* (=7 *stokas*), a *pakṣa* (a day), a *muhūrta* (=70 *lavas*=48 minutes), a day-night (24 hours), a *pakṣa* (15 days), a month (30 days), a season (4 months), a half-year, a year, or any other time-unit of a still longer duration;

Limitation of subjective senses ; of anger, pride, attachment, greed, fear, laughter, affection, hatred, quarrel, calumny, sharp words, meanness, scandal-mongering, pleasure and pain, deceitful falsehood and evil of wrong faith.

The Bhagavân had none of these. 118

से णं भगवं वासा-वास-वज्जं ग्रट्ठ गिम्ह-हेमंतिए मासे गामे एगराइए णगरे
पंच-राइए वासी-चंदण-समाण-कप्पे सम-तिण-मणि-लेट्ठु-कंचणे समदुक्ख-
सुहे इह लोग-परलोग-ग्रप्पडिबद्धे जीविय-मरणे णिरवकंखे संसार-पार-गामी
कम्म-संग-णिग्घायणट्ठाए ग्रब्भुट्ठिए एवं च णं विहरइ। ११९

Monsoon sojourn apart, the Bhagavān spent eight months of summer and winter as follows: if in a village, one night only in one village, and five nights if in a town;

With similar feeling towards excreta and sandal, with similar attitude to hay, jewel, clay and gold, indifferent to pleasure and pain, free from limitation in this world as well as in the next, without a hankering for life and death, destined to overcome the mundane life, born to terminate the bondage of *karma*—thus he spent his time. 119

तस्स णं भगवंतस्स अणुत्तरेणं णाणेणं अणुत्तरेणं दंसणेणं अणुत्तरेणं चरित्तेणं अणुत्तरेणं आलएणं अणुत्तरेणं विहारेणं अणुत्तरेणं वीरियेणं अणुत्तरेणं अज्जवेणं अणुत्तरेणं मद्दवेणं अणुत्तरेणं लाघवेणं अणुत्तराए खंतीए अणुत्तराए मुत्तीए अणुत्तराए गुत्तीए अणुत्तराए तुट्ठीए अणुत्तराए बुद्धीए अणुत्तरेणं सच्च-संजम-तव-सुचरिय-सोवचिय-फलपरिणिव्वाण-मग्गेणं अप्पाणं भावेमाणस्स दुवालस संवच्छराइं विइक्कंताइं तेरसमस्स अंतरा वट्टमाणस्स जे से गिम्हाणं दोच्चे मासे चउत्थे पक्खे वइसाह-सुद्धे तस्स णं वइसाह-सुद्धस्स दसमी-पक्खेणं पाईणा-गामिणीए छायाए पोरिसीए अभिणिवट्टाए पमाणपत्ताए सुव्वएणं दिवसेणं विजएणं मुहुत्तेणं जंभिय-गामस्स णगरस्स वहिया उजुवालियाए णई-तीरे वियावत्तस्स चेइयस्स अदूर-सामंते सामागस्स गाहावइस्स कट्ठ-करणंसि साल-पायवस्स अहे गोदोहियाए उक्कुडुय-णिसिज्जाए आयावणाए आयावेमाणस्स २ छट्ठेणं भत्तेणं आपाणएणं हथ्युत्तराहिं णक्खत्तेणं जोगं उवागएणं झाणं-तरियाए वट्टमाणस्स अणंते अणुत्तरे णिव्वाघाए णिरावरणे कसिणे पडिपुण्णे केवल-वर-णाण-दंसणे समुप्पण्णे । १२०

With supreme knowledge, supreme faith and supreme conduct, in stainless lodgings and blameless wanderings, with extreme valour, extreme uprightness, extreme mildness, extreme dexterity and extreme patience, with utmost caution and utmost satisfaction, with the highest intelligence and the highest truth, restraint and penance, Śramaṇa Bhagavān Mahāvīra passed 12 years in meditation on self on the road to liberation, which was the duly earned outcome of a right conduct.

In the thirteenth year, in the second month of summer, in the fourth fortnight, on the tenth day of the bright half of Vaiśākha, when the shadow had turned eastward, on the expiry of the first quarter, on the day called Subrata, at the hour called Vijaya, outside of the town called Gṛmbhikā-grāma, on the bank of the river Ṛjupālika, not far from a discarded *yakṣa*-abode, on the farm of a householder named Syāmāka, beneath a *sāl* tree, when the moon was in conjunction with the asterism Uttara-phālguni, while, to expose himself to the full blast of the sun, seated was he in a milking posture, with his head erect — and at this time he practised the hard vow of taking meal, devoid of water, every third day (missing in all six meals)—still in meditation, attained he the supreme knowledge and faith, *kevala* by name, unsurpassed unobstructed, unlimited, complete and full. 120

तए णं समणे भगवं मंहावीरे अरहा जाए जिणे केवली सव्वण्णू सव्वदरसी स
देव-मणुयासुरस्स लोगस्स परियायं जाणइ पासइ सव्वलोए सव्वजीवाणं
आगइं गइं ठिइं चवणं उववायं तक्कं मणो माणसियं भुत्तं कडं पडिसेवियं
आवी-कम्मं रहो-कम्मं अरहा अ-रहस्स-भागी तं तं कालं मण-वयण-काय-जोगे
वट्टमाणाणं सव्वलोए सव्वजीवाणं सव्वभावे जाणमाणे पासमाणे विहरइ। १२१

Then Śramaṇa Bhagavân Mahâvîra became the venerable, victor, omniscient, all-knowing, all-observing; knew he and saw he now all categories of gods, men and *asuras* in all the worlds; knew he and saw he the conditions of all the living beings in all the worlds — wherefrom they come, whither they go, where do they stay, when do they slip, where are they born; knew he and saw he the ideas and the thoughts in their mind, their intake, their doings, their open deeds as well as their secret deeds; being the most venerable, from whom nothing could be kept a secret, he knew and he saw, in all respects, the state of mind, words and deeds of all the living beings in all the worlds. 121

तेणं कालेणं तेणं समएणं समणे भगवं मंहावीरे अट्ठिय-ग्गाम[32]-णीसाए पढमं
अंतरावासं वासा-वासं उवागए। चंपं च पिट्ठिचंपंच णीसाए तओ अंतरावासे
वासावासं उवागए। वेसलिं णगरिं वाणियग्गामं च णीसाए दुवालस अंतरावासे[33]
वासावासं उवागए। रायगिहं णगरं णालंदं च वाहिरियं णीसाए चोद्दस अंतरा-
वासे वासावासं उवागए। छ मिहिलियाए दो भद्धियाए एगं आलभियाए
एगं पणिय भूमीए एगं सावत्थीए एगं पावाए मज्झिमाए हत्थिपालस्स रण्णो
रज्जूसभाए अपच्छिमं अंतरावासं वासावासं उवागए। १२२

[तत्थ णं जे से पावाए मज्झिमाए हत्थिपालस्स रण्णो रज्जूसभाए अपच्छिमे
अंतरावासे वासावासं उवागए।] १२३

At that time, in that period, Śramaṇa Bhagavân Mahâvîra selected Asthikā-grāma for his sojourn during the first rainy season, Campā and Pṛṣṭhi-campā during three rainy seasons, Vaiśāli and Vānijya-grāma during 12 rainy seasons, Rājagṛha and the suburbs of Nālanda during 14 rainy seasons, Mithilikā

(Mithilâ) during two, Bhadrikâ during two, Ālavikâ during one, Paṇita-bhūmi during one, Śrâvasti during one, and the writers' building of king Hastipāla in the very heart of Pâvâ one, this being his last sojourn during a rainy season. 122

[He spent his last rainy season at the writers' building of king Hastipāla in the very heart of Pâvâ.] 123

तस्स णं अंतरावासस्स जे से वासाणं चउत्थे मासे सत्तमे पक्खे कत्तिय-बहुले तस्सणं कत्तिय-बहुलस्स पण्णरसी पक्खेणं जा सा चरिमा रयणी तं रयणिं च णं समणे भगवं महावीरे कालगए विइक्कंते समुज्जाए छिण्ण-जाइ-जरा-मरण-बंधणे सिद्धे बुद्धे मुत्ते अंतगडे[34] परिणिव्वुडे सव्व-दुक्ख-प्पहीणे चंदे णामं से दोच्चे संवच्छरे पीइवद्धणे मासे णंदिवद्धणे पक्खे सुव्वयग्गी णामं से दिवसे उवसमि त्ति पवुच्चइ देवाणंदा णामं सा रयणी णिरिति त्ति पवुच्चइ अच्चे लवे मुत्ते पाणू थोवे सिद्धे णागे करणे सव्वथ्थसिद्धे मुहुत्ते साइणा णक्खत्तेणं जोगं उवागएणं कालगए विइक्कंते समुज्जाए छिण्ण-जाइ-जरा-मरण-बंधणे सिद्धे बुद्धे मुत्ते अंतगडे परिणिव्वुडे सव्व-दुक्ख-प्पहीणे । १२४

During this monsoon halt, in the fourth month of the rainy season, in the seventh fortnight, in the dark half Kārttika, on the fifteenth day, that being his last, during the night, Śramaṇa Bhagavān Mahāvīra passed away, went off, quitted the world, cut asunder the ties of birth-oldage-death, became perfected, enlightened and liberated, the maker of the end; he entered into liberation and ended all misery.

This occurred in the year called Candra, being the second year (of the *yuga* or lustrum consisting of five years), in the month called Prīti-vardhana, in the fortnight called Nandi-vardhana, on the day called Subratāgni, also called Upasami, in the night called Devânandâ, also called Nir-ṛti, at a *lava* called Arcya, at a *prāṇa* called Mukta, at a *stoka* called Siddha, at a *karaṇa* called Nāga, at a *muhūrta* called Sarvārtha-siddha, when the moon was in conjunction with the asterism Svāti, (he) passed away, went off, quitted the world, cut asunder the ties of birth-oldage-death, became perfected, enlightened and liberated, the maker of the end, he entered into liberation and terminated all misery. 124

जं रयणिं च णं समणे भगवं महावीरे कालगए जाव· · ·सव्व-दुक्ख-प्पहीणे सा णं रयणी बहूहिं देवेहिं देवीहि य उवयमाणेहि य उप्पयमाणेहि य उज्जोविया यावि होथ्था । १२५

जं रयणिं च णं समणे भगवं महावीरे कालगए जाव· · ·सव्व-दुक्ख-प्पहीणे सा णं रयणीबहूहिं देवेहिं देवीहि य उवयमाणेहि य उप्पयमाणेहि य उप्पिंजलग-भूया कहकहगभूया यावि होथ्था । १२६

During the night when Śramaṇa Bhagavān Mahāvīra passed away,...till ended all misery, during that night, the universe was lit by the ascending and descending of many gods and goddesses. 125

During the night when Śramaṇa Bhagavān Mahāvīra passed away,...till ended all misery, during that night, the universe was filled with confusion by the ascending and descending of many gods and goddesses, and there was an uproar everywhere — 'What's this ?' 'Why this ?' 126

जं रयणिं च णं समणे भगवं महावीरे कालगए जाव· · ·सव्व-दुक्ख-प्पहीणे तं रयणिं च णं जेट्ठस्स गोयमस्स इंदभूइस्स अणगारस्स अंतेवासिस्स णायए पिज्ज-बंधणे वोच्छिण्णे अणंते अणुत्तरे जाव· · ·केवल-वर-णाण-दंसणे समुप्पण्णे। १२७

During the night when Śramaṇa Bhagavān Mahāvīra passed away,...till ended all misery, during that night, his senior disciple-monk, Indra-bhūti, of the Gautama line, was freed from the tie of attachment (towards the Master), and attained the supreme knowledge and faith, *kevala* by name, unprecedented, unobstructed, unlimited, complete and full. 127

जं रयणिं च णं समणे भगवं महावीरे जाव· · ·सव्व-दुक्ख-प्पहीणे तं रयणिं च णं णव मल्लई णव लेच्छइ कासी-कोसलगा अट्ठारस वि गण-रायाणो अमावसाए पाराभोयं पोसहोववास[35] पट्ठवइंसु—गए से भावुज्जोए दव्वुज्जोयं करिस्सामो । १२८

During the night when Śramaṇa Bhagavān Mahāvīra passed away,...till ended all misery, during that night, the night of the new moon, nine Mallaki kings, and nine Licchavi kings, (in all) 18 confederate kings, from Kāśī and Kośala respectively, instituted a spiritual practice name *'pārābhoga-poṣadha'* and said:

"As the light of intellect is gone out, so shall (we) lit the light with material objects." 128

जं रयणिं च समणे जाव... सव्व-दुक्ख-प्पहीणे तं रयणिं च णं खुद्दाए णाम भास-रासी महग्गहे दो-वास-सहस्स-ट्ठिई समणस्स भगवओ महावीरस्स जम्म-णक्खत्तं संकंते । १२९

जप्पभिइं च णं से खुद्दाए भास-रासी-महग्गहे दो-वास-सहस्सट्ठिई समणस्स भगवओ महावीरस्स जम्म-णक्खत्तं संकंते तप्पभिइं च णं समणाणं णिग्गंथाणं णिग्गंथीण य णो उदिए पूया-सक्कारे पवत्तइ । १३०

जया णं से खुद्दाए जाव... जम्म-णक्खत्ताओ विइक्कंते भविस्सइ तया णं णिग्गंथाणं णिग्गंथीण य उदिए पूया-सक्कारे भविस्सइ । १३१

During the night when Śramaṇa Bhagavān Mahāvīra passed away,...till ended all misery, during that night, looking like a heap of ashes, the great planet named Kṣudrātmā, which stays at each asterism for a total span of 2,000 years, contaminated the natal asterism of Śramaṇa Bhagavān Mahāvīra. 129

From the moment the great planet contaminated the natal asterism, etc., the *śramaṇas*, monks and nuns, are not receiving due honour and respect. 130

When that great planet named Kṣudrātmā, *etc.* moves out from the natal asterism, then will be paid to the *śramaṇas*, monks and nuns, due honour and respect. 131

जं रयणिं च णं समणे भगवं महावीरे कालगए जाव... सव्व-दुक्ख-प्पहीणे तं रयणिं च णं कुंथु अणुद्धरी-णामं समुप्पण्णा जा ठिया अचलमाणा छउमत्थाणं णिग्गंथाणं णिग्गंथीण य णो चक्खु-फासं हव्वम् आगच्छइ जा अट्ठिया चलमाणा छउमत्थाणं णिग्गंथाणं णिग्गंथीण य चक्खु-फासं हव्वं आगच्छइ । १३२

जं पासित्ता बहूहिं णिग्गंथेहिं णिग्गंथीहि य भत्ताइं पच्चक्खायाइं ।
से किमाहु भंते !
अज्ज-प्पभिइं दुराराहए संजमे भविस्सइ । १३३

During the night when Śramaṇa Bhagavān Mahāvīra passed away,...till ended all misery, during that night was born the insect called '*kunthu anuddhari*', which, when not moving but at rest, is not easily visible to the young monks and nuns, but when it's moving, and is not at rest, can be easily seen by the young monks and nuns. 132

On seeing this, many monks and nuns had given up food intake. "*Bhante*' Why has this been said ?"

— From now on, restraint would be difficult to observe. 133

तेणं कालेणं तेणं समएणं समणस्स भगवग्रो महावीरस्स इंदभूइ-पामोक्खाग्रो चोद्दस समणसाहस्सीग्रो उक्कोसिया समण-संपया होत्था। १३४

At that time, in that period, Śramaṇa Bhagavān Mahāvīra had an excellent community of 14,000 *śramaṇas* with Indrabhūti at their head. 134

समणस्स णं भगवग्रो महावीरस्स ग्रज्ज-चंदणा[36]-पामोक्खाग्रो छत्तीसं ग्रज्जिया-साहस्सीग्रो उवकोसिया ग्रज्जिया-संपया होत्था। १३५

Śramaṇa Bhagavān Mahāvīra had an excellent community of 36,000 nuns with Candanā at their head. 135

समणस्स णं भगवग्रो महावीरस्स संख-सयग-पामोक्खाणं समणोवासगाणं एगा सय-साहस्सी ग्रउणट्ठिं च सहस्सा उक्कोसिया समणोवासगाणं संपया होत्था। १३६

Śramaṇa Bhagavān Mahāvīra had an excellent community of 1,59,000 male followers with Śaṅkha-śataka at their head. 136

समणस्स णं भगवग्रो महावीरस्स सुलसा-रेवई-पामोक्खाणं समणोवासियाणं तिण्णि सय-साहस्सीग्रो ग्रट्ठारस, सहस्सा उक्कोसिया समणोवासियाणं संपया होत्था। १३७

Śramaṇa Bhagavān Mahāvīra had an excellent community of 3,18,000 female followers with Sulsā and Revatī at their head. 137

समणस्स णं भगवग्रो महावीरस्स तिण्णि सया चउद्दस-पूव्वीणं ग्रजिणाणं

जिण-संकासाणं सव्वक्खर-सण्णिवाईणं जिणोविव अवितहं वागरमाणाणं उक्कोसिया चोद्दस पूव्वीणं संपया होत्था । १३८

Śramaṇa Bhagavān Mahāvīra had an excellent community of 300 *caturdasa-pūrvis* who were masters of the 14 *Pūrvas*, and though not *Jinas* themselves, they came very near to their standard, knew all the combinations of letters and correctly interpreted the truth like a *Jina*. 138

समणस्स णं भगवओ महावीरस्स तेरस सया ओहि-णाणीणं अइ-सेस-पत्ताणं[37] उक्कोसिया ओहि-णाणीणं संपया होत्था । १३९

Śramaṇa Bhagavān Mahāvīra had an excellent community of 1300 *avadhi-jñānins* who were masters of *avadhi* knowledge and had attained the highest limit of it (i.e., only slightly less than omniscience). 139

समणस्स णं भगवओ महावीरस्स सत्त सया केवल-णाणीणं संभिण्ण-वर-णाण-दंसण-धराणं उक्कोसिया केवल-णाणि-संपया होत्था । १४०

Śramaṇa Bhagavān Mahāvīra had an excellent community of 700 omniscients (*kevala-jñānis*) who were masters of supreme and absolute knowledge and faith. 140

समणस्स णं भगवओ महावीरस्स सत्त सया वेउव्वीणं अदेवाणं देवड्ढी-पत्ताणं उक्कोसिया वेउव्वि-संपया होत्था । १४१

Śramaṇa Bhagavān Mahāvīra had an excellent community of 700 *veyuviyas* who were great masters in the art to transform themselves, and even though not gods themselves, they were possessed of the fortune (power) of gods. 141

समणस्स णं भगवओ महावीरस्स पंच सया विउल-मईणं अड्ढाइज्जेसु दीवेसु[38] दोसु य समुद्देसु सण्णीणं पंचिंदियाणं पज्जत्तगाणं मणोगए भावे जाणंताणं उक्कोसिया विउल-मईणं संपया होत्था । १४२

Śramaṇa Bhagavān Mahāvīra had an excellent community of 500 *vipula-matis* who were endowed with the mightiest of intellectual power, who knew the inner thoughts of all the living beings who had full development, mind and five organs of senses and who resided in two islands and a half and in two oceans. 142

समणस्स णं भगवओ महावीरस्स चत्तारि सया वाईणं स देव-मणुयासुराए परिसाए वाए अपराजियाणं उक्कोसिया वाइ-संपया होथा । १४३

Śramaṇa Bhagavān Mahāvīra had an excellent community of 400 *vādis*, logicians (scholars) who were invincible in argument in the assembly of gods, *asuras* and human beings. 143

समणस्स णं भगवओ महावीरस्स सत्त अंतेवासी-सयाइं सिद्धाइं जाव... सव्वदुक्ख-प्पहीणाइं चउद्दस अज्जिया-सयाइं सिद्धाइं । १४४

Śramaṇa Bhagavān Mahāvīra had an excellent community of 700 disciples, who were perfected, till ended all misery, and a similar community of 1400 perfected female disciples. 144

समणस्स णं भगवओ महावीरस्स अट्ठ सया अणुत्तरोववाइयाणं गइ-कल्लाणाणं ठिइ-कल्लाणाणं आगमेसि भद्दाणं उक्कोसिया अणुत्तरोववाइयाणं संपया होथा । १४५

Śramaṇa Bhagavān Mahāvīra had an excellent community of 800 *anuttaropapātikas* who were in their last birth, who had bliss in their life, who had bliss in their movement, and who were lucky as regards their future. They were in possession of excellent allotments in the very highest of celestial abodes like Vijaya and others. 145

समणस्स णं भगवओ महावीरस्स दुविहा अंतगड भूमी होथा । तं जहा-जुगंतकड-भूमी य परियायंत-कड-भूमी य जाव...तच्चाओ पुरिस-जुगाओ जुगंतकड-भूमी चउवास-परियाए अंतं अकासी । १४६

Śramaṇa Bhagavān Mahāvīra had instituted two epochs marking the end, which were as follows: epoch signifying the termination of a generation, and epoch signifying the termination of categories; — till at the third generation, the epoch terminating generation, and till four years from the time of his attainment of supreme knowledge, the epoch terminating categories; and thereafter have closed the categories. 146*

तेणं कालेणं तेणं समएणं समणे भगवं महावीरे तीसं वासाइं अगार-वास-मज्झे वसित्ता साइरेगाइं दुवालस वासाइं छउमथ्थ-परियायं पाउणित्ता देसूणाइं तीसं वासाइं केवलि-परियायं पाउणित्ता बायालीसं वासाइं सामण्ण-परियायं पाउणित्ता बावत्तरिं वासाइं सव्वाउयं पालयित्ता खीणे वेयणिज्जाउय-णाम-गोत्ते इमीसे ओसप्पिणीए दूसम-सुसमाए समाए बहु-विइक्कंताए तीहिं वासेहिं अद्ध-णवमेहि य मासेहिं सेसेहिं पावाए मज्झिमाए हथ्थिपालगस्स ण्णो रज्जू-सभाए एगे अबीए छट्ठेणं भत्तेणं अपाणएणं साइणा णक्खतेणं जोगं उवागएणं पच्चूस-काल-समयंसि संपलियंक[39]-णिसण्ण पणपण्णं उज्झयणाइं पाव-फल-विवागाइं छतीसं च अपुट्ठवागरणाइं वागरित्ता पहाणं णाम अज्झयणं विभावेभाणे २ कालगए विइक्कंते समुज्जाए छिण्ण-जाइ-जरा-मरण-बंधणे सिद्धे बुद्धे मुत्ते अंतकडे परिणिव्वुडे सव्व-दुक्ख-प्पहीणे ।१४७

At that time, in that period, Śramaṇa Bhagavān Mahāvira lived for 30 years, as a householder slightly more than 12 years as a monk, and slightly more than 30 years as an omniscient person, in all 42 years in the order of monks, and 72 years in this world; after which, on the exhaustion of his *vedanīya karma* (which is to be gone through in this world), on the exhaustion of his life-span, name and lineage, in the course of this descension phase, when many years of the non-bracing—bracing phase had rolled down, when there remained 3 years and 8½ months to complete it, in the very heart of Pāvā, at the hall of writers of king Hastipālaka, all alone and without a second person, observing a vow of taking food, devoid of water, once every third day, at the time when the moon was in conjunction with the asterism Svāti, in the hour of day-break, seated in lotus posture (*padmāsana*), reciting 55 courses of study (of the *Vipāka Sūtra*) on the outcome of *karma*, and explaining 36 inadequately explained courses of study (from the *Uttarādhyayana Sūtra*

*"The meaning of this rather dark passage is according to the commentary that after three generations of disciples (Vīra, Sudharman, Jambusvāmin) nobody reached nirvāṇa; and after the fourth year of Mahāvīra's Kevaliship nobody entered the path which ends in final liberation, so that all persons who before that moment had not advanced in the way to final liberation, will not reach that state, though they may obtain the Kevalam by their austerities and exemplary conduct."

— Footnote in Hermann Jacobi's translation of *Kalpa Sūtra*, Sacred Books of the East, Vol. 22 Part I p. 28.

as he was concentrating on the chapter named Pradhâna he passed away, went beyond the bounds of *karma*, was uplifted after having left the world, cut asunder the tie of birth-oldage-death, and became perfected, enlightened and liberated, the maker of the end, and the terminator of all misery. 147

समणस्स भगवओ महावीरस्स जाव···सव्व-दुकख-प्पहीणस्स णव वास-सयाइं विइक्कंताइ दसमस्स य वास-सहस्स अयं असीइमे संवच्छरे काले गच्छइ। वायणंतरे पुण अयं तेणउए संवच्छरे काले गच्छइ इति। १४८

Since the time when Śramaṇa Bhagavân Mahâvīra passed away,...till ended all misery, nine centuries have passed, and of the tenth century, this is the 80th year. As per another redaction, this is the 93rd year, and here ends (the narrative). 148

II

जिण-चरित्तम्

पासे

Biographical Sketch of Arhat Pārśva

Top : Pārśva sporting with his wife
Bottom : Pārśva proceeding to see Kamatha's Five-fire penance

Top : Kamatha performing Five-fire penance
Bottom : Pārśva rescuing the snakes

[facing p. 80

तेणं कालेणं तेणं समएणं पासे अरहा पुरिसदाणीए पंचविसाहे होत्था।
तं जहा—विसाहाहिं चुए चइत्ता गब्भं वक्कंते। विसाहाहिं जाए। विसाहाहिं
मुंडे भवित्ता अगाराओ अणगारियं पव्वइए। विसाहाहिं अणंते अणुत्तरे
णिव्वाघाए णिरावरणे कसिणे पडिपुण्णे केवल-वर-णाण-दंसणे समुप्पण्णे।
विसाहाहिं परिणिव्वुए। १४९

At that time, in that period, the celebrated Arhat Pārśva became a five-viśākhā, as follows :

At the conjunction of the moon with the asterism Viśākhā, he descended (from the celestial abode), and having descended, he entered into the womb;

At the conjunction of the moon with the asterism Viśākhā, he was born;

At the conjunction of the moon with the asterism Viśākhā, he tonsured himself and renounced the household order to join the order of the homeless monks;

At the conjunction of the moon with the asterism Viśākhā, he attained the most excellent, supreme, *kevala* by name, knowledge and faith, infinite, unprecedented, unobstructed, unshrouded, complete and full;

At the conjunction of the moon with the asterism Viśākhā, he entered into his final liberation. 149

तेणं कालेणं तेणं समएणं पासे अरहा पुरिसदाणीए जे से गिम्हाणं पढमे मासे
पढमे पक्खे चित्त-बहुले तस्य णं चित्त-बहुलस्स चउत्थी पक्खेणं पाणयाओ
कप्पाओ वीसं-सागरोवम-ट्ठिइयाओ अणंतरं चयं चइत्ता इहेव जंबुद्दीवे दीवे
भारहे वासे वाराणसीए णयरीए आससेणस्स रण्णो वम्माए देवीए पुव्वरत्ताव-
रत्त-काल-समयंसि विसाहाहिं णक्खत्तेणं जोगमुवागएणं आहार-वक्कंतीए भव-
वक्कंतीए सरीर-वक्कंतीए कुच्छिंसि गब्भत्ताए वक्कंते। १५०

At that time, in that period, the celebrated Arhat Pārśva, having spent a time-span of 20 *ṣāgaropamas*, descended from his celestial abode in the heaven named Praṇata-kalpa, in the first month of summer, in the first fortnight, on the fourth day of the dark half of Caitra, on the exhaustion of his intake, life-span and physical form (in the celestial abode), and when the moon was in conjunction with the asterism Viśākhā, at the confluence of the two halves of the night, entered as an embryo in the womb of Vāmā-devī, the consort of king Aśvasena, in this very island named Jambūdvīpa, in the region named Bhārata-varṣa, in the city of Vārāṇasī. 150

पासे णं अरहा पुरिसदाणीए तिण्णाणोवगए थावि होत्था। तं जहा—चइस्सामि त्ति जाणइ चयमाणे ण जाणइ चुएमि त्ति जाणइ। तेणं चेव अभिलावेणं सुविण-दंसण-विहाणेणं सव्व जाव···णियग-गिहं अणुपविट्ठा (सयं भवणं अणुपविट्ठा) जाव···सुहंसुहेणं तं गब्भं परिवहइ। १५१

The celebrated Arhat Pārśva was in possession of three types of knowledge. They were : he knew — 'I shall descend'; knew he not at the time of descending; knew — 'I have descended.' [Repeat the words previously written after making necessary substitutions, using at appropriate places 'Pārśva' in place of 'Mahāvīra', till entered into her chamber,... till comfortably carried her unborn child.] 151

तेणं कालेणं तेणं समएणं पासे अरहा पुरिसादाणीए जे से हेमंताणं दोच्चे मासे तच्चे पक्खे पोसे-बहुले तस्स णं पोस-बहुलस्स दसमी-पक्खेणं णवण्हं मासाणं बहु-पडिपुण्णाणं अद्धट्ठमाणं राइंदियाणं विइक्कंताणं पुव्वरत्तावरत्त-समयंसि विसासाहिं णक्खत्तेणं जोगं उवागएणं आरोग्गारोग्गं दारयं पयाया। १५२

At that time, in that period, the celebrated Arhat Pārśva, on the completion of full 9 months and 7½ day-nights, was born, in the second month of winter, in the third fortnight, on the tenth day of the dark half of Pauṣa, at the confluence of the two halves of the night, when the moon was in conjunction with the asterism Viśākhā, in a perfectly healthy state, as a son unto Vāmā-devī, who herself was in a healthy state. 152

[जं रयणिं च णं अरहा पुरिसादाणीए जाए तं रयणिं च णं बहूहिं देवेहिं देवीहि य उवयंतेहि य उप्पयंतेहि य उज्जोविया वि होत्था।] जं रयणिं च णं पासे अरहा पुरिसादाणीए जाए तं रयणिं च णं बहूहिं देवेहिं देवीहि य उवयंतेहिं

उप्पयंतेहिं (देवुज्जोए एगालोए लोए देव-सण्णिवाया) उप्पि जलमाण-भूया कह-कहग भूया यावि होथ्था। १५३

During the night when the celebrated Arhat Pārśva was born, the world was lit bright by the descending and ascending of many gods and goddesses. During the night when the celebrated Arhat Pārśva was born, because of the descending and ascending of many gods and goddesses, [the world was lit bright by an array of divine lights,] and was filled with the noise,— 'what's this ?' 'Why this ?' 153

जम्मणं सव्वं पासाभिलावेणं भाणियव्वं जाव...तं होउ णं कुमारे पासे णामेणं। १५४

The details of birth, etc., to be repeated as before, by suitably substituting 'Pārśva',... till "for that reason, this our boy be named Pārśva". 154

पासे णं अरहा पुरिसादाणीए दक्खे दक्ख-पाइण्णे पडिरूवे अल्लीणे भद्दाए विणीए तीसं वासाइं अगारवास-मज्झे वसित्ता पुणरवि लोगंतिएहिं जीय-कप्पियेहिं देवेहिं ताहि इट्ठाहिं जाव...एवं वयासी: १५५

Intelligent by birth, with promise to be intelligent, perfect in beauty, self-controlled, bearing auspicious marks and gentle, the celebrated Arhat Pārśva, having spent 30 years in the household order, was, as per established custom, addressed by the Lokāntika gods in words pleasing, etc.,... till in the following manner: 155

जय २ णंदा। जय २ भद्दा। भद्दं ते खत्तिय-वर-वसभा। बुज्झाहि भगवं लोग णाहा सयल-जगज्जीव-हियं पवत्तेहि धम्म-तित्थं परहिय-सुह-णिस्सेयस-करं सव्व-लोए सव्व-जीवाणं भविस्सइ। त्ति कट्टु जय-जय-सद्दं पउंजंति। १५६

"Victory be to thee, the joy of the world !
Victory be to thee, oh noble one !
Glory be to thee !
Oh bull among the best of kṣatriyas !

Awake oh *Bhagavān*, Master of the world !
Establish now the order
That for all beings in the world
May be most excellent and beneficial,
Oh the giver of highest happiness and bliss."

So saying, (they) repeated the shout of victory. 156

पुव्विं पि णं पासस्स अरहओ पुरिसादाणीयस्स माणुस्सगाओ गिहत्थधम्माओ अणुत्तरे आहोहिए अप्पडिवाई णाण-दंसणो होत्था । तए णं पासे अरहा पुरिसादाणीए तेणं अणुत्तरेणं आहोहिएणं णाण-दंसणेणं अप्पणो णिक्खमण-कालं आभोएइ । आभोएइत्ता चिच्चा हिरण्णं चिच्चा सुव्वन्णं चिच्चा धणं चिच्चा धण्णं चिच्चा रज्जं चिच्चा रट्ठं एवं बलं वाहणं कोसं कोट्ठागारं चिच्चा पुरं चिच्चा अंतेउरं चिच्चा जणवयं चिच्चा धण-कणग-रयण-मणि-मोत्तिय-संख-सिल-प्पवाल-रत्तरयणमाइयं संत-सार-सावएज्जं विच्छड्डइत्ता विग्गोवइत्ता दाणं दायारेहिं परिभाइत्ता ।

Even before the celebrated Arhat Pārśva courted the life of a householder, so coveted by the habits of men, he was in possession of unprecedented, unlimited and unimpeded knowledge and faith. So, with this unprecedented knowledge and faith, the celebrated Arhat Pārśva perceived the time of his renunciation. On perceiving this, he gave up his silver, his gold, his wealth, his granaries, his majesty, his kingdom, his army, his transport, his treasury, his store, his town, his *seraglio* and his subjects, and having given these up, and having discarded riches, gold, precious stones, jewels, pearls, conches, stones, corals, rubies and many other valuable objects, he had them distributed by donors (assistants) among indigent persons.

दाणं दाइयाणं परिभाइत्ता जे से हेमंताणं दोच्चे मासे तच्चे पक्खे पोसबहुले तस्स णं पोस बहुलस्य इक्कारसी दिवसेणं पुव्वण्ह-काल-समयंसि विसालाए सिवियाए स देव-मणुयासुराए परिसाए समणुगम्ममाण-मग्गे संखिय-चक्किय-मंगलिय-मुहमंगलीय-वद्धमाण पूसमाण-घंटिय-गणेहिं ताहिं इट्ठाहिं कंताहि पियाहिं मणुण्णाहिं मणामापहिं ओरालाहिं कल्लाणाहिं सिवाहिं धण्णाहिं मंगल्लाहिं मिय-महुर-सस्सिरियाहिं हियय पल्पाय णिज्जाहिं अट्ठसइयाहिं अपुणरुत्ताहिं वग्गूहिं अभिणंदमाणा २ अभिसंथुणमाणा २ य एवं वयासी :

Having distributed them among indigent persons, in the second month of winter, in the third fortnight, being the eleventh day of the dark half of Pauṣa, in the early hours of the day, riding in a palanquin named Viśālā, he moved out through the city of Vārāṇasī, followed by groups of gods, men and *asuras*, and was surrounded by conch-blowers, bearers of arms, priests, courtiers, carrier-men, heralds, bards, bell-bearers, and these, while moving with him, showered on him praise and hymns with words high, kind, dear, pleasant, noble, helpful, auspicious, fortunate, well-meaning, measured-sweet-decent, heart-pleasing, such 108 words ever-fresh:

जय २ णंदा। जय २ भद्दा। भद्दं ते अभग्गेहिं णाण-दंसण-चरित्तेहिं अजियाइं जिणाहि इंदियाइं जियं च पालेहि समण-धम्मं जिय-विग्घो वि य वसाहि तं देव। सिद्धि-मज्झे। णिहणाहि राग-दोस-मल्ले तवेणं धिइ-धणिय-वद्ध-कच्छे मद्दाहि अट्ठ-कम्म-सत्तू झाणेणं उत्तमेणं सुक्केणं अप्पमत्तो हराहि आराहणा पडागं च वीर। तेलुक्क-रंग-मज्झे पाव य वितिमिरं अणुत्तरं केवल-वर-णाणं गच्छ य मुक्खं परं पयं जिणवरोवइट्ठेण मग्गेणं अकुडिलेणं हंता परीसह-चमुं। जय २ खत्तिय-वर-वसभा। बहुइं दिवसाइं बहुइं पक्खाइं बहुइ मासाइं बहुइं उऊइं बहुइं अयणाइं बहुइं संवच्छराइं अभीए परिसहोवसग्गाणं खंति-खमे भय-भेरवाणं धम्मे ते अविग्घं भवउ। त्ति कट्टु जय-जय-सद्दं पउंजंति।

"Victory be to the joy of the world !
Victory be to one with auspicious marks !
Glory be to thee.
Conquer thy unconquered senses
By unmutilated knowledge, faith and conduct,
Follow thee a *śramaṇa's* life, rightly acquired.
Oh Lord ! Conquering all obstructions,
Live thee in perfection.
By penance, overpower attachment and hatred,—
The two mighty wrestlers.
Vigorously gird thy loin with steadfastness,
Crush the enemy, the eight *karmas*, by meditation —
Best and purest. Being uninfatuated,

Bear the banner of spiritual practices.
Oh hero ! In the arena of the three worlds,
Gain *kevala* knowledge and faith, supreme and best,
With no stain of obscurity.
Attain thee the highest state of liberation
By treading on the straight path,
As advised and chalked out by the best of Jinas.
Bravo ! Ye have beaten the battalion of obstructions,
Victory to thee ! A bull among the kṣatriyas.
By fearing not sundry omens and obstructions,
For many days, fortnights, months and seasons,
For many half-years and years full,
Are thee capable of fortitude and rest
Even when in the midst of fear or danger.
May thy path be harm-free."

तए णं पासे अरहा पुरिसादाणीए णयणमाला-संहस्सेहिं पिच्छिज्जमाणे २ वयणमाला-सहस्सेहिं अभिथुव्वमाणे २ हियय-माला-सहस्सेहिं उण्णंदिज्जमाणे २ मणोरह-माला-सहस्सेहिं विच्छिप्पमाणे २ कंतिरुव-गुणेहिं पच्छिज्जमाणे २ अंगुलिमाला सहस्सेहिं दाइज्जमाणे २ दाहिण-हत्थेणं बहूणं णर-णारी-सहस्साणं अंजलिमाला सहस्साइं पडिच्छमाणे २ भवणपंति-सहस्साइं समइच्छमाणे २ तंति-तल-तुडिय-घण-मुइंग-गीय-वाइय-रवेणं महुरेण य मणहरेण जय-सद्द-घोस-मीसिएणं मंजुमंजुणा घोसेण य पडिबुज्झमाणे २ सव्विड्ढीए सव्व-जूईए सव्व-बलेणं सव्ववाहणेणं सव्व-समुदएणं सव्वायरेणं सव्व-विभूईए सव्व-विभूसाए सव्व-संभमेणं सव्व-संगमेणं सव्व-पगई-एहिं सव्वणाडएणं सव्व-तालयरेहिं सव्वारोहेणं सव्व-पुप्फमल्लालंकार-विभूसाए सव्व-तुडिय-सद्द-संणिणाएणं महया इड्ढीए महया जूईए महया बलेणं महया बाहणेणं महया-वर-तुडिय-जमग-समग-प्पवाइएणं संख-पणव-पडह-भेरि-झल्लरि-खरमुहि-दुंदुहि-णिग्घोस-णाइय-रवेणं वारणसिं णगरिं मज्झं-मज्झेणं णिग्गच्छइ। णिग्गच्छित्ता जेणेव आसम-पए उज्जाणे जेणेव असोग-वर-पायवे तेणेव उवागच्छइ। उवागच्छित्ता असोग-वर-पायस्स अहे सीयं ठावेइ। ठावित्ता सीयाओ पच्चोरुहइ। पच्चोरुहित्ता सयमेव आभरण-मल्लालंकारं ओमुयइ। ओमुइत्ता सयमेव पंच-मुट्ठियं लोयं करेइ। करित्ता अट्ठमएणं भत्तेणं अपाणएणं विसाहाहिं णक्खत्तेणं जोगं उवागएणं एगं देवदूसं आदाय तीहिं पुरिस-सएहिं सद्धिं मुंडे भवित्ता अगाराओ अणगारियं पव्वइए। १५७

Then the celebrated Arhat Pārśva, moving through the city of Vārāṇasī, arrived at the park named Āśramapada, to the place where stood the most excellent *aśoka* tree. On the way he was gazed on by thousands of eyes, praised by thousands of mouths, being the object of thousands of wishes, coveted because of his splendour, beauty and virtues, pointed by thousands of fingers, responding with his right hand (to the greetings from) thousands of folded palms of several thousand men and women, moving on and on by leaving behind rows of thousands of dwellings, greeted by sweet and delightful music of *viṇā*, cymbal, *tūrya*, and great drum, with which were mixed sweet and bracing shouts of victory, and gentle and pleasant murmur of the people; accompanied by all his pomp, all his splendour, all his army, all his train, all his retinue, all his munificence, all his grandeur, all his ornaments, all his majesty, all his men, all his subjects, all his actors, all his attendants. the entire *seraglio*, with all his flowers, wreaths, ornaments and robes on; attended by the sound of all *tūryas*, with great pomp and great splendour, great army, great train, and the best of instruments, such as *tūrya*, *yamaka*, *samaka*, conch, *paṇava*, *paṭaha*, *verī*, *jhallari*, *kharamukhī*, *dundubhi* and many others.

Having moved (out of the city), he reached the most excellent *aśoka* tree in the park named Āśramapada, and ordered his palanquin to be placed beneath it. Then he came out of the palanquin. Thereafter, with his own hands, he took off his wreaths, fineries and ornaments. Having taken them off, he himself tonsured his head in five handfuls. Having done so, he courted the vow of taking food, without water, once every fourth day, missing eight meals at a time, and then having put on a divine robe, and in the company of 300 men, at the hour when the moon was in conjunction with the asterism Viśākhā, he, having given up the household order and having tonsured, joined the order of the homeless monks. 157

पासे णं अरहा पुरिसदाणीए तेसीइं राइंदियाइं णिच्चं वोसट्ठकाए चियत्तदेहे जे केइ उवसग्गा उप्पज्जंति तं जहा—दिव्वा वा माणूसा वा तिरिक्खजोणिया वा अणुलोमा वा पडिलोमा वा—ते उप्पण्णे सम्मं सहइ तितिक्खइ खमइ अहियासेइ। १५८

The celebrated Arhat Pârśva gave up the care of the body for the whole time for 83 day-nights and exposed the body to hard life. Whatever the hardship, he bore it in all respects, forgave it, overlooked it, believed it to be no hardship, howsoever severe, maybe it was created by the divine agency, or by men, animals, forces of nature, or by any other adverse forces. 158

तए णं से पासे भगवं अणगारे जाए। इरिया-समिए भासा-समिए एसणा-समिए आयाण-भंड-मत्त-णिक्खेवण-समिए उच्चार-पासवण-खेल-सिंधाण-जल्ल-पारिट्ठावणीया-समिए मण-समिए वय-समिये काय-समिए मण-गुत्ते वय-गुत्ते काय-गुत्ते गुत्तिदिए गुत्तं-बंभयारी अकोहे अमाणे अमाए अलोहे संते पसंते उवसंते परिणिव्वुडे अण सवे अममे अकिंचणे छिण्णग्गंथे णिरुवलेवे। कंस-पाईव मुक्क-तोए संखो इव णिरंजणे जीवे इव अप्पडिहयगई गगणमिव णिरवलंबणे वायुरिव अप्पडिबद्धे सारय-सलिलं व सुद्ध-हियए पुक्खर-पत्तं पिव णिरुवलेवे कुम्मो इव गुत्तिदिए खग्गि-विसाणं व एग-जाए विहग इव विप्पमुक्के भारुंड-पक्खीं इव अप्पमत्ते कुजरो इव सोडीरे वसभो इव जाय-थामे सीहो इव दुद्धरिसे मंदरो इव अप्पकंपे सागरो इव गंभीरे चंदो इव सोमलेसे सूरो इव दित्ततेए जच्च कणगं व जाय-रुवे वसुंधरा इव सव्व-फास-विसहे सुहुय-हुयासणो इव तेयसा जलंते।

Then Bhagavân Pârśva became the truly homeless: careful in movement, careful in words, careful in desires, careful in acceptance-accumulation-renunciation, careful in depositing stool, urine, phlegm, body-dirt;

Restrained in mind, restrained in words, restrained in physical activities;

Guarding his thought, guarding his words, guarding his physical activities, guarding his organs of senses, guarding his chastity;

Without anger, without pride, without attachment, without greed, calm, grave, devoid of attachment, desisted from everything, freed from compulsion;

Without ego, without possession, with the tie (of worldly bondage) cut, free from any stain of worldliness;

Liberated by giving up suffering, like bell-metal unstained by water;

Sin-free like a conch taking a black dot, without obstruction like the course of life, without support like the firmament, without bound like the wind, pure at heart like water in autumn, without a smear like the lotus leaf, with organs of senses withdrawn like a tortoise, solitary like the rhino's horn, free like the birds, ever alert like the monstrous *bhāruṇḍa*, with a high status like an elephant, born strong like an ox, invincible like a lion, steadfast like Mount Mandara, deep like an ocean, mild like the moon, effulgent in prowess like the sun, pure like fine gold, bearing (with unconcern) all touches like the earth, like fire well-fed by offerings.

णत्थि णं तस्स भगवंतस्स कत्थइ पडिबंधे। से य चउव्विहे पण्णत्ते। तं जहा—दव्वग्रो खित्तग्रो। कालग्रो, भावग्रो दव्वग्रो—सचित्ताचित्त-मीसएसु दव्वेसु। खित्तग्रो—गामे वा णगरे वा ग्ररण्णे वा खित्ते वा खले वा ग्रंगणे वा। कालग्रो—समए वा ग्रावलियाए वा ग्राणा-पाणुए वा थोवे वा खणे वा लवे वा मुहुत्ते वा ग्रहोरत्ते वा पक्खे वा मासे वा उऊए वा ग्रयणे वा संवच्छरे वा ग्रण्णयरे वा दीह-काल-संजोए। भावग्रो—कोहे वा माणे वा मायाए वा लोभे वा भये वा हासे वा पिज्जे वा दोसे वा कलहे वा ग्रबभक्खाणे वा पेसुण्णे वा पर-परिवाए वा ग्ररइ-रई वा माया-मोसे वा मिच्छा-दंसण-सल्ले वा। तस्स णं भगवंतस्स णो एवं भवइ।

No more limitation was there for him, the Venerable One. Limitations have been stated to be four: limitation of objects, limitation of space, limitation of time, limitation of subjective senses.

Limitation of objects: of animate objects, of inanimate objects, and of those in a mixed state;

Limitation of space: of a village, a town, a forest, a farm, a house or a yard;

Limitation of time : of a unit called *samaya*, of one called *āvalika*, one called *ānāpānaka* or deep-breath/respiration, of one called *stoka*, one called *kṣaṇa*, *lava*, *pakṣa*, *muhūrta*, day-night, fortnight, month, season, half-year, year, or any other time unit of a longer duration;

Limitation of subjective senses: of anger, pride, attachment, greed, fear, laughter, affection, hatred, quarrel, calumny, sharp words, meanness, scandal-mongering, pleasure and pain, deceitful falsehood and evil of wrong faith. The Bhagavān had none of these.

से णं भगवं वासा-वास-वज्जम् अट्ठ गिम्हहेमंतिए मासे—गामे एगराइए—णगरे पंच-राइए वासीचंदण-समाण-कप्पे सम-तिण-मणि-लेट्ठु-कंचणे समदुक्खसुहे इहलोग-परलोक-अप्पडिबंधे जीविय-मरणे णिरवकंखे, संसार-पारगामी, कम्म-संग-णिग्घायणट्ठाए अब्भुट्ठिए एवं च णं विहरइ।

Monsoon sojourn apart, the Bhagavān spent eight months of summer and winter as follows: if in a village, one night only in a village, five nights if in a town;

With a similar feeling towards excreta and sandal, with similar attitude to hay, jewel, clay and gold, indifferent to pleasure and pain, free from limitation in this world as well as in the next, without a hankering for life and death, destined to overcome the mundane life, born to terminate the bondage of *karma* — thus he spent his time.

तस्स णं भगवंतस्स अणुत्तरेणं णाणेणं अणुत्तरेणं दंसणेणं अणुत्तरेणं चरित्तेणं अणुत्तरेणं आलएणं अणुत्तरेणं विहारेणं अणुत्तरेणं वीरिएणं अणुत्तरेणं अज्जवेणं अणुत्तरेणं मद्दवेणं अणुत्तरेणं लाघवेणं अणुत्तराए कंतीए अणुत्तराए मुत्तीए अणुत्तराए गुत्तीए अणुत्तराए तुट्ठीए अणुत्तराए बुद्धीए अणुत्तरेणं सच्च-संजम - तव - सुचरिय - सोवचिय - फल - परिणिव्वाण - मग्गेणं अप्पाणं भावेमाणस्स तेसीइं राइंदियाइं विइक्कंताइं। चउरासीइमस्स राइंदियस्स अंतरा वट्टमाणस्स जे से गिम्हाणं पढमे मासे पढमे पक्खे चित्त-बहुले तस्स णं चित्त-बहुलस्स चउत्थी-पक्खेणं पुव्वण्ह-काल समयंसि धायइ-पायवस्स अहे छट्ठेणं भत्तेणं अपाणएणं विसाहाहिं णक्खत्तेणं जोगमुवागएणं झाणंतरियाए वट्टमाणस्स अणंते अणुत्तरे णिव्वाघाए णिरावरणे कसिणे पडिपुण्णे केवलवर-णाण-दंसणे समुप्पण्णे।

With supreme knowledge, supreme faith, supreme conduct, in stainless lodgings and blameless wanderings, with extreme valour, extreme uprightness, extreme mildness, extreme dexterity, and extreme patience, with utmost caution and utmost satisfaction, with the highest intelligence and the highest truth, restraint and penance, the Bhagavān (Arhat Pārśva) passed 83 day-nights in meditation on self on the road to liberation, which was the duly earned outcome of a right conduct. On the 84th day-night, in the first month of summer, in the first fortnight, on the fourth day of the dark half of Caitra, in the early part of the day, when the moon was in conjunction with the asterism Viśākhā, under the *dhātakī* tree, while practising the vow of taking food without water once in three days (missing in all six full meals in between), while in meditation, he attained the supreme knowledge and faith, *kevala* by name, unsurpassed, unobstructed, unlimited, complete and full.

तए णं पासे अरहा पुरिसदाणीए अरहा जाए जिणे केवली-सव्वण्णु सव्वदरिसी सदेव-मणुया-सुरस्स लोगस्स परियायं जाणइ पासइ सव्वलोए सव्व-जीवाणं आगइं गइं थिइं चवणं उववायं तक्कं मणो माणसियं भुत्तं कडं पडिसेवियं आवी-कम्मं रहो-कम्मं अरहा अ-रहस्स-भागी तं तं कालं मण-वयण-कायजोगे वट्टमाणाणं सव्व-लोए सव्व-जीवाणं सव्वभावे जाणमाणे पासमाणे विहरइ। १५९

Then the celebrated Arhat Pārśva became the venerable, victor, omniscient, all-knowing, all-observing;

Knew he and saw he now all categories of gods, men and *asuras* in all the worlds;

Knew he and saw he the conditions of all the living beings in all the worlds, — wherefrom they came, whither they go, where do they stay, when do they slip, where are they born; he knew and saw he the ideas and the thoughts in their minds, their intake, their doings, their open deeds as well as their secret deeds;

Being the most venerable from whom nothing could be kept a secret, he knew and he saw, in all respects, the state of mind, words and deeds of all the living beings in all the worlds. Thus by knowing and seeing the inner feeling of all beings in all the worlds, he lived on. 159

पासस्स णं अरहओ पुरिसदाणीयस्स अट्ठ गणा अट्ठ गणहरा[40] होत्था। तं जहा —

सुभे य अज्जघोसे य वसिट्ठे बंभयारी य।
सोमे सिरिहरे चेव वीरभद्दे जसेवी य॥ १६०

पासस्स णं अरहओ पुरिसदाणीयस्स अज्जदिण्ण-पामुक्खाओ सोलस-समण-साहस्सीओ उक्कोसिया समण-संपया होत्था। १६१

पासस्स णं अरहस्रो पुरिसादाणीयस्स पुप्फचूल-पामोक्खाओ अट्ठतीसं अज्जिया-साहस्सीओ उक्कोसिया अज्जिया-संपया होत्था। १६२

पासस्स णं अरहओ पुरिसादाणीयस्स सुव्वय-पामुक्खाणं समणोवासगाणं एगा सयसाहस्सी चउसट्ठिं च सहस्सा उक्कोसिया समणोवासगाणं संपया होत्था।। १६३

पासस्स णं अरहओ पुरिसादाणीयस्स सुणंदा-पामुक्खाणं समणोवासियाणं तिण्णि सयसाहस्सीओ सत्तवीसं च सहस्सा उक्कोसिया समणोवासियाणं संपया होत्था। १६४

The celebrated Arhat Pārśva had eight *gaṇas* and eight *gaṇadharas*. They were :

Śubha, Aśvaghoṣa, Vaśiṣṭha, Brahmacāri,
Saumya, Śrīdhara, Vīrabhadra and Yaśasvī. 160

The celebrated Arhat Pārśva had an excellent community of 16,000 *śramaṇas*, with Āryadatta at their head. 161

The celebrated Arhat Pārśva had an excellent community of 38,000 nuns, with Puṣpacūlā at their head. 162

The celebrated Arhat Pārśva had an excellent community of 1,64,000 male followers, with Subrata at their head. 163

The celebrated Arhat Pārśva had an excellent community of 3,27,000 female followers, with Sunandā at their head. 164

पासस्स णं अरहओ पुरिसदाणीयस्स अद्धुट्ठसया चउद्दस-पुव्वीणं अजिणाणं जिण-संकासाणं सव्वक्खर-संणिवाईणं जिणोविव अवितहं वागरमाणाणं उक्कोसिया चउद्दस पुव्वीणं संपया होत्था। १६५

पासस्स णं अरहओ पुरिसादाणीयस्स चउद्दससया ओहीणाणीणं दससया केवल-णाणीणं एक्कारससया वेउव्वियाणं छस्सया रिउ-मईणं दससया सिद्धा वीसं अज्जिया-सया सिद्धा अद्धट्ठम-सया विउल-मईणं छस्सया वाईणं वारस-सया अणुत्तरोव वाइयाणं। १६६

The celebrated Arhat Pārśva had an excellent community of 350 monks who were the masters of the 14 Pūrvas. Though not *Jinas*, they came very near to them, knew all combinations of letters and correctly interpreted the truth like the *Jinas* themselves. 165

The celebrated Arhat Pārśva had an excellent treasure of 1400 monks who possessed *avadhi* knowledge, 1000 who possessed the *kevala* knowledge, 1100 who could transform themselves, 600 with straight intellect, 1000 perfected males, 2000 perfected nuns, 750 with *vipula-mati* or vast intellect, 600 logicians and 1200 in their last birth. 166

पासस्स एां अरहश्रो पुरिसादाणीयस्स दुविहा अंतगड-भूमि होत्था । तं जहा—जुगंतकड-भूमि य परियायंतकड भूमि य जाव···चउत्थाश्रो पुरिस-जुगाश्रो जुगंतकड-भूमि ति-वास-परियाए अंतं अकासी । १६७

The celebrated Arhat Pārśva had instituted two epochs marking termination, one terminating a generation and the other terminating categories; the epoch terminating generation, till the fourth generation (after Pārśva); and the epoch terminating categories for three years (after his attainment of the state of omniscience). 167

तेणं कालेणं तेणं समएणं पासे अरहा पुरिसादाणीए तीसं वासाइं अगार-वास-मज्झे वसित्ता तेसीइं राइंदियाइं छउमथ्थ-परियायं पाउणित्ता देसूणाइं सत्तरि वासाइं केवलि—परियायं पाउणित्ता पडिपुण्णाइं सत्तरि वासाइं सामण्ण परियायं पाउणित्ता एक्कं वास-सयं सव्वाउयं पालइत्ता खीणे वेयणिज्जाउय-णाम-गोत्ते इमीसे श्रोसप्पणीए दूसम-सुसमाए बहु-विइक्कंताए जे से वासाणं पढमे मासे दोच्चे पक्खे सावण-सुद्धे तस्स णं सावण-सुद्धस्स अट्ठमी-पक्खेणं उप्पि सम्मेय-सेल-सिहरंसि अप्प-चउत्तीसइमे मासिएणं भत्तेणं अपाणएणं विसाहाहिं णक्खत्तेणं जोगमुवागएणं पुव्वण्ह-काल-समयंसि वग्घारिय-पाणी काल-गए जाव···सव्व-दुक्ख-प्पहीणे । १६८

In that period, at that time, the celebrated Arhat Pārśva lived as a householder for 30 years, as a monk 83 day-nights, and slightly less than 70 years as an omniscient being—full 70 years in the order of *śramaṇas,* and a hundred years on the whole. Then on the exhaustion of his *vedanīya karma,* life-span, name and lineage, when a good part of the unbracing-bracing epoch in the flow of this descension phase had passed, in the first month of the rainy season, in the second fortnight, on the eighth day of the bright half of Śrāvaṇa, when the moon was in conjunction with the asterism Viśākhā, in the early part of the day, atop Mount Sammeta, by courting the vow of taking food without water once at the end of the month, he passed away, went beyond the bounds of *karma*, was uplifted after having left the world, cut asunder the tie of birth, oldage and death, and became perfected, enlightened and liberated, the maker of the end, the liberated, the terminator of all misery. 168

पासस्स णं अरहओ पुरिसादाणीयस्स सव्व-दुक्ख-प्पहीणस्स दुवालस वास-सयाइं विइक्कंताइं तेरसमस्स य वास-सयस्स अयं तीसइमे संवच्छरे काले गच्छइ। १६९

Since the time when the celebrated Pārśva passed away, till he became the terminator of all misery, twelve centuries have passed, and of the thirteenth century, this is the thirtieth year. 169

III

जिण-चरित्तम्
अरिट्ठणेमी

Biographical Sketch of Ariṣṭanemī

Top : Ariṣṭanemi blowing Kṛṣṇa's Conch
Bottom : Kṛṣṇa trying in vain to bend Ariṣṭanemi's arm

तेणं कालेणं तेणं समएणं अरहा अरिट्ठणेमी पंच-चित्ते होत्था । तं जहा—
चित्ताहिं चुए चइत्ता गब्भं वक्कंते । चित्ताहिं जाए । चित्ताहिं मुंडे भवित्ता
अगाराओ अणगारियं पव्वइए । चित्ताहिं अणंते अणुत्तरे णिव्वाधाए
णिरावरणे कसिणे पडिपुण्णे केवल-वर-णाण-दंसणे समुप्पण्णे । चित्ताहिं
परिणिव्वुए । १७०

In that period, at that time, Ariṣṭanemi became a five-Citra. They are : at the conjunction of the moon with the asterism Citrā, he descended from the celestial abode, and entered into the womb;
At the conjunction of the moon with the asterism Citrā, he was born;
At the conjunction of the moon with the asterism Citrā, he tonsured himself, and by giving up the life of a householder, he courted the life of a homeless monk;
At the conjunction of the moon with the asterism Citrā, he attained the supreme knowledge and faith, infinite, unprecedented, unobstructed, complete and full; and
At the conjunction of the moon with the asterism Citrā, he entered into liberation. 170

तेणं कालेणं तेणं समएणं अरहा अरिट्ठणेमी जे से वासाणं चउत्थे मासे
सत्तमे पक्खे कत्तिय-बहुले तस्स णं कत्तिय-बहुलस्स बारसी पक्खेणं
अपराजियाओ महाविमाणाओ छत्तीसं सागरोवम-ट्ठिइयाओ अणंतरं चयं
चइत्ता इहेव जंबुद्दीवे दीवे भारहे वासे सोरियपुरे णयरे समुद्दविजयस्स
रण्णो भारियाए सिवाए देवीए पुव्व-रत्तावरत्त-कालसमयंसि चित्ताहिं
णक्खत्तेणं जोगमुवागएणं आहार-वक्कंतीए भव-वक्कंतीए सरीर-वक्कंतीए
कुच्छिंसि गब्भत्ताए वक्कंते । [सव्वं तहेव सुविण-दंसण-दविण-संहरणाइयं
एत्थ भाणियव्वं ।] १७१

In that period, at that time, in the fourth month of the rainy season, in the seventh fortnight, on the 12th day of the dark half of Kārttika, Ariṣṭanemi, having spent a time-span of 36 *sāgaropamas* in the great celestial abode named Aparājita, descended, and thereon, in this very isle named Jambūdvīpa, in the region named Bhārata-varṣa, he, who had exhausted his intake, his life-span, his title to the body (at the celestial abode), at the confluence of the two halves of the night, entered into the womb of Śivā devī, consort of Samudravijaya, king of Śauripura.

[The dreams, accumulation of riches, etc., to be repeated here as before.] 171

तेणं कालेणं तेणं समएणं अरहा अरिट्ठणेमी, जे से वासाणं पढमे मासे दोच्चे पक्खे सावण-सुद्धे, तस्स णं सावणसुद्धस्स पंचमी पक्खेणं णवण्हं मासाणं बहुपड़िपुण्णाणं अद्धट्ठमाणं राइंदियाणं विइक्कंताणं [उच्चट्ठाण-गएसु गहेसु पढमे चंद-जोगे सोमासु दिसासु वितिमिरासु विसुद्धासु जइएसु सव्व-सउणेसु, पयाहिणाणुकूलंसि भूमि-सप्पिंसि मारुयंसि पवायंसि णिप्फण्ण-मेयणियंसि कालंसि पमुइय-पक्किलिएसु सव्व-जाणवएसु] पुव्वरत्तावरत्त-काल-समयंसि चित्ताहिं नक्खत्तेणं जोगमुवागएणं आरोग्गारोग्गं दारयं पयाया। जम्मणं समुद्दविजयाभिलावेणं णेयव्वं जाव···तं होउ कुमारे अरिट्ठणेमी णामेणं।

In that period, at that time, after the expiry of full 9 months and 7½ days, in the first month of the rainy season, in the second fortnight, on the fifth day of the bright half of Śrāvaṇa, [when the planets had attained high positions, with the rise of the new moon, when all the directions were calm, pure and free from darkness, when as per the science of astronomy there were all good omens, when the southern wind was mildly blowing touching the ground, and when the people were happy and at play,] at the confluence of the two halves of the night, when the moon was in conjunction with the asterism Citrā, Ariṣṭanemi was born in a perfectly good health, of Śivā devī who herself was in a perfectly good health.

The account of the birth is to be repeated *in toto*, substituting the name Samudravijaya at proper places, all down to "this our boy be named Ariṣṭanemi."

अरहा अरिट्ठणेमी दक्खे पडिरूवे आलीणे भद्दए विणीए···अम्मापिईहिं देवत्त-गएहिं गुरुमहत्तरएहिं अब्भुणुण्णताए समत्त-पइण्णे पुणरवि लोयंतिएहिं जीयकप्पिएहिं देवेहिं ताहिं इट्ठाहिं कंताहिं पियाहिं मणुण्णाहिं मणामाहिं ओरालाहिं कल्लाणाहिं सिवाहिं धण्णाहिं मंगल्लाहिं मिय-महुर-सस्सिरीयाहिं अपुणरुत्ताहिं वग्गूहिं अणवरयं अभिणंदमाणा य अभिथ्थुणमाणा य एवं

वयासि ॥ "जय णंदा । जय भद्दा । भद्दं ते खत्तिय-वर-वसभा । बुज्झाहि भगवं लोग-णाहा, सयल-जगज्-जीव-हियं पवत्तेहि धम्मतिथ्थं परहिय-सुह-निस्सेयस-करं सव्वलोए सव्वजीवाणं भविस्सइ !" त्ति कट्टु जय-जय-सद्दं पउंजंति ॥ पुव्वि पि णं अरहओ अरिट्ठणेमिस्स माणुस्साओ गिहथ्थ-धम्माओ अणुत्तरे आभोइए अप्पडिवाइ णाण-दंसणे होथ्था । तए णं अरहा अरिट्ठणेमी तेणं अणुत्तरेणं आहोइएणं णाण-दंसणेणं अप्पणो णिक्खमणकालं आभोइए । त्ता चिच्चा हिरण्णं चिच्चा सुवण्णं चिच्चा धणं चिच्चा धण्णं चिच्चा रज्जं चिच्चा रट्ठं एवं वलं वाहणं कोणं कोट्ठागारं चिच्चा पुरं चिच्चा अंतेउरं चिच्चा जणवयं चिच्चा धण-कणग-रयण-मणि-मोत्तिय-संख-सिल-प्पवाल-रत्तरयणमाइयं संत-सार-सावएज्जं विच्छड्डइत्ता विग्गोव-इत्ता दाणं दायारेहिं परिभाइत्ता दाणं दाइयाणं परिभाइत्ता । १७२

Intelligent, promising, the very perfection of beauty, with full controls, bearing auspicious marks, polite... Ariṣṭanemi, at the death of his parents, with the permission of his elders and superiors, fulfilled his mission. As per the established custom, the *lokāntika* gods incessantly praised him and hymned him with these high, kind, dear, pleasant, pleasing, noble, helpful, auspicious, fortunate, well-meaning, measured-sweet-decent, heart-appealing, heart-pleasing, serious and ever-fresh words:

"Victory be to the joy of the world !
Victory be to one with auspicious marks !
Glory be to thee, oh bull among the best of kṣatriyas.
Awake oh Lord, Master of the Universe,
Establish religion and order
For the well-being of all living beings.
These will bring supreme benefit,
The best of welfare and happiness,
To all beings in all the worlds."

So saying, they shouted 'victory' again and again.

Even before Arhat Ariṣṭanemi courted the life of a householder, so coveted by the habits of men, he was in possession of unprecedented, unlimited and unimpeded knowledge and faith. So with this unprecedented and unlimited knowledge and faith, Arhat Ariṣṭanemi perceived the time of his renunciation. On perceiving this, he gave up his silver, his gold, his wealth, his granaries, his majesty, his kingdom, his army, his transport, his treasury, his store, his town, his *seraglio* and his subjects, and having given them up, having discarded riches, gold, precious stones, corals, rubies and many other valuable objects, he had them distributed by assistants among the indigent persons. 172

जे से वासाणं पढमे मासे दोच्चे पक्खे सावण-सुद्धे तस्स णं सावण-सुद्धस्स चट्ठी-पक्खेणं पुव्वण्ह-काल-समयंसि उत्तर-कुराए सीयाए सदेव-मणुयासुरेए परिसाए अणुगम्ममाण-मग्गे [संखिय-चक्किय-मंगलिय-मुह-मंगलिय वद्धमाण-पूसमाण-घंटिय-गणेहिं ताहि इट्ठाहिं कंताहिं पियाहिं मणुण्णाहिं मणामाहिं ओरालाहिं कल्लाणाहि सिवाहिं धण्णाहिं मंगल्लाहिं मिय-महुर-सस्सिरीयाहिं हियय-पल्हायणिज्जाहिं अट्ठ-सइयाहिं अपुणरुत्ताहिं वग्गूहिं गिराहिं अणवरयं अभिणंदमाणा अभिसंथुणमाणा य एवं वयासी :

In the first month of the rainy season, in the second fortnight, on the sixth day of the bright half of Śrāvaṇa, in the early part of the day, having ascended on a palanquin named Uttarakuru, he moved through the city of Dvārāvatī, followed on the way by groups of gods, men and *asuras*, and [was surrounded by conch-blowers, bearers of arms, priests, courtiers, carrier-men, heralds, bards, bell-bearers, and these showered on him praise and hymns, with words high, kind, dear, pleasant, noble, helpful, auspicious fortunate, well-meaning, measured-sweet-decent, heart-delighting 108 unrepeated (words) :

जय णंदा। जय भद्दा। भद्दं ते अभग्गेहिं णाण-दंसण-चारित्तेहिं अजियाइं जिणाहिं इंदियाइं जियं च पालेहि समण-धम्मं जियविग्घो वि य वसाहिं तं देव! सिद्धि-मज्झे णिहणाहि राग-दोस-मल्ले तवेणं धिइ-धणिय-बद्ध-कच्छे मद्दाहि अट्ठ-कम्म-सत्तू झाणेणं उत्तमेणं सुक्केणं अप्पमत्तो हराहि आराहणा-पडागं च वीर! तेलुक्क-रंग-मज्झे पाव य वितिमिरं अणुत्तरं केवल-वर-णाणं गच्छ य मुक्खं परं पयं जिण-वरोवइट्ठेण मग्गेणं अकुटिलेणं हंतापरि-सह-चमुं। जय खत्तिय-वर-वसभा। बहूइं दिवसाइं बहूइं पक्खाइं बहूइं उऊइं बहूइं अयणाइं बहुइं संवच्छराइं अभीए परीसहोवसग्गाणं खंति-खाम-भय-भेरवाणं धम्मे ते अविग्घं भवउ। -त्ति कट्टु जय-जय सद्दं पउंजंति।

"Victory be to the joy of the world !
Victory to one with auspicious marks !
Glory be to thee !

Conquer thy unconquered senses
By unmutilated knowledge, faith and conduct,
Follow thee a *śramaṇa's* life, rightly acquired.
Oh Lord ! Conquering all obstructions,
Live thee in perfection,
By penance, overpower attachment and hatred, —
The two mighty wrestlers,
Vigorously gird thy loin with steadfastness,
Crush the enemy, the eight *karmas*, by meditation —
Best and purest. Being uninfatuated,
Bear the banner of spiritual practices.
Oh hero ! In the arena of the three worlds,
Gain *kevala* knowledge and faith, supreme and best,
With no stain of obscurity.
Attain thee the highest state of liberation
By treading on the straight path,
As advised and chalked out by the best of *Jinas*.
Bravo ! You have beaten the battalion of obstructions,
Victory to thee ! A bull among the kṣatriyas.
By fearing not sundry omens and obstructions,
For many days, fortnights, months and seasons.
For many half-years and years full
Are thee capable of fortitude and rest
Even when in the midst of fear or danger.
May thy path be harm-free."

So saying they shouted 'victory' incessantly.

तए णं अरहा अरिट्ठणेमी णयण-माला-सहस्सेहिं पिच्छिज्जमाणे २ वयण-माला-सहस्सेहिं अभिथुव्वमाणे २ हियय-माला-सहस्सेहिं उण्णंदिज्जमाणे २ मणोरह-माला-सहस्सेहिं विच्छिप्पमाणे २ कंति-रूव-गुणेहिं पच्छिज्जमाणे २ अंगुलि-माला-सहस्सेहिं दाइज्जमाणे २ दाहिण-हत्थेणं बहूणं णर-णारि-सहस्साणं अंजलि-माला-सहस्साइं पडिच्छमाणे २ भवण-पंति-सहस्सेहिं समइच्छमाणे २ तंति-तल-ताल-तुडियं-घण-मुइंग-गीय-वाइय-रवेणं महुरेण य मणहरेणं जय-सद्द-घोस-मीसिएणं मंजु-मंजुणा घोसेण य पडिबुज्झमाणे सव्विड्ढीए सव्वजुईए सव्वबलेणं सव्व-वाहणेणं सव्व-समुदयेणं सव्वायरेणं सव्व-विभूईए सव्व-विभूसाए सव्व-संभमेणं सव्व-संगमेणं सव्व-पगईएहिं सव्व-णाडएणं सव्व-तालयरेहिं सव्वारोहेणं सव्व-पुप्फ-मल्लालंकार-विभूसाए

सव्व-तुडिय-सद्द-संणिणाएणं महया इड्ढीए महया जुईए महया बलेणं महया बाहणेणं महया वर-तुडिय-जमग-समग-प्पवाईएणं संख-पणव-पडह-भेरि-झल्लरि-खरमुहि-दुंदुहि-णिग्घोस-णाइय-रवेणं बारवए णगरीए मज्झं-मज्झेणं णिग्गच्छइ । -त्ता जेणेव रेवइथ उज्जाने तेणेव उवागच्छइ ॥ -त्ता असोग-वर-पायवस्स अहे सीयं ठावेइ । -त्ता सीयाओ पच्चोरुहइ । -त्ता सयमेव आभरण-मल्लालंकारं ओमुयइ । -त्ता सयमेव पंच-मुट्ठियं लोयं करेइ । -त्ता छट्ठेणं भत्तेणं अपाणएणं चित्ताहिं णक्खत्तेणं जोगमुवागएणं एगं देवदूसं आदाय एगेणं पुरिस-सहस्सेणं सद्धिं मुंडे भवित्ता अगाराओ अणगारियं पव्वइय । १७३

Then Arhat Ariṣṭanemi, gazed on by thousands of eyes, praised by thousands of mouths, extolled by thousands of hearts, being the object of thousands of wishes, coveted because of his splendour, beauty and virtues, pointed by thousands of fingers, responding with his right hand (to the greetings from) thousands of folded palms of several thousand men and women, moving on and on by leaving behind rows of thousands of dwellings;

Greeted by sweet and delightful music of *viṇā*, cymbaḷ, *tūrya* and great drum, with which were mixed sweet and bracing shouts of victory, and gentle and pleasant murmur of the people ;

Accompanied by all his pomp, all his splendour, all his army, all his train, all his retinue, all his munificence, all his grandeur, all his ornaments, all his majesty, all his men, all his subjects, all his actors, all his attendants, the entire *seraglio*, with all his flowers, wreaths, ornaments and robes on :

With the sound of all *tūryas*, with great pomp and great splendour, great army, great train, and the best of instruments, such as *tūrya*, *vamaka*, *samaka*, conch, *paṇava*, *paṭaha*, *verī*, *jallari*, *kharamukhi*, *dundubhi* and many others,] moved through the city of Dvāravāti and came outside the city.

Having come out, he ordered the palanquin to be placed beneath an excellent *aśoka* tree in a park named Revatikā. Then he came out of the palanquin. Thereafter, with his own hand, he took off his wreaths, fineries and ornaments. Having taken them off, he tonsured himself in five handfuls. Having done so, he courted the vow of taking food, devoid of water, every third day, missing in all six meals (between one meal and the other), ... till the moon was in conjunction with the asterism Citrā, at which, with a divine robe on, with one thousand men in his train, he tonsured, and having given up the household order, he entered the order of the homeless monks. 173

से अरहा णं अरिट्ठणेमी चउप्पण्णं राइंदियाइं णिच्चं वोसट्ठ-काए चियत्त-देहे—[वासी-चंदण-समाण-कप्पे सम-तिण-मणि-लेट्ठु-कंचणे सम-दुक्ख-सुहे इहलोग-परलोग-अप्पडिबद्धे जीविय-मरणे णिरवकंखे संसार-पारगामी कम्म-संग-णिग्घायणट्ठाए अब्भुट्ठिए एवं च णं विहरइ। तस्स णं भगवंतस्स] पणपण्णइमस्स राइंदियस्स अंतरा वट्टमाणस्स जे से वासाणं तच्चे मासे पंचमे पक्खे आसोय-बहुले तस्स णं आसोय-बहुलस्स पण्णरसी पक्खेणं दिवसस्स पच्छिमे भागे उज्जिंत-सेल-सिहरे वेडसपायवस्स अहे अट्ठमेणं भत्तेणं अपाणएणं चित्ताहिं णक्खत्तेणं जोगमुवागएणं झाणं-तरियाए वट्टमाणस्स अणंते अणुत्तरे णिव्वाधाए णिरावरणे कसिणे पडिपुण्णे केवल-वर-णाण-दंसणे समुप्पण्णे। [तए णं भगवं अरिट्ठणेमी अरहा जाए जिणे केवली सवण्णु सव्वदरिसी सव्व-देव-मणुयासुरस्स लोगस्स परियायं जाणइ पासइ, सव्व-लोए सव्व-जीवाणं आगइं गइं थिइं चवणं उववायं तक्कं मणो माणसियं भुत्तं कडं पडिसेवियं आवी-कम्मं रहो-कम्मं अरहा अरहस्सभागी तं तं कालं मणवयण-काय-जोगे वट्टमाणाणं] सव्व-लोए सव्व-जीवाणं भावे जाणमाणे पासमाणे विहरइ। १७४

For 54 day-nights, Arhat Ariṣṭanemi neglected the care of his body and exposed it to hardship. [Thus he lived, indifferent alike to stool and sandal, to hay, gems, pebbles and gold, to pleasure and pain, untied by this world and the next, careless of life and death, started to terminate the mundane life, and determined to end the bondage of *karma*. The said Bhagavān] on the 55th day, in the third month of the rainy season, in the fifth fortnight, on the 15th, the new moon, day of the month of Āśvina, in the later part of the day, atop Mount Ujjinta, at the foot of the *betasa* (banyan, in some reading) tree, taking food without water once every fourth day, missing in all eight meals (between one meal and the other), at the conjunction of the moon with the asterism Citrā, while in meditation, attained the supreme, *kevala* knowledge and faith, infinite, unprecedented, unobstructed, complete and full.

[Then Arhat Ariṣṭanemi became venerable, victor, omniscient, all-knowing and all-observing. Knew he and saw he all categories of gods, men and *asuras* in all the worlds. Knew he and saw he the conditions of all the living beings in all the worlds — wherefrom they come, whither they go, where do they stay, when do they slip, where are they born. Knew he and saw he the ideas, the thoughts in their mind, their intake, their doings, their open deeds as well as their secret deeds. Being the most venerable from whom nothing could be kept a secret, he knew and he saw, in all respects, the state of mind, words and deeds of all the living beings in all the worlds.] Knowing and seeing the mental state of all the beings in all the worlds, he lived and moved (on the earth). 174

अरहओ णं अरिट्ठणेमिस्स अट्ठारस गणा अट्ठारस गणहरा होत्था १७५

अरहओ णं अरिट्ठणेमिस्स वरदत्त-पामोक्खाओ अट्ठारस समण-साहस्सीओ उक्कोसिया समण-संपया होत्था । १७६

अरहओ णं अरिट्ठणेमिस्स अज्ज-जक्खिणी-पामोक्खाओ चत्तालीसं अज्जिया-साहस्सीओ उक्कोसिया अज्जिया-संपया होत्था । १७७

अरहओ णं अरिट्ठणेमिस्स णंद-पामोक्खाणं समणोवासगाणं एगा सय-साहस्सी अउणत्तरिं च सहस्सा उक्कोसिया समणोवासग-संपया होत्था । १७८

अरहओ णं अरिट्ठणेमिस्स महासुव्वय-पामोक्खाणं तिण्णि सय-साहस्सीओ अउणत्तरिं च सहस्सा उक्कोसिया समणोवासियाणं संपया होत्था । १७९

Arhat Ariṣṭanemi had 18 *gaṇas* and 18 *gaṇadharas*. 175

Arhat Ariṣṭanemi had an excellent community of 18000 monks, with Varadatta at their head. 176

Arhat Ariṣṭanemi had an excellent community of 40000 nuns, with Arya Yakṣiṇī at their head. 177

Arhat Ariṣṭanemi had an excellent community of 1,69,000 men followers, with Nanda at their head. 178

Arhat Ariṣṭanemi had an excellent community of 3,69,000 female followers, with Mahāsubrata at their head. 179

अरहओ णं अरिट्ठणेमिस्स चत्तारि सया चउद्दस-पुव्वीणं अजिणाणं जिण-संकासाणं सव्वक्खर-सण्णिवाईणं जिणो विव अवितहं वागरमाणाणं उक्कोसिया चउद्दस-पुव्वीणं संपया होत्था । १८०

Ariṣṭanemi's Marriage procession

[facing p. 104

पण्णरस सया ओहि-णाणीणं पण्णरस सया वेउव्वियाणं दस सया विउल-मईणं अट्ठसया वाईणं सोलससया अणुत्तरोववाइयाणं पण्णरस समणसया सिद्धा तीसं अज्जिया-सयाइं सिद्धाइं। अरहओ णं अरिट्ठणेमिस्स दुविहा अंतगड-भूमी होथ्था तं जहा—जुगंतगड-भूमीय परियायंतगड-भूमी य। जाव···अट्ठमाओ पुरिस-जुगाओ जुगंत-कड-भूमी दुवालस-परियाए अंतमकासी। १८१

Arhat Ariṣṭanemi had an excellent community of 400 monks who were masters of the 14 *Pūrvas*, and though not *Jinas* themselves, they were very near to them, knew well all the combinations of letters and correctly interpreted the truth like the *Jinas* themselves. 180

(He had an excellent community of) 1500 monks who had mastered *avadhi* knowledge, 1500 with power to transform, 1000 with mighty intellect, 1800 who were logicians, 1600 in their last birth, 1500 perfected *śramaṇas* and 3000 perfected nuns. Arhat Ariṣṭanemi had instituted two epochs marking termination — one terminating a generation, and the other terminating categories, — the epoch terminating generation ... till the eighth generation and the one terminating category, ... till 12 years after his attainment of supreme knowledge. 181

तेणं कालेणं तेणं समएणं अरहा अरिट्ठणेमी तिण्णि वास-सयाइं कुमार-वास-मज्झे वसित्ता चउपण्णं राइंदियाइं छउमथ्थ-परियायं पाउणित्ता देसूणाइं सत्तवास-सयाइं केवलि-परियायं पाउणित्ता एगं वास-सहस्सं सव्वाउयं पालइत्ता खीणे वेयणिज्जाउय-णाम-गोत्ते इमीसे ओसप्पिणीए दूसम-सूसमाए समाए बहुविइक्कंताए जे से गिम्हाणं चउथ्थे मासे अट्ठमे पक्खे आसाढ-सुद्धे तस्स णं आसाढ-सुद्धस्स अट्ठमी-पक्खेणं उप्पिं उज्जित-सेल-सिहरंसि पंचहिं छत्तीसेहिं अणगार-सएहिं सद्धिं मासिएणं भत्तेणं अपाणएणं चित्ता-णक्खत्तेणं जोगमुवागएणं पुव्व-रत्तावरत्त-काल--समयंसि णेसज्जिए कालगए विइक्कंते समुज्जाए छिण्ण-जाइ-जरा-मरण-बंधणे सिद्धे वुद्धे मुत्ते अंतगडे परिणिव्वुडे सव्व-दुक्ख-प्पहीणे। १८२

In that period, at that time, Arhat Ariṣṭanemi lived for 300 years as a bachelor, 54 days as a monk, and slightly less than 700 years as an omniscient being, 1000 years on the whole. On the completion of this life-span, on the exhaustion of his *vedanīya karma*, name and lineage, in the flow of time of this descension phase, on the expiry of many years of the unbracing-bracing phase, in the fourth month of summer, in the eighth fortnight, on the 8th day of the bright half of Āṣāḍha, on the top of Mount Ujjinta, in the company of 536 monks, taking food without water once at the expiry of a month, when the moon was in conjunction with the asterism Citrā, at the confluence of the two halves of the night, he passed away, went beyond the bounds of *karma*, was uplifted after having left the world, cut asunder the tie of birth, oldage and death, and became perfected, enlightened and liberated, the maker of the end and the terminator of all misery. 182

अरहओ णं अरिट्ठणेमिस्स कालगयस्स विइक्कंतस्स समुज्जाअस्स छिण्ण-जाइ-जरा-मरण-बंधणस्स सिद्धस्स बुद्धस्स मुत्तस्स अंतगडस्स परिणिव्वुडस्स सव्व-दुक्खप्पहीणस्स चउरासीइं वास-सहस्साइं विइक्कंताइं, पंचासीइमस्स वास-सहस्सस्स णव वास-सयाइं विइक्कंताइं, दसमस्स य वास-सयस्स अयं असीइमे संवच्छरे काले गच्छइ । १८३

Since the time when Arhat Ariṣṭanemi passed away, went beyond the bounds of *karma*, was uplifted after having left the world, cut asunder the tie of birth, oldage and death, and became perfected, enlightened and liberated, the maker of the end, the terminator of all misery, 84,000 years have elapsed, and of the 85th millennium, nine centuries have elapsed, and of the tenth century, this is the eightieth year. 183

IV

जिणचरित्तम्
वीसं तित्थगराणं

On Twenty Tirthaṅkaras

णमिस्स णं अरहओ कालगयस्स विइक्कंतस्स समुज्जाअस्स छिण्ण-जरा-जाइ-मरण-बंधणस्स सिद्धस्स बुद्धस्स मुत्तस्स अंतगडस्स परिणिव्वुडस्स सव्वदुक्ख-प्पहीणस्स पंच-वास-सय-सहस्साइं चउरासीइं च वास-सहस्साइं विइक्कंताइं, णव च वास-सयाइं विइक्कंताइं। दसमस्स य वास-सयस्स अयं असीइमे संवच्छरे काले गच्छइ। १८४

Since the passing away of Arhat Nami, since his going beyond the bounds of *karma*, since his being uplifted after having left the world, since he cut asunder the tie of birth-oldage-death, and became perfected, enlightened and liberated, the maker of the end and the terminator of all misery, 5,84,900 years have passed : thereafter, of the tenth century, this is the 80th year. 184

मुणिसुव्वयस्स णं अरहओ कालगयस्स जाव…सव्वदुक्खप्पहीणस्स एक्कारस वास-सय-सहस्साइं चउरासीइं च वाससहस्साइं णव य वास-सयाइं विइक्कंताइं। दसमस्स य वाससयस्स अयं असीइमे संवच्छरे काले गच्छइ। १८५

Since the passing away of Muni Subrata, ... till he became the terminator of all misery, 11,84,900 years have passed : thereafter, of the tenth century, this is the 80th year. 185

मल्लिस्स णं अरहओ काल-गयस्स विइक्कंतस्स समुज्जाअस्स छिण्ण-जरा-जाइ-मरण-बंधणस्स सिद्धस्स बुद्धस्स मुत्तस्स अंतगडस्स पडिणिव्वुडस्स सव्व-दुक्ख-प्पहीणस्स पण्णट्ठिं वास-सय-सहस्साइं चउरासीइं च वास-सहस्साइं णव य वाससयाइं विइक्कंताइं। दसमस्स य वास-सयस्स अयं असीइमे संवच्छरे काले गच्छइ। १८६

Since the passing away of Arhat Malli, since his going beyond the bounds of *karma*, since his being uplifted after having left the world, since he cut asunder the tie of birth-oldage-death, and became perfected, enlightened and liberated, the maker of the end, the terminator of all misery, 65,84,900 years have passed; and thereafter, of the tenth century, this is the 80th year. 186

अरस्स णं अरहओ कालगयस्स जाव···सव्व-दुक्ख-प्पहीणस्स एगे वास-कोडि-सहस्से विइक्कंते। पण्णट्ठिं वास-सय-सहस्साइं चउरासीइं च वास-सहस्साइं णव य वास-सयाइं विइक्कंताइं दसमस्स य वास-सयस्स अयं असीइमे संवच्छरे काले गच्छइ। तं च एयं : पंच-सट्ठिं लक्खा चउरासीइं सहस्सा विइक्कंता तंमि समए महावीरो णिव्वुओ। तओ परं णव य विइक्कंता दसमस्स य वास-सयस्स असीइमे संवच्छरे काले गच्छइ। [एवं अग्गओ जाव सेयंसो ताव दट्ठव्वं।] १८७

Since the passing away of Arhat Ara, ... till he became the terminator of all misery, a thousand times 65,84,900 years have passed ; thereafter, of the tenth century this is the 80th year. On the completion of his 65,84,900 years, Mahavīra passed away. Nine centuries have elapsed since then. Of the tenth century, this is the 80th year.
(To be stated like this till Śreyāṅsa.) 187

कुंथुस्स णं अरहओ जाव···-प्पहीणस्स एगे चउभागे पलिओवमे विइक्कंते पंचसट्ठिं च सय-सहस्सा चउरासीइं च वास-सहस्सा विइक्कंता। तंमि समये महावीरो णिव्वुओ। तओ परं णव य विइक्कंताइं वास-सयाइं। दसमस्स य वास-सयस्स अयं असीइमे संवच्छरे काले गच्छइ। १८८

Since the passing away of Arhat Kunthu, ... till he became the terminator of all misery, a quatrer of a *palyopama* has elapsed; thereafter, 65,84,900 years have elapsed when, Mahavīra passed away. Since then, nine centuries have elapsed, and of the tenth century, this is the 80th year. 188

संतिस्स णं अरहओ जाव···-प्पहीणस्स एगे चउभाग-ऊणे पलिओवमे विइक्कंते। पण्णट्ठिं च सय-सहस्सा चउरासीइं च वास-सहसाइं णव य वास-सयाइं। दसमस्स य वास-सयस्स अयं असीइमे संवच्छरे काले गच्छइ। १८९

Since the passing away of Arhat Śānti, ... till he became the terminator of all misery, three quarters of a *palyopama* have elapsed. After that, 65,84,900 years have passed, and of the tenth century, this is the 80th year. 189

धम्मस्स णं अरहओ जाव···-प्पहीणस्स तिण्णि सागरोवमाइं विइक्कंताइं
पण्णट्ठिं च सय-सहस्सा चउरासीइं च वास-सहस्साइं णव य वास-सयाइं ।
दसमस्स य वास-सयस्स अयं असीइमे संवच्छरे काले गच्छइ । १९०

Since the passing away of Arhat Dharma, ... till he became the terminator of all misery, time of the span of three *sāgaropamas* has elapsed ; and thereafter 65,84,900 years have passed; and of the tenth century, this is the 80th year. 190

अणंतस्स णं अरहओ जाव···-प्पहीणस्स सत्त सागरोवमाइं विइक्कंताइं
पण्णट्ठिं च सय-सहस्सा चउरासीइं च वास-सहस्साइं णव य वास-सयाइं ।
दसमस्स य वास-सयस्स अयं असीइमे संवच्छरे काले गच्छइ । १९१

Since the passing away of Arhat Ananta, ... till he became the terminator of all misery, time of the span of seven *sāgaropamas* has elapsed ; and thereafter, 65,84,900 years have passed; and of the tenth century, this is the 80th year. 191

विमलस्स णं अरहओ जाव···-प्पहीणस्स सोलस सागरोवमाइं विइक्कंताइं
पण्णट्ठिं च सय-सहस्सा चउरासीइं च वास-सहस्साइं णव य वास-सयाइं ।
दसमस्स य वास-सयस्स अयं असीइमे संवच्छरे काले गच्छइ । १९२

Since the passing away of Arhat Vimala, ... till he became the terminator of all misery, time of the span of 16 *sāgaropamas* has elapsed ; and thereafter, 65,84,900 years have passed; and of the tenth century, this is the 80th year. 192

वासुपुज्जस्स णं अरहओ जाव···-प्पहीणस्स छायालीसं सागरोवमाइं
विइक्कंताइं पण्णट्ठिं च सय-सहस्सा चउरासीइं च वास-सहस्साइं णव
य वास-सयाइं दसमस्स य वास-सयस्स अयं असीइमे संवच्छरे काले गच्छइ ।
१९३

Since the passing away of Arhat Vāsupūjya, ... till he became the terminator of all misery, time of the span of 46 *sāgaropamas* has elapsed; and thereafter, 65,84,900 years have passed; and of the tenth century, this is the 80th year. 193

सेज्जंसस्स णं अरहओ जाव···-प्पहीणस्स एगे सागरोवम-सए विइक्कंते

पण्णट्ठिं च सय-सहस्सा चउरासीइं च वास-सहस्साइं णव य वास-सयाहिं। दसमस्स य वास-सयस्स अयं असीइमे संवच्छरे काले गच्छइ। १९४

Since the passing away of Arhat Śreyânsa, till he became the terminator of all misery, time of the span of 100 *sāgaropamas* has elapsed ; and thereafter 65,84,900 years have passed; and of the tenth century, this is the 80th year. 194

सीयलस्स णं अरहओ जाव···-प्पहीणस्स एगा सागरोवम-कोडी-तिवास-अद्धणव-मासाहिय बायालीस-वास-सहस्सेहिं ऊणिया विइक्कंता। एयंमि समए वीरे णिव्वुए तओ वि य णं परं णव-वास-सयाइं विइक्कंता। दसमस्स य वास-सयस्स अयं असीइमे संवच्छरे काले गच्छइ। १९५

Since the passsing away of Arhat Sītala, ... till he became the terminator of all misery, time of the span of one crore *sāgaropamas*, less 42003 years and 8½ months, elapsed, when Vīra (i.e., Mahāvīra) passed away. Thereafter nine centuries have passed ; and of the tenth century, this is the 80th year. 195

सुविहिस्स णं अरहओ पुप्फदंतस्स जाव··प्पहीणस्स दस सागरोवम-कोडीओ विइक्कंताओ तिवास-अद्धणव-मासाहिय बायालीस-वास-सहस्सेहिं ऊणिया। एयंमि समए वीरे णिव्वुए। तओ वि य णं परं णव-वास-सयाइं विइक्कंताइं। दसमस्स य वास-सयस्स अयं असीइमे संवच्छरे काले गच्छइ। १९६

Since the passing away of Arhat Subidhi Puṣpadanta, ... till he became the terminator of all misery, time of the span of 10 crores of *sāgaropamas*, less 42003 years and 8½ months, elapsed, when Vīra passed away. Thereafter nine centuries have passed, and of the tenth century, this is the 80th year. 196

चंदप्पहस्स णं अरहओ जाव ··-प्पहीणस्स एगं सागरोवम-कोडी-सयं विइक्कंतं तिवास-अद्धणव-मासाहिय-बायालीस वास-सहस्सेहिं ऊणगं। एयंमि समए वीरे णिव्वुए। तओ वि य णं परं णव-वास-सयाइं विइक्कंताइं। दसमस्स य वास-सयस्स अयं असीइमे संवच्छरे काले गच्छइ। १९७

Since the passing away of Arhat Candraprabha, ... till he became the terminator of all misery, time of the span of 100 crores of *sāgaropama*, less 42003 years and 8½ months, elapsed, when Vīra passed away. Thereafter nine centuries have passed; and of the tenth century, this is the 80th year. 197

सुपासस्स णं अरहओ जाव ···-पहीणस्स एगे सागरोवमकोडी-सहस्सा विइक्कंता तिवास-अद्धणव-मासाहिय-बायालीस-सहस्सेहिं ऊणिया । एयंमि समए वीरे णिव्वुए। तओ वि य णं परं णव-वास-सयाइं विइक्कंताइं । दसमस्स य वास-सयस्स अयं असीइमे संवच्छरे काले गच्छइ । १९८

Since the passing away of Arhat Supārśva, ... till he became the terminator of all misery, time of the span of 1000 crores of *sāgaropamas*, less 42003 years and 8½ months, elapsed, when Vīra passed away. Thereafter, nine centuries have passed ; and of the tenth century, this is the 80th year. 198

पउमप्पभस्स णं अरहओ जाव ···-पहीणस्स दस सागरोवम-कोडि-सहस्सा विइक्कंता तिवास-अद्धणव-मासाहिय-बायालिस-सहस्सेहिं ऊणिया । एयंमि समए वीरे णिव्वुए। तओ वि य णं परं णव-वास-सयाइं विइक्कंताइं । दसमस्स य वास-सयस्स अयं असीइमे संवच्छरे काले गच्छइ । १९९

Since the passing away of Arhat Padmaprabha, ... till he became the terminator of all misery, time of the span of 10,000 crores of *sāgaropamas*, less 42003 years and 8½ months, elapsed, when Vīra passed away. Thereafter nine centuries have passed; and of the tenth century, this is the 80th year. 199

सुमइस्स णं अरहओ जाव ···-पहीणस्स एगे सागरोवमकोडि-सय-सहस्से विइक्कंते तिवास-अद्धणव-मासाहिय-बायालिस सहस्सेहिं ऊणगे । एयंमि समए वीरे णिव्वुए ; तओ वि य णं परं णव-वास-सयाइं विइक्कंताइं । दसमस्स य वास-सयस्स अयं असीइमे संवच्छरे काले गच्छइ । २००

Since the passing away of Arhat Sumati, ... till he became the terminator of all misery, time of the span of 100,000 crores of *sāgaropamas*, less 42003 years and 8½ months, elapsed, when Vīra passed away. Thereafter, nine centuries have passed ; and of the tenth century, this is the 80th year. 200

अभिणंदणस्स णं अरहओ जाव···-पहीणस्स दस सागरोवम कोडि-सय-सहस्सा विइक्कंता तिवास-अद्धणव-मासाहिय-बायालिस-सहस्सेहिं ऊणिया । एयंमि

समए वीरे णिव्वुए। तम्रो वि य णं परं णव-वास-सयाइं विइक्कंताइं।
दसमस्स य वास-सयस्स अयं असीइमे संवच्छरे काले गच्छइ। २०१

Since the passing away of Arhat Abhinandana, ... till he became the terminator of all misery, time of the span of 10,00,000 crores of *sāgaropamas*, less 42003 years and 8½ months, elapsed, when Vira passed away. Thereafter, nine centuries have passed ; and of the tenth century, this is the 80th year. 201

संभवस्स णं अरहओ जाव -पहीणस्स वीसं-सागरोवमकोडि-सय-सहस्सा विइक्कंता तिवास-अद्धणव-मासाहिय-वायालिस-सहस्सेहिं ऊणिया। एयंमि समए वीरे णिव्वुए। तओ वि य णं परं णव-वास-सयाइं विइक्कंताइं।
दसमस्स य वास-सयस्स सयं असीइमे संवच्छरे काले गच्छइ। २०२

Since the passing away of Arhat Sambhava, ... till he became the terminator of all misery, time of the span of 20,00,000 crores of *sāgaropamas*, less 42003 years and 8½ months, elapsed, when Vīra passed away. Thereafter, nine centuries have passed ; and of the tenth century, this is the 80th year. 202

अजियस्स णं अरहओ जाव···पहीणस्स पन्नासं सागरोवमकोडि-सय-सहस्सा विइक्कंता तिवास-अद्धणव-मासाहिय-वायालिस-सहस्सेहिं ऊणिया। एयंमि समए वीरे णिव्वुए। तयो वि य णं परं णव-वास-सयाइं विइक्कंताइं।
दसमस्स य वास-संयस्स अयं असीइमे संवच्छरे काले गच्छइ। २०३

Since the passing away of Arhat Ajita, ... till he became the terminator of all misery, time of the span of 50,00,000 crores of *sāgaropamas*, less 42003 years 8½ months elapsed, when Vīra passed away. Thereafter nine centuries have passed; and of the tenth century, this is the 80th year. 203

V

जिण-चरित्तम्
उसभे

Biographical Sketch of Arhat Ṛṣabha

तेणं कालेणं तेणं समएणं उसभे अरहा कोसलिए चउ-उत्तरासाढे अभीइ-
पंचमे होत्था । २०४

तं जहा—उत्तरासाढाहि चुए चइत्ता गब्भं वक्कंते । उत्तरासाढाहिं जाए । उत्तरासाढाहिं मुंडे भवित्ता अगाराओ अणगारियं पव्वइए । उत्तरासाढाहिं अणंते अणुत्तरे णिव्वाधाए णिरावरणे कसिणे पडिपुण्णे केवल-वर-णाण-दंसणे समुप्पण्णे । अभीइणा परिणिव्वए । २०५

In that period, at that time, four auspicious events in the life of Arhat Ṛṣabha took place when the moon was in conjunction with the asterism Uttarāṣāḍha, and the fifth one took place when it was in conjunction with the asterism Abhijit. 204

They are :

When the moon was in conjunction with the asterism Uttarāṣāḍha, he descended from the celestial abode and entered into the womb ;

When the moon was in conjunction with the asterism Uttarāṣāḍha, he was born ;

When the moon was in conjunction with the asterism Uttarāṣāḍha, he tonsured, and by giving up the life of a householder, courted the life of a homeless monk ;

When the moon was in conjunction with the asterism Uttarāṣāḍha, he attained the supreme knowledge and faith, infinite, unprecedented, unobstructed, unshrouded, complete and full;
(But) when the moon was in conjunction with the asterism Abhijit, he entered into liberation. 205

तेणं कालेणं तेणं समएणं उसभे णं अरहा कोसलिए जे से गिम्हाणं चउत्थे मासे सत्तमे पक्खे आसाढ-बहुले तस्स णं आसाढ-बहुलस्स चउत्थीपक्खेणं सव्वट्ठसिद्धाओ महाविमाणाओ तित्तीसं-सागरोवम-ट्ठिइयाओ अणंतरं चयं चइत्ता इहेव जंबुद्दीवे दीवे भारहे वासे इक्खाग-भूमीए णाभिस्स कुलगरस्स मारुदेवीए भारियाए पुव्वरत्तावरत्त-काल-समयंसि आहार-वक्कंतीए भव-वक्कंतीए सरीर-वक्कंतीए उत्तरासाढानक्खत्तेणं जोगमुवागएणं कुच्छिंसि गब्भत्ताए वक्कंते । २०६

In that period, at that time, Arhat Ṛṣabha of Kośala, in the fourth month of summer, in the seventh fortnight, on the fourth day in the dark half of Āṣāḍha, having spent a time-span of 33 *sāgaropamas* in the celestial abode named Sarvārthasiddhi, descended, and as he had already exhausted there his intake, his life-span and the use of his physical body, at the confluence of the two halves of the (aforesaid) night, he entered into the womb of Māru devī, consort of patriarch Nābhi, in the land of the Ikṣvākus, in the region named Bhāratavarṣa, in this isle named Jambūdvīpa. 206

उसभे णं अरहा कोसलिए तिण्णाणोवगए होथ्था। तं जहा—चइस्सामि त्ति जाणइ, चयमाणे ण जाणइ चुएमि त्ति जाणइ। जं रयणिं च णं अरहा उसभे णाभिस्स कुलगरस्स भारियाए मारु-देवीए कुच्छिसि गब्भत्ताए वक्कंते तं रयणिं णं सा मारुदेवी सयणिज्जंसि सुत्त-जागरा ओहीरमाणी २ इमे एयारुवे ओराले कल्लाणे सिवे धण्णे मंगले सस्सिरीए चोद्दस महासुमिणे पासइ। तं जहा—गय वसह गाहा। [सव्वं तहेव णवरं पढमं उसहं मुहेण आइंतं पासइ सेसाओ गयं। णाभिकुलगरस्स साहइ। सुविणपाढ़गा णथ्थि। णाभि-कुलगरो सयमेव वागरेइ] २०७

Arhat Ṛṣabha was the master of three types of knowledge. Knew he, 'I shall descend' ; knew he not at the time of descending ; knew he, 'I have descended'. The night during which Arhat Ṛṣabha of Kośala entered as an embryo into the womb of Māru devī, consort of patriarch Nābhi, during that night, she, lying half asleep and half awake, saw 14 great dreams, noble, beautiful, blissful, blest, auspicious and fortunate. They are : an elephant, an ox, etc., [all as aforesaid, difference being, at first an ox, with its face uplifted, as if ready to make a charge, and an elephant last of all. Māru devī narrated the dreams to patriarch Nābhi. There being at that time no interpreters of the dreams, the patriarch himself interpreted them.] 207

तेणं कालेणं तेणं समएणं उसभे णं जे से गिम्हाणं पढमे मासे पढमे पक्खे चित्त-बहुले तस्स णं चित्तबहुलस्स अट्ठमी-पक्खेणं णवण्हं मासाणं बहु-पडिपुण्णाणं अद्धट्ठमाणं राइंदियाणं विइक्कंताणं (उच्चट्ठाण-गएसु गहेसु जइएसु सव्व-सउणेसु पयाहिणाणुकुलंसि भूमी-सप्पिंसि मारुयंसि पवायंसि

णिप्फण्ण-मेयणींसि कालंसि पमुइय पक्कीलिएसु सव्य-जणवएसु] पुव्वरत्ताव-
रत्त-काल-समयंसि उत्तरासाढाहिं नक्खत्तेणं जोगमुवागएणं आरोग्गारोग्गं
दारगं पयाया। २०८

In that period, at that time, in the first month of summer, in the first fortnight, on the eighth day of the dark half of Caitra, on the expiry of full 9 months and 7½ days (of stay in the womb), [when the planets were located high, the stars gave out good omens, the favourable south wind was blowing touching the ground, and the earth being full of grains, people were happy and at play,] at the confluence of the two halves of the night, when the moon was in conjunction with the asterism Uttarāṣāḍha, Māru devī, who was in perfect health, gave birth to a son, who was also in perfect health 208

जं रयणिं च णं उसभे जाए तं रयणिं च णं बहूहिं देवेहिं देवीहि य
उवयंतेहिं उप्पयंतेहि य [देवुज्जोए एगालोए लोए देव-संणिवाया] उप्पिं-
जलमाण-भूया कह-कहग-भूया यावि होत्था।

जं रयणिं च णं उसभे जाए तं रयणिं च णं बहवे वेसमण-कुंड-धारि-तिरिय
जंभगा देवा देवीओ य णाभिकुलगरस्स भवणंसि हिरण्ण-वासं च सुवण्ण वासं च
वइर-वासं च वथ्थ-वासं च आभरण-वासं च पत्त-वासं च पुप्फ-वासं च फल-वासं
च वीय-वासं च मल्ल-वासं च गंध-वासं च वण्ण-वासं च चुण्ण-वासं च वसुहार-
वासं च वासिंसु। [सेसं तहेव चारग-सोहणं माणुम्माणवद्धणं उस्सुंकमाइयं
ठिइ-पडिय-जव-वज्जं सव्वं भाणियव्वं]। २०९

During the night when Ṛṣabha was born, because of the ascending and descending of many gods and goddesses, [the glitter of the *vimānas* of gods mingling with that of the abodes of men, lighting the whole universe, because of this movement] the world became terror-stricken, and everywhere there was a confusion and uproar — 'What's this ?' 'Why this ?' During the night when Ṛṣabha was born, many order-bearers of Vaiśramaṇa, the gods from the animal and *jṛmbhaka* worlds, showered in the abode of patriarch Nābhi silver and gold, jewels, garments, ornaments, leaves, flowers, fruits, seeds, wreaths, perfumes, sandal-wood, powder and riches. [The rest as aforesaid. Not to be stated are: the release of the prisoners, remisssion of excises and customs, increase in weight and measures, and the performance of the rites of *sthiti-pratijyā* and *yūpa.*) 209

उसभेणं अरहा कोसलिए कासवे गोत्तेणं । तस्स णं पंच णामधेज्जा एवमाहिज्जंति। तं जहा—उसभे इ वा पढम-राया इ वा पढम-भिक्खाचरे इ वा पढम-जिणे इ वा पढम-तिथ्थयरे इ वा । २१०

Arhat Ṛṣabha of Kośala belonged to the line of Kāśyapa and was known by five names : Ṛṣabha, First Monarch, First Mendicant, First *Jina*, First *Tīrthaṅkara.* 210

उसभे णं अरहा कोसलिए दक्खे दक्ख-पइण्णे पडिरुवे अल्लीणे भद्दए विणीए वीसं पुव्व-सय-सहस्साइं कुमार-वास-मज्झे वसइ । वसित्ता तेवट्ठिं पुव्व-सय-सहस्साइं रज्ज-वास-मज्झे वसइ तेवट्ठिं पुव्व-सय-सहस्साइं रज्ज-वास-मज्झे वसमाणे लेहाइयाओ गणिय-प्पहाणओ सउण-रुय-पज्जवसाणाओ वावत्तरिं कलाओ चउसट्ठिं च महिला-गुणे सिप्प-सयं च, कम्माणं तिन्नि वि पया-हियाए उवदिसइ उवदिसइत्ता पुत्त-सयं रज्ज-सए अभिसिंचइ अभिसिंचइत्ता पुणरवि लोयंतिएहिं जिय-कप्पि-एहिं देवेहिं ताहिं इट्ठाहिं कंताहिं पियाहिं मणुण्णाहिं मणंमाहिं ओरालाहिं कल्लाणाहिं सिवाहिं धण्णाहिं मंगल्लाहिं मिय-महुर-सस्सिरीयाहिं हियय-गमणिज्जाहिं हियय-पल्हायणिज्जाहिं गंभीराहिं अपुणरुत्ताहिं वग्गूहिं अणवरयं अभिणण्दमाणा य अभिथ्थुणमाणा य एवं वयासि ।

Intelligent, promising, perfect in beauty, wholly self-controlled, gentle and polite, Arhat Ṛṣabha of Kośala lived as a prince for 20,00,000 *pūrvas* and as a monarch for 63,00,000 *pūrvas.** During his reign, he taught, for the good of his people, 72 arts, 64 feminine accomplishments, 100 crafts and 3 professions. Of the 72 arts, the first one is writing, the most important is arithmetic, and the last one is the knowledge of the meaning of omens. Having imparted these to his people, he anointed his one hundred sons as kings. After they had been so anointed/enthroned, as per the established customs and practices, the *lokāntika* gods appeared and incessantly praised and hymned him with these high, kind, dear, pleasant, pleasing, noble, helpful, auspicious, fortunate, well-meaning, measured-sweet-decent, heart-appealing, heart-pleasing, grave and ever-fresh words:

*According to Hermann Jacobi, "They are those long periods by which the length of the early *tīrthaṅkara's* life is measured."—*Ācārāṅga Sūtra* I-6, 3, §2 Note 1.

"जय जय णंदा ! जय जय भद्दा ! भद्दं ते खत्तिय-वर वसभा ! बुजझाहि भगवं लोग-णाहा ! सयल-जगज्-जीव-हियं पवत्तेहि धम्म-तित्थं पर-हिय-सुह-णिस्सेयस-करं सव्व-लोए सव्व-जीवाणं भविस्सइ !" त्ति कट्टु जय-जय-सद्दं पउंजंति।

"Victory be to the joy of the world !
Victory be to one with auspicious marks !
Glory be to thee, oh bull among the best of kṣatriyas.
Awake oh Lord, Master of the Universe,
Establish religion and order
For the well-being of all living beings.
These will bring supreme benefit,
The best of welfare and happiness,
To all beings in all the worlds."

So saying, they shouted victory again and again.

पुव्विं पि णं अरहओ उसभस्स कोसलियस्स माणुस्साओ गिहत्थ-धम्माओ अणुत्तरे आभोइए अप्पडिवाई णाण-दंसणे होत्था। तए णं उसभे तेणं अणुत्तरेणं आभोइएणं णाण-दंसणेणं अप्पणे णिक्खमणकालं आभोइए, आभोएइत्ता चिच्चा हिरण्णं चिच्चा सुवण्णं चिच्चा धणं चिच्चा रज्जं चिच्चा रट्ठं एवं बलं वाहणं कोसं कोट्ठागारं चिच्चा पुरं चिच्चा अंतेउरं चिच्चा धण-कणग-रयण-मणि-मोत्तिय-संख-सिल-प्पवाल-रत्तरयणमाइयं संत-सार-साव-एज्जं विच्छाडइत्ता विग्गोवइत्ता दाणं दायारेहिं परिभाइत्ता दाणं दाइयाणं परिभाइत्ता।

Even before Arhat Ṛṣabha courted the life of a householder, so coveted by the habits of men, he was in possession of unprecedented, unlimited and unimpeded knowledge and faith. So with this unprecedented and unlimited knowledge and faith, Arhat Ṛṣabha perceived the time of his renunciation. On perceiving this, he gave up his silver, his gold, his wealth, his granaries, his majesty, his kingdom, his army, his transport, his treasury, his store, his town, his *seraglio* and his subjects; and having given these up, and having discarded riches, gold, precious stones, jewels, pearls, conches stones, corals, rubies, and many other valuable objects, he had them distributed by the assistants among indigent persons.

जे से गिम्हाणं पढमे मासे पढमे पक्खे चित्त-बहुले तस्स णं चित्तवहुलस्स अट्ठमी पक्खेणं दिवसस्स पच्छिमे भागे सुदंसणाए सिवियाए सदेव-मणुया-सुराए परिसाए समणुगम्ममाणमग्गे संखिय-चक्किय-मंगलिय-मुह-मंगलिय-वद्धमाण-पूसमाण-घंटिय-गणेहिं ताहिं इट्ठाहिं कंताहिं पियाहिं मणुण्णाहिं मणामाहिं ओरालाहिं कल्लाणाहिं सिवाहिं धण्णाहिं मंगल्लाहि मिय-महुर-सस्सिरीयाहिं हियय-पल्हायणिज्जाहिं अट्ठसइयाहिं अपुणरुत्ता हिं वग्गूहिं अभिणंद-माण अभिसंथुणमाणा य एवं वयासी :

(Having done so), in the first fortnight of the first month of summer, on the eighth day of the dark half of Caitra, towards the latter part of the day, having ascended a palanquin named Sudarśanā, he set out through the city of Vinitā and arrived outside the city in the park named Siddhārthavana under the most excellent *aśoka* tree. He was followed on the way by groups of men, gods and *asuras*, and was surrounded by conch-blowers, bearers of arms, priests, courtiers, carrier-men, heralds, bards, bell-bearers, and these showered on him praise and hymns with 108 words high, kind, dear, pleasant, noble, helpful, auspicious, fortunate, well-meaning, measured-sweet-decent, heart-appealing, heart-pleasing, grave and ever-fresh.

जय जय णंदा ! जय जय भद्दा ! भद्दं ते ! अभग्गेहिं नाण-दंसण-चरित्तेहिं अभियाइं जिणाहिं इंदियाइं जियं च पालेहि समणधम्मं जिय-विग्धो वि-य वसाहिं तं देव ! सिद्धिमज्झे, निहणाहिं राग-दोस-मल्ले तवेणं धिइ-धणिय-बद्ध-कच्छे मद्दाहि अट्ठ-कम्म-सत्तू झाणेणं उत्तमेणं सुक्केणं, अप्पमत्तो हराहि आराहणापडागं च, वीर ! तेल्लोक्क-रंगमज्झे पाव य वितिमिरं अणुत्तरं केवल-वर-णाणं गच्छ य मुक्खं परं पयं जिण-वरोवइट्ठेण मग्गेणं अकुडिलेणं हंता परीसह-चमुं । जय जय खत्तिय-वर-वसभा ! बहूइं दिवसाइं बहूइं पक्खाइं बहूइं मासाइं बहूइं उऊइं बहूइं अयणाइं बहूइं संवच्छराइं अभीए परीसहोवसग्गाणं खंति-खमे भय-भेखाणं धम्मे ते अविग्ध भवउ ! त्ति कटटु जय-जय सद्दं पउंजंति ।

"Victory be to the joy of the world !
Victory to one with auspicious marks !
Glory be to thee !
Conquer thy unconquered senses
By unmutilated, knowledge, faith and conduct,

Follow thee a *śramaṇa's* life, rightly acquired.
Oh Lord ! Conquering all obstructions,
Live thee in perfection,
By penance, overpower attachment and hatred, —
The two mighty wrestlers.
Vigorously gird thy loin with steadfastness,
Crush the enemy, the eight *karmas*, by meditation —
Best and purest. Being uninfatuated,
Bear the banner of spiritual practices.
Oh hero ! In the arena of the three worlds,
Gain *kevala* knowledge and faith, supreme and best,
With no stain of obscurity.
Attain thee the highest state of liberation
By treading on the straight path,
As advised and chalked out by the best of *Jinas*.
Bravo ! You have bitten the battalion of obstructions.
Victory to thee ! A bull among the kṣatriyas.
By fearing not sundry omens and obstructions,
For many days, fortnights, months and seasons,
For many half-years and years full
Are thee capable of fortitude and rest
Even when in the midst of fear and danger.
May thy path be harm free ! "

So saying, they shouted victory again and again.

तए णं उसभे कोसलिए णयण-माला-सहस्सेहिं पिच्छिज्जमाणे पिच्छिज्जमाणे वयण-माला-सहस्सेहिं अभिथुव्वमाणे अभिथुव्वमाणे हियय-माला-सहस्सेहिं उण्णंदिज्जमाणे उण्णंदिज्जमाणे मणोरहमाला-सहस्सेहिं विच्छिप्पमाणे विच्छिप्पमाणे कंति-रूव-गुणेहिं पच्छिज्जमाणे पच्छिज्जमाणे अंगुलि-माला-सहस्सेहिं दाइज्जमाणे दाइज्जमाणे दाहिण-हथ्थेणं बहूणं णर-णारी-सहस्साणं अंजलि-माला-सहस्साइं पडिच्छमाणे पडिच्छमाणे भवण-पंति-सहस्साइं समइच्छमाणे समइच्छमाणे तंति-तल-ताल-तुडिय-घण-मुइंग-गीय-वाइय-खेणं महुरेण य मणहरेणं जय-सद्द-घोस-मीसिएणं मंजु-मंजुणा घोसेण य पडिबुज्झमाणे पडिबुज्झमाणे सव्विड्ढीए सव्वजुईए सव्व-बलेणं सव्व-वाहणेणं सव्व-समुदएणं सव्वायरेणं सव्व-विभूइए सव्व-विभूसाए सव्व-संभमेणं सव्व-संगमेणं सव्व-पगईएहिं सव्व-णाडएणं सव्व-तालायरेहिं सव्वो-रोहेणं सव्व-पुप्फमल्लालंकार-विभूसाए सव्व-तुडिय-सद्द-संणिणाएणं महया

इड्ढीए महया जुईए महया बलेगं महया वाहणेणं महयावर-तुडिय-जमग-समग-प्पवाइएणं संख-पणव-पडह-भेरि-झल्लरि-खरमुहि-दुंदुहि-णिग्घोस-णाइय-रवेणं विणीयं-रायहाणि मज्झंमज्झेणं णिग्गच्छइ ।

Then Arhat Ṛṣabha, gazed on by thousands of eyes, praised by thousands of mouths, extolled by thousands of hearts, being the object of thousands of wishes, coveted because of his splendour, beauty and virtues, pointed by thousands of fingers, responding with his right hand (to the greetings from) thousands of folded palms of several thousand men and women, moving on and on by leaving behind rows of thousands of dwellings;

Greeted by sweet and delightful music of *viṇā*, cymbal, *tūrya*, and the great drum, with which were mixed sweet and bracing shouts of victory, and gentle and pleasant murmur of the people;

Accompanied by all his pomp, all his splendour, all his army, all his train, all his retinue, all his munificence, all his grandeur, all his ornaments, all his majesty, all his men, all his subjects, all his actors, all his attendants, the entire *seraglio*, with all his flowers, wreaths, ornaments and robes on;

With the sound of all *tūryas*, with great pomp and great splendour, great army, great train, and the best of musical instruments, such as, *verī*, *jhallari*, *kharamukhi*, *dundubhi* and many others, (he) passed through the city filling it with noise and sound of music.

णिग्गच्छित्ता जेणेव सिद्धत्थ-वणे उज्जाणे जेणेव असोग-वर पायवे तेणेव उवागच्छइ । उवागच्छित्ता असोग-वर-पायवस्स अहे सीयं ठावेइ । ठावित्ता सीयाओ पच्चोरुहइ । पच्चोरुहित्ता सयमेव आभरण-मल्लालंकारं ओमुयइ ओमुयित्ता सयमेव चउ-मुट्ठियं लोयं करेइ । लोयं करित्ता छट्ठेणं भत्तेणं अपाणएणं उत्तरासाढाहिं णक्खत्तेणं जोगमुवागएणं उग्गाणं भोगाणं राइण्णाणं च खत्तियाणं च चउहिं सहस्सेहिं सद्धि एगं देव-दूसमादाय मुंडे भवित्ता अगाराओ अणगारियं पव्वइए । २११

Having moved out, he went to the park named Siddhārtha-vana, and reached the most excellent *aśoka* tree. On reaching the most excellent *aśoka* tree, he ordered his palanquin to be placed beneath it. Then he came out of the palanquin. Thereafter, with his own hand, he took off his wreaths, fineries and ornaments. Having taken them off, he tonsured his head by four handfuls, and taking food without water once in three days, when the moon came in conjunction with the asterism Uttarāṣāḍha, in the company of 4000 men of noble families, affluent families, royal families and kṣatriya families, he gave up the household order and entered into the order of the homeless monks. 211

उसभे णं अरहा कोसलिए एगं वास-सहस्सं णिच्चं वोसट्ठकाये चियत्त-देहे जे केइ उपसग्गा उप्पज्जंति तं जहा—दव्वा वा माणुसा वा तिरिक्ख-जोणिया वा अणुलोमा वा पंडिलोमा वा—ते उप्पण्णे सम्मं सहइ खमइ तितिक्खइ अहियासेइ ।

Arhat Ṛṣabha of Kośala gave up the care of his body for a thousand years and exposed it, regularly like an unfurled flag, to hardships. During this period, whenever any hardship came, he bore it in all respects, forgave it, overlooked it, believed it to be no hardship, howsoever severe, maybe due to divine wrath, or caused by men, animals or forces of nature or from any other adverse agents.

तएणं उसभे अरहा कोसलिए अणगारे जाए इरिया-समिए भासा-समिए एसणा-समिए आयाण-भंड-मत्त-णिक्खेवणा-समिए मण-समिए वय-समिए काय-समिए मणगुत्ते वय-गुत्ते काय-गुत्ते गुत्तिदिए गुत्त-बंभयारी अकोहे अमाणे अभाए अलोहे संते पसंते उवसंते परिणिव्वुडे अणासवे अममे अकिंचणे छिण्ण-ग्गंठे णिरुवलेवे ।

Then Arhat Ṛṣabha became homeless; circumspect in movement, circumspect in words, circumspect in desires, circumspect in acceptance-accumulation-renunciation, circumspect in throwing-out stool, urine, saliva and body dirt; restrained in mind, restrained in words, restrained in physical activities; guarding his thoughts, guarding his words, guarding his physical activities, guarding his organs of senses, guarding his chastity; without anger, without pride, without attachment, desisted from everything, freed from compulsion; without ego, without possession, with the tie (of worldly bondage) cut, free from any stain of worldliness.

कंस-पाईव मुक्क-तोए संखो इव णिरंजणे जीवे इव अप्पडिहयगई गगणमिव णिरालंबणे वायुरिव अप्पडिबद्धे सारयसलिलं सुद्ध-हियए पुक्खर-पत्तं पिव णिरुवलेवे कुम्मो इव गुत्तिदिये खग्गि-विसाणं व एग-जाए विहग इव विप्पमुक्के भारुंड-पक्खी व अप्पमत्ते कुंजर इव सोडीरे वसभो इव जाय-थामे सीहो इव दुद्धरिसे मंदरो इव अप्पकंपे सागरो इव गंभीरे चंदो इव सोमलेसे सूरो इव दित्ततेए जच्च-कणगं व जाय-रुवे वसुंधरा इव सव्व-फास-विसहे सुहय-हुयासणो इव तेयसा जलंते ।

He became liberated by giving up suffering, like bell-metal pot unstained by water, sinfree like a conch taking no black dot, without obstruction like the course of life, without support like the firmament, without bound like the wind, purest at heart like water in autumn, without a smear like a lotus leaf, with organs of senses withdrawn like tortoise, solitary like the rhino's horn, free like the birds, ever alert like the monstrous *bhāruṇḍa*, with a high status like an elephant, born strong like an ox, invincible like a lion, steadfast like Mount Mandara, deep like an ocean, mild like the moon, refulgent in glory like the sun, pure like fine gold, bearing (with unconcern) all touches like the earth, like a fire well-fed by offerings, he shone in his own splendour.

णत्थि णं तस्स अरहओ उसभस्स कोसलियस्स कथ्थइ पडिबंधे । से य चउव्विहे पण्णत्तो तं जहा—दव्वओ खित्तओ कालओ भावओ । दव्वओ सचित्ताचित्त-मीसएसु दव्वेसु । खित्तओ गामे वा णगरे वा अरण्णे वा खित्ते वा खले वा अंगणे वा । कालओ समए वा आवलियाए वा आणा-पाणुए वा योवे वा खणे वा लवे वा मुहुत्ते वा अहोरत्ते वा पक्खे वा मासे वा उऊए वा अयणे वा संवच्छरे वा अण्णयरे वा दीहकाल-संजोए । भावओ कोहे वा माणे वा मायाए वा लोभे वा भए वा हासे वा पिज्जे वा दोसे वा कलहे वा अब्भक्खाणे वा पेसुण्णे वा पर-परिवाए वा अरइ-रई वा माया-मोसे वा मिच्छा-दंसणसल्ले वा तस्स एां अरहओ उसभस्स णो एवं भवइ ।

Arhat Ṛṣabha of Kośala had no more limitations. Limitations have been stated to be four : limitation of objects, limitation of space, limitation of time and limitation of subjective senses. Limitation of objects : of animate objects, of inanimate objects, and of those in a mixed state :

Limitation of space : of a village, a town, a forest, a farm, a house or a yard;
Limitation of time : of a unit called *samaya,* of one called *āvalikā*, one called *ānāpānaka* (deep-breath / respiration), one called a *stoka*, one called a *kṣaṇa*, one called a *lava*, a *pakṣa*, a *muhūrta*, a day-night, a fortnight, a month, a season, a half-year, a year, or any other time-unit of a still longer duration;
Limitation of subjective senses : of anger, pride, attachment, greed, fear, laughter, affection, hatred, quarrel, calumny, sharp words, meanness, scandal-mongering, pleasure and pain, deceitful falsehood and evil of wrong faith. Arhat Ṛṣabha had none of these.

से णं अरहा उसभे वासा-वास-वज्जं अट्ठ गिम्ह-हेमंतिए मासे गामे एगराइए णगरे· पंच-राइए वासी-चंदण-समाण-कप्पे सम-तिण-मणि-लेट्ठु-कंचणे समदुक्ख-सुहे इहलोग-परलोग-अप्पडिबद्धे, जीवियमरणे णिरवकंखे, संसार-पार-गामी कम्म-संग-णिग्घायणट्ठाए अब्भुट्ठिए एवं च णं विहरइ ।

Monsoon sojourn apart, Arhat Ṛṣabha spent eight months of summer and winter as follows: if in a village, one night only in one village, and five nights if in a town;

With similar feeling towards excreta and sandal wood, with similar attitude to hay, jewel, clay and gold, indifferent to pleasure and pain, free from limitation in this world as well as in the next, without a hankering for life and death, destined to overcome the mundane life, born to terminate the bondage of *karma*—thus he spent his time.

तस्स णं अरहओ उसभस्स अणुत्तरेणं णाणेणं अणुत्तरेणं दंसणेणं अणुत्तरेणं चरित्तेणं अणुत्तरेणं आलएणं अणुत्तरेणं वीरिएणं अणुत्तरेणं अज्जवेणं अणुत्तरेणं मद्दवेण अणुत्तरेणं लाधवेणं अणुत्तराए खंतीए अणुत्तराए बुद्धीए अणुत्तरेणं सच्च-संजम-तव-सुचरिय-सोवचिय-फल-परिणिव्वाण-मग्गेणं अप्पाणं भावेमाणस्स एक्कं वास-सहस्सं विइक्कंतं ।

With supreme knowledge, supreme faith and supreme conduct, in stainless lodgings and blameless wanderings, with extreme valour, extreme uprightness, extreme mildness, extreme dexterity and extreme patience, with utmost caution and utmost satisfaction, with the highest intelligence and highest truth, restraint and penance, Arhat Ṛṣabha spent a thousand years in meditating on self on the road to liberation, which was the duly earned outcome of right conduct.

तश्रो णं जे से हेमंताणं चउथ्थे मासे सत्तमे पक्खे फग्गुण-बहुले तस्स णं फग्गुण-बहुलस्स एगारसी-पक्खेणं पुव्वण्ह-काल-समयंसि पुरिम-तालस्स णगरस्स बहिया सगडमुहंसि उज्जाणंसि णिग्गोह-वर-पायवस्स श्रहे श्रट्ठमेणं भत्तेणं श्रपाणएणं श्रासाढाहिं-नक्खत्तेणं जोगमुवागएणं झाणंतरियाए वट्टमाणस्स श्रणंते श्रणुत्तरे णिव्वाधाए णिरावरणे कसिणे पडिपुण्णे केवल-वर-नाण-दंसणे समुप्पण्णे ।

Thereon, in the seventh fortnight of the fourth month of winter, on the eleventh day of the dark half of Phālguna, in the earlier part of the day, outside the city of Purimātāla, in a park named Śakaṭamukha, under the shade of an excellent *nyagrodha* tree, taking food without water once in four days, when the moon was in conjunction with the asterism Uttarāṣāḍha, while in meditation, he became the master of *kevala* knowledge and faith, infinite, unsurpassed, unobstructed, complete and full.

तए णं उसभे श्ररहा कोसलिए जिणे केवली सव्वण्णू सव्य-दरिसी स देव-मणुयासुरस्स लोगस्स परियायं जाणइ पासइ । सव्वलोए सव्वजीवाणं श्रागइं गइं थिइं चवणं उव्वायं तक्कं मणो माणसियं भूत्तं कडं पडिसेवियं श्रावी-कम्मं रहो-कम्मं श्र-रहा-श्र-रहस्सभागी तं तं कालं मण-वयण-काय-जोगे वट्टमाणाणं सव्वलोए सव्वजीवाणं सव्वभावे जाणमाणे पासमाणे विरहइ । २१२

Then Arhat Ṛṣabha became the venerable, the victor, omniscient all-knowing, all-observing;

Knew he and saw he all categories of gods, men and *asuras in* all the worlds;

Knew he and saw he the conditions of all the living beings in all the worlds — wherefrom they come, whither they go, where do they stay, when do they slip, where are they born; knew he and saw he their ideas, the thoughts in their mind, their intake, their doings, their open deeds as well as their secret deeds;

Maru Devi (Ṛṣabha's Mother) attains Omniscience

[facing p. 128

being the most venerable, from whom nothing could be kept a secret, he knew and he saw, in all respects, the state of mind, words and deeds, of all the living beings in all the worlds. 212

उसभस्स णं अरहओ कोसलियस्स चउरासीइ गण चउरासीइ गणहरा य होत्था। २१३

उसभस्स णं अरहओ कोसलियस्स उसभसेण-पामोक्खाओ चउरासीइ समण-साहस्सीओ उक्कोसिया समण-संपया होत्था। २१४

उसभस्स णं अरहओ कोसलियस्स बंभिसुंदरी-पामोक्खाणं अज्जियाणं तिण्णि सय-साहस्सीओ उक्कोसिया अज्जिया-संपया-होत्था। २१५

उसभस्स णं अरहओ कोसलियस्स सेज्जंस-पामोक्खाणं समणोवासयाणं तिण्णि सय-साहस्सीओ पंच सहस्सा उक्कोसिया समणोवासग-संपया होत्था। २१६

उसभस्स णं अरहओ कोसलियस्स सुभद्दा-पामोक्खाणं समणोवासियाणं पंच सय-साहस्सीओ चउपण्णं च सहस्सा उक्कोसिया समणोवासियाणं संपया होत्था। २१७

Arhat Ṛṣabha of Kośala had 84 *gaṇas* and 84 *gaṇadharas*. 213
Arhat Ṛṣabha of Kośala had an excellent community of 84,000 monks with Ṛṣabhasena at its head. 214
Arhat Ṛṣabha of Kośala had an excellent community of 3,00,000 nuns with Brāhmī-Sundarī at its head. 215
Arhat Ṛṣabha of Kośala had an excellent community of 3,05,000 male followers with Śreyānsa at its head. 216
Arhat Ṛṣabha of Kośala had an excellent community of 5,54,000 female followers with Subhadrā at its head. 217

उसभस्स णं अरहओ कोसलियस्स चत्तारि सहस्सा सत्त सया पण्णासा चउद्दसपुव्वीणं अजिणाणं जिण-संकासाणं उक्कोसिया चउद्दसपुव्वी-संपया होत्था। २१८

उसभस्स णं अरहओ कोसलियस्स णव सहस्सा ओहिणाणीणं उक्कोसिया संपया होत्था। २१९

उसभस्स णं अरहओ कोसलियस्स बीस सहस्सा केवलणाणीणं उक्कोसिया संपया होत्था। २२०

Arhat Ṛṣabha of Kośala had an excellent community of 4,750 monks who were masters of 14 *Pūrvas*, who, though not *Jinas* themselves, were very much near them, who knew all the combinations of letters and correctly interpreted the truth like a *Jina*. 218

Arhat Ṛṣabha of Kośala had an excellent community of 9,000 masters of *avadhi* knowledge. 219

Arhat Ṛṣabha of Kośala had an excellent community of 20,000 omniscients. 220

उसभस्स णं अरहओ कोसलियस्स वीस सहस्सा छच्च सया वेउव्वियाणं उक्कोसिया संपया होत्था। २२१

उसभस्स णं अरहओ कोसलियस्स बारस सहस्सा छच्च सया पण्णासा विउलमईणं उड्ढाइज्जेसु दीवसमुद्देसु सण्णीणं पंचिंदियाणं पज्जत्तगाणं मण्णोगए भावे जाणमाणाणं उक्कोसिया संपया होत्था। २२२

उसभस्स णं अरहओ कोसलियस्स बारस सहस्सा छच्च सया पण्णासा वाइणं उक्कोसियां संपया होत्था। २२३

Arhat Ṛṣabha of Kośala had an excellent community of 20,600 monks who were great masters in the art of transforming their bodies. 221

Arhat Ṛṣabha of Kośala had an excellent community of 12,650 monks who were endowed with the highest intellectual power, who knew the inner thoughts of all the living beings who had full development, mind and five organs of senses and who resided in two islands and a half and in two oceans. 222

Arhat Ṛṣabha of Kośala had an excellent community of 12,650 logicians. 223

उसभस्स णं अरहओ कोसलियस्स वीसं अंतेवासि-सहस्सा सिद्धा चत्तालीसं अज्जिया-साहस्सीओ सिद्धाओ। २२४

उसभस्स णं अरहओ कोसलियस्स बावीस सहस्सा णवसया अणुत्तरोववाइयाणं गइ-कल्लाणाणं उक्कोसिया संपया होत्था। २२५

उसभस्स णं अरहओ कोसलियस्स दुविहा अंतगड-भूमी होत्था तं जहा—जुगंतकड-भूमी य परियायंतकड-भूमी य। जाव असंखिज्जाओ पुरिस-जुगाओ जुगंतकड-भूमी अंतो-मुहुत्त-परियाए अंतं अकासी। २२६

Arhat Ṛṣabha of Kośala had 20,000 male disciples and 40,000 female disciples who had been perfected. 224

Arhat Ṛṣabha of Kośala had an excellent community of 22,900 who were in their last birth. All of them had attained a blissful state. 225

Arhat Ṛṣabha had instituted two epochs marking the end, which were as follows : epoch signifying the termination of a generation, and epoch signifying the termination of categories, the former having terminated after innumerable generations had lived through and the latter within less than a 48-minute time-span after his attainment of omniscience. 226

तेणं कालेणं तेणं समएणं उसभे अरहा कोसलिए वीसं पुव्व-सय-सहस्साइं कुमार-वास-मज्झे वसित्ताणं तेसीइं पुव्व-सय-सहस्साइं अगार-वास-मज्झे वसित्ताणं एगं वास-सहस्सं छउमत्थ-परियायं पाउणित्ता एगं पुव्व-सय-सहस्सं वास-साहस्सूणं केवलि-परियायं पाउणित्ता पडिपुण्णं पुव्व-सय-सहस्सं सामण्ण-परियायं पाउणित्ता चउरासीइं पुव्व-सय-सहस्साइं सव्वाउयं पालइत्ता खीणे वेयणिज्जाउय-णाम-गोत्ते इमीसे ओसप्पिणीए सुसम-दुस्समाए समाए विइक्कंताए तीहिं वासेहिं अद्ध-णवमेहि य मासेहिं सेसेहिं जे से हेमंताणं तच्चे मासे पंचमे पक्खे माह-बहुले तस्स णं माह-बहुलस्स तेरसी पक्खेणं उप्पिं अट्ठावय-सेल-सिहरंसि दसहिं अणगार-सहस्सेहिं सद्धिं चउद्दमेणं भत्तेणं अपाणएणं अभीइणा णक्खत्तेणं जोगमुवागएणं पुव्वण्ह-काल-समयंसि संपलियंक-णिसण्णे कालगए विइक्कंते समुज्जाए छिण्ण-जाइजरा-मरण-बंधणे सिद्धे बुद्धे मुत्ते अंतगडे परिणिव्वुडे सव्व-दुक्ख-प्पहीणे । २२७

In that period, at that time, Arhat Ṛṣabha was a prince for 20,00,000 *pūrvas*, then he reigned for 63,00,000 *pūrvas*, in all 83,00,000 *pūrvas* in the household state; he was a monk for 1000 years and lived as an omniscient for 1,00,000 *pūrvas* 1000 years; altogether full 1,00,000 *pūrvas* in the order of a monk, and 84,00,000 *pūrvas* on this earth. Then on the exhaustion of his *karma*, giving experience name and lineage, at the termination time of the bracing-unbracing part of the descension phase of the cycle, less 3 years and 8½ months, in the fifth fortnight of the third month of winter, on the 13th day of the dark half of Māgha, atop Mount Aṣṭāpada, in the company of 10,000 monks, and courting the vow of taking food without water once in seven days, when the moon was in conjunction with the asterism Abhijit, in the early part of the day, seated in the *samparyaṅka* posture, he passed away, went beyond the bounds of *karma*, was uplifted after having left the world, cut asunder the tie of birth-oldage-death, and became perfected, enlightened and liberated, the maker of the end, and the terminator of all misery. 227

उसभस्स णं अरहओ कोसलियस्स कालगयस्स जाव...सव्व-दुक्ख-प्पहीणस्स तिण्णि वासा अद्धणव मासा विइक्कंता तओ वि परं एगा य सागरोवम-कोडाकोडी तिवास-अद्धणव-मासाहिय-बायालीसाए वास-सहस्सेहिं ऊणिया विइक्कंता एयंसि समए समणे भगवं महावीरे परिणिव्वुए तओवि परं णव-वास-सया विइक्कंता दसमस्स य वास-सयस्स अयं असीइमे संवच्छरे काले गच्छइ। २२८

Since the time when Arhat Ṛṣabha passed away, till he became the terminator of all misery, 3 years and 8½ months have elapsed, and thereafter have elapsed one crore times one crore *sāgaropamas*, less 2003 years, and 8½ months, when Śramaṇa Bhagavān Mahāvīra passed away. Since then, nine centuries have elapsed, and of the tenth century, this is the 80th year. 228

VI

जिण-चरित्तं

थेरावली

List of Senior Monks

तेणं कालेणं तेणं समएणं समणस्स भगवओ महावीरस्स णव गणा इक्कारस गणहरा होत्था । से केणट्ठेणं भंते ! एवं वुच्चइ: समणस्स भगवओ महावीरस्स णव गणा इक्कारस गणहरा होत्था ? समणस्स भगवओ महावीरस्स जेट्ठे इंदभूई अणगारे गोयमगोत्तेणं पंच समण-सयाइं वाएइ । मज्झिमे अग्गिभूई अणगारे गोयम गोत्तेणं पंच समण-सयाइं वाएइ । कणीयसे अणगारे वाउभूई णामेणं गोयमगोत्तेणं पंच समण-सयाइं वाएइ । थेरे अज्ज-वियत्ते भारद्दाएगोत्तेणं पंच समण-सयाइं वाएइ । थेरे अज्ज-सुहम्मे अग्गिवेसायण-गोत्तेणं पंच समण-सयाइं वाएइ । थेरे मंडियपुत्ते वासिट्ठ-गोत्तेणं अदघुट्ठाइं समण-सयाइं वाएइ । थेरे मोरियपुत्ते कासव-गोत्तेणं अद्धुट्ठाइं समण-सयाइं वाएइ । थेरे अकंपिए[11] गोयम-गोत्तेणं थेरे अयल-भाया हरियायण-गोत्तेणं ते दुण्णि वि थेरा तिण्णि-तिण्णि समण-सयाइं वाएंण्णि । थेरे मेयज्जे थेरे पभासे एए दुण्णि वि थेरा कोडिण्ण-गोत्तेणं तिण्णि तिण्णि समण-सयाइं वाएंति । से तेणं अट्ठेणं अज्जो ! एवं वुच्चई: समणस्स भगवओ महावीरस्स णव गणा इक्कारस गणहरा होत्था । १

In that period, at that time, Śramaṇa Bhagavān Mahāvīra had nine *gaṇas* and eleven *gaṇadharas*.

—*Bhante*! Why has it been said that Śramaṇa Bhagavān Mahāvīra had nine *gaṇas* and eleven *gaṇadharas* ?

The seniormost disciple of Śramaṇa Bhagavān Mahāvīra was Indrabhūti of the Gautama line* who imparted lessons in the sacred texts to 500 monks.

The middle disciple Agnibhūti of the Gautama line imparted lessons in the sacred texts to 500 monks.

The youngest disciple Vāyubhūti of the Gautama line imparted lessons in the sacred texts to 500 monks.

Sthavira Ārya Vyakta of the Bhāradvāja line imparted lessons in the sacred texts to 500 monks.

Sthavira Ārya Sudharmā of the Agni Vaiśāyana line imparted lessons in the sacred texts to 500 monks.

Sthavira Mandika-putra of the Vasiṣṭha line imparted lessons in the sacred texts to 250 monks.

Sthavira Maurya-putra of the Kāśyapa line imparted lessons in the sacred texts to 250 monks.

---

* In this Chapter, *Gotra* has been translated as 'line'.

Sthavira Akampita of the Gautama line and *sthavira* Acalabhrātā of the Hāritāyana line, each imparted lessons in the sacred texts to 300 monks.

Sthavira Maiṭārya and *sthavira* Prabhāsa, both of the Kauṇḍinya line, each imparted lessons in the sacred texts to 300 monks.

—*Ārya*! It is for this (did I say as above), and so it is said that Śramaṇa Bhagavān Mahāvīra had nine *gaṇas* and eleven *gaṇadharas*. 1

सव्वे एए समणस्स भगवओ महावीरस्स इक्कारस वि गणहरा दुवालसंगिणो चउद्दस-पुव्विणो समत्त-गणि-पिडगा-धारगा रायगिहे णगरे मासिएणं भत्तेणं अपाणएणं कालगया विइक्कंता 'समुज्जाया छिण्ण-जाइ-जरा-मरण-बंधण सिद्धा मुत्ता अंतगडा परिणिव्वुडा सव्व-दुक्ख-प्पहीणा। थेरे इंदभूइ थेरे अज्ज-सुहम्मे सिद्धिगए महावीरे पच्छा दुण्णि वि थेरा परिणिव्वुया। जे इमे अज्जत्ताए समणा णिग्गंठा एए सव्वे अज्ज सुहम्मस्स अणगारस्स अवच्चेज्जा, अवसेसा गणहरा निरवच्चा वोच्छिन्ना। २

Of these eleven *gaṇadharas* of Śramaṇa Bhagavān Mahāvīra, all were masters of the 12 *Aṅgas*, 14 *Pūrvas* and all the spiritual treasures created by the *gaṇis*, all (but two) courted the vow of taking food without water once after a month and passed away in Rājagṛha, died, were uplifted, cut asunder the ties of birth-oldage-death, had been perfected, enlightened and liberated, were (when on this earth) in their last birth, had entered into liberation, and became the terminators of all misery. *Sthavira* Indrabhūti and *sthavira* Ārya Sudharmā entered into liberation after the passing away of Mahāvīra. The *nirgrantha* monks of the present times are all the spiritual descendants of *sthavira* Ārya Sudharmā. The rest of the *gaṇadharas* are without (spiritual) progeny, and hence they are uprooted (i.e., have left no line). 2

समणे भगवं महावीरे कासव-गोत्तेणं। समणस्स भगवओ महावीरस्स कासव-गोत्तस्स अज्ज-सुहम्मे थेरे अंतेवासी अग्गिवेसायण-सगोत्ते। थेरस्स णं अज्ज-सुहम्मस्स अग्गिवेसायण-सगोत्तस्स अज्ज-जंबु-णामे थेरे अंतेवासी कासवगोत्ते। थेरस्स णं अज्ज-जंबु-णामस्स कासव-गोत्तस्स अज्ज-प्पभवे थेरे अंतेवासी कच्चायण-सगोत्ते। थेरस्स णं अज्ज-सिज्जंभवे थेरे अंतेवासी मणग-

पिया वच्छ-सगोत्ते। थेरस्स णं अज्ज-सिज्जंभवस्स मणग-पिउणो वच्छ-
सगोत्तस्स थेरे अंतेवासी अज्ज-जसभद्दे तुंगियायण-सगोत्ते। ३

Śramaṇa Bhagavān Mahāvīra belonged to the Kāśyapa line. *Sthavira* Ārya Sudharmā who was the disciple of Śramaṇa Bhagavān Mahāvīra was of the Agni-vaiśāyana line.

Sthavira Ārya Jambu who was the disciple of Ārya Sudharmā of the Agni-vaiśāyana line belonged to the Kāśyapa line.

Sthavira Ārya Prabhava who was the disciple of *sthavira* Ārya Jambu of the Kāśyapa line belonged to the Kātyāyana line. Ārya Sayyambhava, the father of Māṇaka, who was the disciple of the *sthavira* (Ārya Prabhava), belonged to the Vātsya line. *Sthavira* Ārya Yaśobhadra who was the disciple of *sthavira* Ārya Sayyambhava of the Vātsya line, the father of Māṇaka, belonged to the Tungikāyaṇa line. 3

संखित्त-वायणाए अज्ज-जसभद्दाए अग्गओ एवं थेरावली भणिया तं जहा— थेरस्स णं अज्ज-जसभद्दाओ तुंगियायण-सगोत्तस्स अंतेवासी दुवे थेरा। थेरे अज्ज-संभूयविजए माढर-सगोत्ते थेरे अज्ज-भद्दबाहू पाईण-सगोत्ते। थेरस्स णं अज्ज-संभूयविजयस्स माढर-सगोत्तस्स अंतेवासी थेरे अज्ज-थूलभद्दे गोयम-सगोत्ते। थेरस्स णं अज्ज-थूलभद्दस्स गोयमसगोत्तस्स अंतेवासी दुवे थेरा। थेरे अज्ज महागिरी एलावच्च-सगोत्ते, थेरे अज्ज-सुहत्थी वासिट्ठ-सगोत्ते। थेरस्स णं अज्ज-सुहत्थिस्स वासिट्ठ-सगोत्तस्स अंतेवासी दुवे थेरा सुट्ठिय-सुप्पडि-बुद्धा कोडिय-काकंदगा वग्धावच्च-सगोत्ता। थेराणं सुट्ठिय-सुप्पडिबुद्धाणं कोडिय-काकंदगाणं वग्धावच्च-सगोत्ताणं अंतेवासी थेरे अज्ज इंददिण्णे कोसिय-सगोत्ते। थेरस्स णं अज्ज-इंददिण्णस्स कोसिय-सगोत्तस्स अंतेवासी अज्ज-दिण्णे गोयम-सगोत्ते। थेरस्स णं अज्ज-दिण्णस्स गोयम-सगोत्तस्स अंतेवासी थेरे अज्जसीहगिरी जाईसरे कोसिय-सगोत्ते। थेरस्स णं अज्जसीहगिरिस्स जाईसरस्स कोसिय-सगोत्तस्स अंतेवासी थेरे अज्ज-वइरे गोयम-सगोत्ते। थेरस्स णं अज्ज-वइरस्स गोयम-सगोत्तस्स (अंतेवासी थेरे अज्ज-वइरसेणे उक्कोसिय-गोत्ते। थेरस्स णं अज्ज-वइर-सेणस्स उक्कोसिय-गोत्तस्स) अंतेवासी चत्तारि थेरा। थेरे अज्ज-णाइले, थेरे अज्ज-वोमिले, थेरे अज्ज-जयंते थेरे अज्ज-तावसे। थेराओ अज्ज-णाइलाओ अज्जणाइला साहा णिग्गया। थेराओ अज्ज-वोमिलाओ अज्ज-

वोमिला साहा णिग्गया। थेराश्रो श्रज्ज-जयंताश्रो श्रज्ज-जयंती साहा णिग्गया। थेराश्रो श्रज्ज-तावसाश्रो श्रज्ज-तावसी साहा णिग्गया त्ति ४

In a precise redaction, the list of the *sthaviras* after Ārya Yaśobhadra would read as follows :

Sthavira Yaśobhadra of the Tungikāyaṇa line had two disciples: *sthavira* Ārya Sambhūta-vijaya of the Māṭhara line, and *sthavira* Ārya Bhadrabāhu of the Prācīna line.

Sthavira Ārya Sambhūta-vijaya of the Māṭhara line had a disciple in *sthavira* Ārya Sthūlabhadra who belonged to the Gautama line.

Sthavira Ārya Sthūlabhadra of the Gautama line had two disciples : *sthavira* Ārya Mahāgiri of the Ailāpatya line, and *sthavira* Ārya Suhasti of the Vasiṣṭha line.

Sthavira Ārya Suhasti of the Vasiṣṭha line had two disciples : *sthaviras* Susthita and Supratibuddha, *alias* Kotika and Kākandaka respectively, both belonging to the Byāghrāpatya line.

Sthaviras Susthita and Supratibuddha, *alias* Kotika and Kākandaka, both of the Byāghrāpatya line, had a disciple in *sthavira* Indradatta who belonged to the Kauśika line.

Sthavira Ārya Indradatta of the Kauśika line had a disciple in Āryadatta of the Gautama line.

Sthavira Āryadatta of the Gautama line had a disciple in *sthavira* Ārya Singhagiri Jātismara who belonged to the Kauśika line.

Sthavira Ārya Singhagiri Jātismara of the Kauśika line had a disciple in *sthavira* Ārya Vajra of the Gautama line.

Sthavira Ārya Vajra of the Gautama line had (a disciple in *sthavira* Ārya Vajrasena of the Utkṛṣṭa line; and *sthavira* Ārya Vajrasena of the Utkṛṣṭa line had) four disciples : *sthavira* Ārya Nagila, *sthavira* Ārya Bomila, *sthavira* Ārya Jayanta and *sthavira* Ārya Tāpasa.

From *sthavira* Ārya Nagila branched out the Ārya-Nagilā *śākhā** From *sthavira* Bomila branched out the Arya-Bomilā *śakhā*. From *sthavira* Ārya Jayanta branched out the Ārya-Jayanti *śākhā*. From *Sthavira* Ārya Tâpasa branched out the Ārya-Tâpasi *śākhā*. 4

विथ्थर-वायणाए पुण अज्ज-जसभद्दाओ परओ थेरावली एवं पलोइज्जइ तं जहा-थेरस्स णं अज्ज-जसभद्दस्स इमे दो थेरा अंतेवासी अहावच्चा अभिण्णाया होथ्था तं जहा-थेरे अज्ज-भद्दबाहू पाइण-सगोत्ते, थेरे संभूय-विजए माढर-सगोत्ते। थेरस्स णं अज्ज-भद्दबाहूस्स पाइण-सगोत्तस्स इमे चत्तारि थेरा अंतेवासी अहावच्चा अभिण्णाया[42] होथ्था तं जहा-थेरे गोदासे थेरे अग्गिदत्ते थेरे जणदत्ते थेरे सोमदत्ते कासव-गोत्तेणं। थेरेहितो णं गोदासेहिंतो कासव-गोत्तेहिंतो एथ्थ णं गोदास-गणे णामं गणेणिग्गए; तस्स णं इमाओ चत्तारि साहाओ एवमाहिज्जंति तं जहा-तामलित्तिया कोडिवरि-सिया पोंडवद्धणिया दासीखब्बडिया। थेरस्स णं अज्ज-संभूयविजयस्स माढर-सगोत्तस्स इमे दुवालस थेरा अंतेवासी अहावच्चा अभिण्णाया होथ्था तं जहा-

णंदणभद्दे थेरे
उवणंदे तीसभद्द जसभद्दे।
थेरे य सुमणभद्दे
मणिभद्दे पुण्णभद्दे य।१।
थेरे य थूलभद्दे
उज्जुमई जंबुनामधिज्जे य।
थेरे य दीहभद्दे
थेरे तह पंडुभद्दे ।।२।।

थेरस्स णं अज्ज-संभूयविजयस्स माढर-सगोत्तस्स इमाओ सत्त अंतेवासिणीओ अहावच्चाओ अभिण्णायाओ होथ्था तं जहा-

---

*Hermann Jacobi writes: "It is not clear what is meant by *gaṇa*, *kula* and *śākhā*. *Gaṇa* designates the school which is derived from one teacher; *kula* the succession of teachers in one line, *śākhā* the lines which branch off from each teacher. The modern *gaccha* appears equivalent with the ancient *gaṇa*.

—*Kalpa Sūtra*, in Sacred Books of the East, Vol. XXII, p. 288.

जक्खा य जक्खदिण्णा
भूया तह चेव भूयदिण्णा य।
सेणा वेणा रेणा
भगिणीओ थुलभद्दस्स।३। ५

In an exhaustive redaction, the list of the *sthaviras* after Ārya Yaśobhadra would read as follows :

Sthavira Ārya Yaśobhadra had two disciples in *sthavira* Ārya Bhadrabāhu of the Prācīna line and *sthavira* Sambhūta-vijaya of the Māṭhara line, who were progeny-like and very dear to him. *Sthavira* Ārya Bhadrabāhu of the Prācīna line had four progeny-like and very dear disciples in *sthavira* Godāsa, *sthavira* Agnidatta, *sthavira* Janadatta and *sthavira* Somadatta—all of the Kāśyapa line.

From *sthavira* Godāsa of the Kāśyapa line branched out a *gaṇa* named Godāsa *gaṇa*, of which the four *śākhās* were Tāmraliptikā, Koṭivarsiā, Puṇḍra-vardhaniā and Dāsi-kharvāṭikā. *Sthavira* Ārya Sambhūta-vijaya of the Māṭhara line had 12 progeny-like and very dear disciples as follows :

Nandana-bhadra *sthavira*
Upananda, Tiṣya-bhadra, Yaśo-bhadra
Sthavira Sumana-bhadra
Maṇi-bhadra Puṇya-bhadra 1

Sthavira Sthūla-bhadra
Ṛjumati and one Jambu by name
Sthavira Dīrgha-bhadra
And *Sthavira* Paṇḍu-bhadra. 2

Sthavira Ārya Sambhūta-vijaya of the Māṭhara line had the following progeny-like and very dear female disciples :

Yakṣā, Yakṣadattā
Bhūtā, Bhūta-dattā
Senā (Enā ?), Benā, Renā—
Sisters of Sthūla-bhadra. 3 5

थेरस्स णं अज्ज-थूलभद्दस्स गोयम-सगोत्तस्स इमे दो थेरा अहावच्चा अभिण्णाया होत्था तं जहा-थेरे अज्ज-महागिरी एलावच्च-सगोत्ते थेरे अज्ज-सुहत्थी वासिट्ठ-सगोत्ते। थेरस्स णं अज्ज-महागिरीस्स एलावच्च-

सगोत्तस्स इमे अट्ठ थेरा अंतेवासी अहावच्चा अभिण्णाया होथ्था तं जहा– थेरे उत्तरे थेरे बलिस्सहे थेरे धणड्ढे थेरे सिरिड्ढे थेरे कोडिण्णे थेरे णागे थेरे णागमित्ते थेरे छलुए रोहगुत्ते कोसिय-गोत्तेणं। थेरेहिंतो णं छलुएहिंतो रोहगुत्तेहिंतो कोसिय-गोत्तेहिंतो तथ्थ णं तेरासिया साहा णिग्गया। थेरेहिंतो णं उत्तर-बलिस्से-हिंतो तथ्थ णं उत्तर बलिस्सहगणे णामं गणे णिग्गए। तस्स णं इमाओ चत्तारि साहाओ एवमाहिज्जंति तं जहा– कोसंबिया सोइत्तिया कोड्डवाणी चंदणागरी। थेरस्स णं अज्ज-सुहथ्थि-स्स वासिट्ठ-सगोत्तस्स इमे दुवालस थेरा अंतेवासी अहावच्चा अभिण्णाया होथ्था तं जहा–

थेरज्ज-रोहणे य
द्दजसे मेहे गणी य कामिड्ढी।
सुट्ठिय-सुप्पडिबुद्धे
रक्खिय तह रोहगुत्ते य।४।

इसिगुत्ते सिरिगुत्ते
गणी य बंभे गणी य तह सोमे।
दस दो य गणहरा खलु
एए सीसा सुहथ्थिस्स।५। ६

Sthavira Ārya Sthūla-bhadra had two progeny-like and very dear disciples in *sthavira* Ārya Mahâgiri of the Ailâpatya line, and *sthavira* Ārya Suhasti of the Vasiṣṭha line.

Sthavira Ārya Mahâgiri had the following eight progeny-like and very dear disciples : *sthavira* Uttara, *sthavira* Balissaha, *sthavira* Dhanāḍhya, *sthavira* Sirardhi, *sthavira* Kodinna, *sthavira* Nāga, *sthavira* Nāgamitra and *sthavira* Chāluka Rohagupta (the last one being) of the Kauśika line.

From *sthavira* Chāluka Rohagupta of the Kauśika line branched out the Trairāśika *śākhā*.

From *sthavira* Uttara and *sthavira* Balissaha branched out a *gaṇa* named Uttara-Balissaha *gaṇa*, of which four *śākhās* were Kauśambikā, Sautaptikā, Kauṭumbinī and Candra-nagari. *Sthavira* Ārya Suhasti of the Vasiṣṭha line had the following 12 progeny-like and very dear disciples :

Sthavira Ārya Rohana
Bhadrayasah, Megha, Kāmardhi
Susthita, Supratibuddha
Rakṣita and Rohagupta 4

Ṛṣigupta, Śrīgupta
Gaṇi Brahma and *gaṇi* Soma
These ten plus two, *gaṇadharas* (12 in all)
All disciples of Suhasti. 5 6

थेरेहिंतो णं अज्ज-रोहणेहिंतो कासव-गोत्तेहिंतो तथ्थ णं उद्देहगणे णामं गणे णिग्गए। तस्स इमाओ चत्तारि साहाओ णिग्गयाओ छच्च कुलाइं एवं आहिज्जंति। से किं तं साहाओ ? साहाओ एवमाहिज्जंति तं जहा– उडुंबरिज्जियां, मासपूरिया, मइपत्तिया, सुण्णपत्तिया। से तं साहाओ। से किं तं कुलाइं ? कुलाइं एवमाहिज्जंति तं जहा –

पढमं च णागभूयं
बीयं पुण सोमभूइयं होइ।
अह उल्लगच्छ तइयं
चउथ्थयं हथ्थिलिज्जं तु ।६।

पंचमगं णंदिज्जं
छट्ठं पुण पारिहासयं होइ।
उद्देह गणस्सेए
छच्च कुला होंति णायव्वा ।७।

थेरेहिंतो णं सिरिगुत्तेहिंतो हारिय-सगोत्तेहिंतो एथ्थ णं चारण-गणे णामं गणे णिग्गए; तस्स णं इमाओ चत्तारि साहाओ सत्त य कुलाइं एवमाहिज्जंति। से किं तं साहाओ ? साहाओ एवमाहिज्जंति तं जहा– हारियमालागारी संकासिया गवेधुया वज्जणागरी। से तं साहाओ। से किं तं कुलाइं ? कुलाइं एवमाहिज्जंति तं जहा–

पढमेथ्थ वच्छलिज्जं
बीयं पुण पीइधम्मियं होइ।
तइयं पुण हालिज्जं
चउथ्थं पूसमित्तिज्जं ।८।

पंचमगं मलिज्जं
छट्ठं पुण अज्ज-चेडयं होइ ।
सत्तमगं कण्हसहं
सत्त कुला चारणगणस्स ।९। ७

From *sthavira* Ārya Rohana of the Kāśyapa line branched out a *gaṇa* named Uddeha *gaṇa*, of which four *śākhās* and six *kulas* were stated to be as follows. What were the *śākhās* ? They were : Audumbariā, Māsapuriyā, Mati-prāptikā and Śūnya-prāptikā. These are the *sākhās*. What were the *kulas* ? They were :

First was Nagabhūta
Second, Somabhūtikā
Ullagaccha (Ardra-kaccha ?) the third
And fourth Hastiliya 6

Fifth was Nandiya
And sixth Parihāsaka—
Of the Uddeha *gaṇa*, to be noted,
These were the six *Kulas*. 7

From *sthavira* Śri-gupta of the Hārīta line branched out a *gaṇa* named Cārana *gaṇa*, of which four *śākhās* and seven *kulas* had been as follows. What were the *śākhās* ? They were : Hārīta-mālākari, samkāsyā (Saṁkāsika ?), Gavedhukā and Vajra-nāgari, And what were the *kulas* ? They were :

First was Vatsaliyā
And second Prīti-dharmikā
Third was Hāliya (Haligga ?)
And fourth Pausa-maitreya (mittigga ?) 8
Fifth was Maleya (Maligga ?)
And sixth Ārya-Cetaka
And the seventh Kṛṣṇa-śākha (Kanhasaha ?)—
Such were seven *kulas* of the Cārana *gaṇa*. 9 7

थेरेहिंतो भद्दसेहिंतो भारद्दाय-सगोत्तेहिंतो एत्थ णं उडुवाडियगणे णामं गणे णिग्गए । तस्स णं इमाओ चत्तारि साहाओ तिण्णि य कुलाइं एव-माहिज्जंति । से किं तं साहाओ ? साहाओ एवमाहिज्जंति तं जहा—चंपि-

ज्जिया भद्दिज्जिया काकंदिया मेहलिज्जिया। से तं साहाओ। से किं तं कुलाइं ? कुलाइं एवमाहिज्जंति तं जहा–

भद्दजसियं तह भद्द–
गुत्तिय तइयं च होइ जसभद्दं।
एयाइं उडुवाडिय–
गणस्स तिण्णेव य कुलाइं।१०।

थेरेहिंतो णं कामिड्ढीहिंतो कुंडल-सगोत्तेहिंतो एत्थ णं वेसवाडियगणे णाम गणे णिग्गए। तस्स णं इमाओ चत्तारि साहाओ चत्तारि कुलाइं एवमाहिज्जंति। से किं तं साहाओ ? साहाओ एवमाहिज्जंति ? तं जहा–सावत्थियारज्जपालिया अंतरिज्जिया खेमलिज्जिया। से तं साहाओ। से किं तं कुलाइं ? कुलाइं एवमाहिज्जंति तं जहा–

गणियं मेहिय कामिड्
ढियं च तह च होइ इंदपुरगं च।
एयाइ वेसवाडिय
गणस्स चत्तारि य कुलाइं।११। ८

From *sthavira* Bhadrayaśāh of the Bhāradvāja line branched out a *gaṇa* named Udubadiya *gaṇa*, which in turn branched out into four *śākhās* and three *kulas*. What were these *śākhās* ? They were Campiyā, Bhadriyā, Kākandiā and Mekhaliā. Such were the *śākhās*. And what were the *kulas* ? The *kulas* were :

Bhadra-yasasya and Bhadra-
Guptīya, third Yaśo-bhadra—
These are the *kulas*
Of *gaṇa* named Uduvadīya. 10

From *sthavira* Kāmardhi of the Kuṇḍala (Kauṇḍinya, in alternative reading) line branched out a *gaṇa* named Vesavādiya, which in turn branched out in four *śākhās* and four *kulas*. What were these *śākhās* ? They were Śrāvastikā, Rājyapālikā, Antariyā and Kṣemaliyā. Such were the *śākhās*. And the *kulas*? They were :

Gaṇika, Maighika, Kāmardhika
And the fourth was Indrapuraka—
Such were the *kulas*
Of *gaṇa* named Vesavādiya. 11 8

Top : Sthūlabhadra as a lion with his sisters
Bottom : Sthūlabhadra's sisters with Bhadrabāhu (or Sthūlabhadra)

[facing p. 144

थेरेहिंतो णं इसिगुत्तेहिंतो काकंदियेहिंतो वासिट्ठ-सगोत्तेहिंतो एत्थ णं माणव-गणे णामं गणे णिग्गए। तस्स णं इमाओ चत्तारि साहाओ तिण्णि य कुलाइं एवमाहिज्जंति। से किं तं साहाओ? साहाओ एवमाहिज्जंति तं जहा—कासविज्जिया गोयमिज्जिया वासिट्ठिया सोरट्ठिया। से तं साहाओ। से किं तं कुलाइं? कुलाइं एवमाहिज्जंति तं जहा—

इसिगुत्तियत्थ पढमं
बिइयं इसिदत्तेयं मुणेयव्वं।
तइयं च अभिजसं तं
तिण्णि कुला माणवगणस्स।१२।

थेरेहिंतो सुट्ठिय-सुप्पडिबुद्धेहिंतो कोडिय-काकंदएहिंतो वग्घावच्च-सगोत्तेहिंतो एत्थ णं कोडियगणे णामं गणे णिग्गए। तस्स णं इमाओ चत्तारि साहाओ चत्तारि कुलाइं एवमाहिज्जंति। से किं तं साहाओ? साहाओ एवमाहिज्जंति तं जहा—

उच्चणागरी विज्जा
हरी य वइरी य मज्झिमिल्ला य।
कोडियगणस्स एया
हवंति चत्तारि साहाओ।१३।

से तं साहाओ। से किं तं कुलाइं? कुलाइं एवमाहिज्जंति तं जहा—

पढमित्थ बंभलिज्जं
बिइयं णामेण वच्छलिज्जं तु
तइयं पुण वाणिज्जं
चउत्थयं पण्हवाहणयं।१४। ९

From *sthavira* Ṛṣigupta Kākandika of the Vasiṣṭha line branched out a *gaṇa* named Mānava *gaṇa,* which in turn had four *śākhās* and three *kulas.* What were the *śākhās*? They were Kāśyapīyā, Gautamīyā, Vāsiṣṭhīyā and Saurāṣṭrīyā. Such were the *śākhās.* And the *kulas*? They were:

First was Ṛṣiguptīya
Second to be noted was Ṛṣidattīya
And the third—Abhijasā—
The three *kulas* of Mānava *gaṇa.* 12

From the two *sthaviras* of the Byâghrāpatya line, Susthita (*alias* Kotika) and Supratibuddha (*alias* Kâkandaka) branched out a *gaṇa* named Kotika *gaṇa*, which had four *śākhās* and four *kulas*. What were the *śākhās* ? They were :

First was Uccanâgari, and then
Vidyâdhari; Vajri, Mâdhyamila—
Such were the four *śākhās*
Of the *gaṇa* named Kotika. 13

Such were the *śākhās* ? And what about the *kulas* ? They were :

Brahmaliyâ was the first
The second was Vātsaliyâ
The third was Vānijya
And the fourth Praśna-vâhanaka. 14 9

थेराणं सुट्ठिय-सुप्पडिबुद्धाणं कोडिय-काकंदगाणं वग्घावच्च-सगोत्ताणं इमे पंच थेरा अंतेवासी अहावच्चा अभिण्णाया होथ्था तं जहा—थेरे अज्ज-इंददिण्णे थेरे पियगंठे थेरे विज्जाहरगोवाले कासव-गोत्तेणं थेरे इसिदत्ते थेरे अरिहदत्ते। थेरेहिंतो णं पियगंठेहिंतो एथ्थ णं मज्झिमा साहा णिग्गया। थेरेहिंतो विज्जाहरगोवालेहिंतो तथ्थ णं विज्जाहरी साहा णिग्गया। थेरस्स णं अज्ज-इंददिण्णस्स कासव-गोत्तस्स अज्ज-दिण्णे थेरे अंतेवासी गोयम-सगोत्ते। थेरस्स णण अज्ज-दिण्णस्स गोयम-सगोत्तस्स इमे दो थेरा अंतेवासी अहावच्चा अभिण्णाया होथ्था। थेरे अज्ज-संतिसेणिए माढर-गोत्ते। सथेरे अज्ज-सीहगिरी जाईसरे कोसियगोत्ते। थेरेहिंतो णं अज्ज-संतिसेणिएहिंतो माढर-सगोत्तेहिंतो एथ्थ णं उच्चणागरी साहा णिग्गया। १०

The two *sthaviras* of the Byâghrāpatya line, Susthita *alias* Kotika and Supratibuddha *alias* Kâkandaka had five progeny-like and very dear disciples in *sthavira* Ārya Indradatta, *sthavira* Priyagrantha, *sthavira* Vidyâdhara-gopâla of the Kâśyapa line, *sthavira* Ṛṣidatta and *sthavira* Arhadatta.

From *sthavira* Priyagrantha branched out the Madhyamâ *śākhā*. From *sthavira* Vidyâdhara-gopâla branched out the Vidyādhari *śākhā*.

Sthavira Ārya Indradatta of the Kâśyapa line had a disciple in *sthavira* Āryadatta of the Gautama line.

Sthavira Āryadatta of the Gautama line had two, progeny-like and very dear disciples in *sthavira* Śānti-sainika of the Māṭhara line, and *sthavira* Ārya Singhagiri Jātismara of the Kauśika line. From *sthavira* Ārya Śānti-sainika of the Māṭhara line branched out the Uccanāgari *śākhā*. 10

थेरस्स णं अज्ज-संतिसेणियस्स माढर-सगोत्तस्स इमे चत्तारि थेरा अंतेवासी अहावच्चा अभिण्णाया होथ्था तं जहा—थेरे अज्ज-सेणिए थेरे अज्ज-तावसे थेरे अज्ज-कुबेरे थेरे अज्ज-इसिपालिए । थेरेहिंतो णं अज्ज-सेणिएहिंतो एथ्थ णं अज्जसेणिया साहा णिग्गया । थेरेहिंतो णं अज्ज-तावसेहिंतो एथ्थ णं अज्ज-तावसी साहा णिग्गया । थेरेहिंतो णं अज्ज-कुबेरेहिंतो एथ्थ णं अज्ज-कुवेरा साहा णिग्गया । थेरेहिंतो णं अज्ज-इसपालिएहिंतो एथ्थ णं अज्ज-इसिपालिया साहा णिग्गया । थेरस्स णं अज्ज सिहगिरिस्स जाइसरस्स कोसिय-गोत्तस्स इमे चत्तारि थेरा अंतेवासी अहावच्चा अभिण्णाया होथ्था तं जहा—थेरे धणगिरि थेरे अज्ज-वइरे थेरे अज्ज-समिए थेरे अरिहदिण्णे । थेरेहिंतो णं अज्ज-समिएहिंतो गोयम-सगोत्तेहिंतो एथ्थ णं बंभदीविया साहा णिग्गया । थेरेहिंतो णं अज्ज-वइरेहिंतो गोयम-सगोत्तेहिंतो एथ्थ णं अज्ज-वइरा साहा णिग्गया । थेरस्स णं अज्ज-वइरस्स गोयम-सगोत्तस्स इमे तिण्णि थेरा अंतेवासी अहावच्चा अभिण्णाया होथ्था तं जहा—थेरे अज्ज-वइरसेणिए थेरे अज्ज-पउमे थेरे अज्ज-रहे । थेरेहिंतो णं अज्ज-वइरसेणिएहिंतो एथ्थ णं अज्ज-णइली साहा णिग्गया । थेरेहिंतो णं अज्ज-पउमेहिंतो एथ्थ णं अज्ज-पउमा साहा णिग्गया । थेरेरितो णं अज्ज-रहेहिंतो एथ्थ णं अज्ज-जयंती साहा णिग्गया । थेरस्स णं अज्ज-रहस्स वच्छ-सगोत्तस्स अज्ज-पूसगिरी थेरे अंतेवासी कोसिय-सगोत्ते । थेरस्स णं अज्ज-पूसगिरिस्स कोसिय-सगोत्तस्स अज्ज-फग्गुमित्ते थेरे अंतेवासी गोयम सगोत्ते । ११

Sthavira Ārya Śānti-sainika of the Māṭhara line had four progeny-like and very dear disciples in *sthavira* Ārya Sainika, *sthavira* Ārya Tāpasa, *sthavira* Ārya Kuvera and *sthavira* Ṛṣipālita.

From *sthavira* Ārya Sainika branched out the Ārya-Sainika *śākhā*. From *sthavira* Arya Tāpasa branched out the Ārya-Tāpasi *śākhā*. From *sthavira* Ārya Kuvera branched out the Ārya-Kuverā *śākha*. From *sthavira* Ārya Ṛṣi-pālita branched out the Ārya Ṛṣi-pālita *śākhā*.

Sthavira Ārya Singhagiri Jātismara of the Kauśika line had progeny-like and very dear disciples in *sthavira* Dhanagiri, *sthavira* Ārya Vajra, *sthavira* Ārya Samita and *sthavira* Arhaddatta.

From *sthavira* Ārya Samita of the Gautama line branched out the Brahmadīpikā *śākhā*. From *sthavira* Ārya Vajra of the Gautama line branched out the Ārya-Vajra *śākhā*.

Sthavira Ārya Vajra of the Gautama line had three progeny-like and very dear disciples in *sthavira* Ārya Vajra-sainika, *sthavira* Ārya Padma and *sthavira* Ārya Ratha.

From *sthavira* Ārya Vajra-sainika branched out the Ārya-naili *śākhā*.

From *sthavira* Ārya Padma branched out the Arya-Padmā *śākhā*. From *sthavira* Ārya Ratha branched out the Ārya-Jayanti *śākhā*. *Sthavira* Ārya Ratha of the Vātsya line had a disciple in Ārya Pauṣyagiri of the Kauśika line.

Sthavira Ārya Pauṣyagiri of the Vātsya line had a disciple in *sthavira* Ārya Phalgumitra of the Gautama line. 11

[थेरस्स णं अज्ज-फग्गुमित्तस्स गोयम-सगुत्तस्स अज्ज-धणगिरी थेरे अंतेवासी वासिट्ठ-सगोत्ते । थेरस्स णं अज्ज-धणगिरीस्स वासिट्ठ-सगोत्तस्स अज्ज-सिवभूई थेरे अंतेवासी कुच्छ-सगोत्ते । थेरस्स णं अज्ज-सिवभूइस्स कुच्छ-सगोत्तस्स अज्ज-भद्दे थेरे अंतेवासी कासव-गोत्ते । थेरस्स णं अज्ज-भद्दस्स कासव-गोत्तस्स अज्ज-णक्खत्ते थेरे अंतेवासी कासव-गोत्ते । थेरस्स णं अज्ज-णक्खत्तस्स कासव-गोत्तस्स अज्ज-रक्खे थेरे अंतेवासी कासव-गोत्ते । थेरस्स णं अज्ज-रक्खस्स कासव-गोत्तस्स अज्ज-णागे थेरे अंतेवासी गोयम-सगोत्ते । थेरस्स णं अज्ज-णागस्स गोयम-सगोत्तस्स अज्ज-जेहिले थेरे अंतेवासी वासिट्ठ-सगोत्ते । थेरस्स णं अज्ज-जेहिलस्स वासिट्ठ-सगोत्तस्स अज्ज-विण्हु थेरे अंतेवासी माढर-सगोत्ते । थेरस्स णं अज्ज-विण्हुस्स माढर-सगोत्तस्स अज्ज-कालए थेरे अंतेवासी गोयम-सगोत्ते । थेरस्स णं अज्ज-कालगस्स गोयम-सगोत्तस्स इमे दो थेरा अंतेवासी गोयम-सगोत्ता थेरे अज्ज-संपलिए थेरे अज्ज-भद्दे । एएसिं दुण्ह वि थेराणं गोयम-सगोत्ताणं अज्ज-वुड्ढे थेरे अंतेवासी गोयम-सगोत्ते । थेरस्स णं अज्ज-वुड्ढस्स गोयम-सगोत्तस्स अज्ज-संघपालिए थेरे अंतेवासी गोयम-सगोते । थेरस्स णं अज्ज-संघपालियस्स गोयम-सगोत्तस्स अज्ज-हत्थी थेरे अंतेवासी कासव-गोत्ते ।

थेरस्स णं अज्ज-हत्थिस्स कासव-गोत्तस्स अज्ज-धम्मे थेरे अंतेवासी सुव्वय-मेगोत्ते । थेरस्स णं अज्ज-धम्मस्स सुव्वय-गोत्तस्स अज्ज-सीहे थेरे अंतेवासी कासव-गोत्ते । थेरस्स णं अज्ज-सीहस्स कासव-गोत्तस्स अज्ज-धम्मे थेरे अंतेवासी कासव-गोत्ते । थेरस्स णं अज्ज-धम्मस्स कासव-गोत्तस्स अज्ज-संडिल्ले थेरे अंतेवासी ।] १२

[*Sthavira* Ārya Phalgumitra of the Gautama line had a disciple in *sthavira* Ārya Dhanagiri of the Vasiṣṭha line.

Sthavira Ārya Dhanagiri of the Vasiṣṭha line had a disciple in *sthavira* Ārya Śivabhūti of the Kautsa line.

Sthavira Ārya Śivabhūti of the Kautsya line had a disciple in *sthavira* Āryabhadra of the Kāśyapa line.

Sthavira Āryabhadra of the Kāśyapa line had a disciple in *sthavira* Ārya Nakṣatra of the Kāśyapa line.

Sthavira Ārya Nakṣatra of the Kāśyapa line had a disciple in *sthavira* Ārya Rakṣa of the Kāśyapa line.

Sthavira Ārya Rakṣa of the Kāśyapa line had a disciple in *sthavira* Ārya Nāga of the Gautama line.

Sthavira Ārya Nāga of the Gautama line had a disciple in *sthavira* Ārya Jehila (Jetthila, also Jyeṣṭha in other readings) of the Vasiṣṭha line.

Sthavira Ārya Jehila of the Vasiṣṭha line had a disciple in *sthavira* Ārya Viṣṇu of the Māṭhara line.

Sthavira Ārya Viṣṇu of the Māṭhara line had a disciple in *sthavira* Ārya Kālaka of the Gautama line.

Sthavira Ārya Kālaka of the Gautama line had two disciples in *sthavira* Ārya Sampālita and *sthavira* Āryabhadra, both of the Gautama line.

These two *sthaviras* of the Gautama line had a disciple in *sthavira* Āryabṛddha of the Gautama line.

Sthavira Āryabṛddha of the Gautama line had a disciple in *sthavira* Ārya Saṅgha-pālita of the Gautama line.

Sthavira Ārya Saṅgha-pālita of the Gautama line had a disciple in *sthavira* Ārya Hasti of the Kāśyapa line.

Sthavira Ārya Hasti of the Kāśyapa line had a disciple in *sthavira* Ārya Dharma of the Subrata line.

Sthavira Ārya Dharma of the Subrata line had a disciple in *sthavira* Ārya Siṅgha of the Kāśyapa line.

Sthavira Ārya Siṅgha of the Kāśyapa line had a disciple in *sthavira* Ārya Dharma of the Kāśyapa line.

Sthavira Ārya Dharma of the Kāśyapa line had a disciple in *sthavira* Ārya Śāṇḍilya.] 12

वंदामि फग्गुमित्तं
च गोयमं धणगिरिं च वासिट्ठं ।
कुच्छं सिवभूइं पिय
कोसिय दुज्जिंत–कण्हे य ।१।

तं वंदिऊण सिरसा
भद्दं वंदामि कासवं गोत्तम् ।
णक्खं कासव गोत्तं
रक्खं पि य कासवं वंदे ।२।

वंदामि अज्ज-णागं
च गोयमं जेहिलं च वासिट्ठं ।
विण्हुं माढर-गोत्तं
कालगं अवि गोयमं वंदे ।३।

गोयम-गोत्त-कुमारं
संपलियं तह य भद्दयं वंदे ।
थेरं च अज्ज-वुड्ढं
गोयम-गोत्तं नमंसामि ।४।

तं वंदिऊण सिरसा
थिर-सत्त-चरित्त-णाण-संपण्णं ।
थेरं च संधवालिय
कासव-गोत्तं पणिवयामि ।५।

वंदामि अज्ज-हथ्थिं
च कासवं खंति-सागरं धीरं ।
गिम्हाण पढ़म मासे
कालगयं चित्त-सुद्धस्स ।६।

वंदामि अज्ज.धम्मं
च सुव्वयं सील-लद्धि-संपण्णं ।
जस्स णिक्खमणे देवो
छत्तं वरं उत्तमं वहइ ।७।

हत्थं कासव-गोत्तं
धम्मं सिव-साहगं पणिवयामि ।
सीहं कासव-गोत्तं
धम्मं पि य कासवं वंदे ।८।

तं वंदिऊण सिरसा
[थिर-सत्त-चरित्त-णाण-संपण्णं ।
थेरं च अज्ज-जंबु
गोयम-गोत्तं णमंसामि ।९।

मिउ-मद्दव-संपण्णं
उवउत्तं णाण-दंसण-चरित्ते ।
थेरं च णंदियं पि य
कासव-गोत्तं पणिवयामि ।१०।

तत्तो अथिर-चरित्तं
उत्तम-संमत्त-सत्त-संजुत्तं ।
देसिगणि-खमासमणं
कासव-गोत्तं णमंसामि ।११।

तत्तो अणुओगधरं
धीरं मइ-सागरं महासत्तं ।
थिरिगुत्त-खमासमणं
वच्छ-सगोत्तं पणिवयामि ।१२।

तत्तो अणाण-दंसण
चरित्त-तव-सुट्ठियं-गुण-महंतं ।
थेरं कुमारं धम्मं
वंदामि गणिं गुणोवेयं ।१३।]

सुत्तत्थ-रयण-भरिए
खम-दम-मद्दव-गुणेहि संपण्णे ।
देविड्ढि-खमासमणे
कासव-गोत्ते पणिवयामि ।१४। १३

I pay homage to Phalgumitra of Gautama line
To Dhanagiri of the line of Vasiṣṭha
I pay homage to Śivabhūti of the Kautsya line
To Durdānta-kṛṣṇa of the line of Kauśika. Śl. 1

I pay homage to Bhadra of Kāśyapa line
With my head bent low.
To Nakṣa of the Kāśyapa line
To Rakṣa of Kāśyapa line (again). Śl. 2

Bow I to Ārya Nâga of the Gautama line
To Jehila of the line of Vasiṣṭha
To Viṣṇu of Māṭhara line
To Kālaka of the line of Gautama. Sl. 3

Bow I to Kumâra Sampālita and to Bhadraka
Both of the line of Gautama
Bow I to *sthavira* Ārya Bṛddha
Who (also) belongs to the line of Gautama. Śl. 4

Having paid obeisance to them
With head bent low
Do I bow to *sthavira* Sanghapālita of Kāśyapa line
Fixed in equanimity and master of knowledge and conduct. Śl. 5

Obeisance to Ārya Hasti of the Kāśyapa line
Calm was he, an ocean of fortitude
Passed he away in the first month of summer
In the bright half of the month of Caitra. Śl. 6

Obeisance to Ārya Dharma of Subrata line
Rich in quietude and spiritual fortune
When he was on his wandering missions
Gods held an excellent umbrella (on his head). Śl. 7

Obeisance to Hasta of Kāśyapa line
To Dharma, master of bliss and welfare
To Singha, to Dharma, bow I in obeisance,
Both of whom are of the line of Kāśyapa. Śl. 8

[Placing my head on the ground
Pay I homage and obeisance to *sthavira* Jambu
Who is in the line of Gautama,
Master of equanimity, of knowledge and conduct. Śl. 9

Bow I to Upagupta, with clemency great,
Master of knowledge, faith and conduct
To *sthavira* Nandita of the Kāśyapa line
Do I bow in deep reverence. Śl. 10

Even more steadfast in conduct
High in equanimity, with merit great
Do I bow to Deśigaṇi Kṣamāśramaṇa
Who is in the line of Kāśyapa. Śl. 11

To the great preserver of the sacred lore
Wise, an ocean of wisdom, with merit great
Do I bow to Deśigaṇi Sthiragupta
Who belongs to the line of Vātsya. Śl. 12

Then I adore the *sthavira*-prince Dharma
A *gaṇadhara* with merits great
Rich in virtue, with posture high
In knowledge, faith, conduct and penance. Śl. 13]

Bow I to Devardhi Kṣamāśramaṇa
Who belongs to the line of Kāśyapa
Full of gems — the meaning of the *śrutas*
And adorned with clemency, patience and restraint. Śl. 14 13

VII

पज्जोसवणा-कप्पो

Prescription for the Parjuṣaṇā (Rules for the monks)

तेणं कालेणं तेणं समएणं समणे भगवं महावीरे वासाणं स-वीसइ-राए मासे विइक्कंते वासावासं पज्जोसवेइ। से केणट्ठेणं भंते! एवं वुच्चइ: समणे भगवं महावीरे वासाणं स-वीसइ-राए मासे विइक्कंते वासावासं पज्जोसवेइ? १

In that period, at that time, Śramaṇa Bhagavân Mahâvîra performed the *parjuṣaṇā* rites during the monsoon sojourn when a month and 20 nights of the rainy season had elapsed. —*Bhante*! In what sense is it said that Śramaṇa Bhagavân Mahâvîra performed the *parjuṣaṇā* rites during the monsoon sojourn when one month and 20 nights of the rainy season had elapsed? 1

जओ णं पाएणं अगारिणं अगाराइं कडियाइं उक्कंपियाइं छण्णाइं लित्ताइं घट्ठाइं मट्ठाइं संपधूमियाइं खाओदगाइं खायणिद्धमणाइं अप्पणो अट्ठाए कडाइं परिभुत्ताइं परिणामियाइं भवंति से तेणट्ठेणं एवं वुच्चइ: समणे भगवं महावीरे वासाणं स-वीसइ-राए मासे विइक्कंते वासावासं पज्जोसवेइ। २

Since (about this time) the householders usually repair their houses, white-wash them, thatch them, smear them, level them, smoothen them, perfume them, dig pits and drains in them, furnish their houses, render them comfortable and rid them of all defects and inconveniences, so has it been said that Śramaṇa Bhagavân Mahâvîra performed the *parjuṣaṇā* rites during the monsoon sojourn when one month and 20 nights of the rainy seasons had elapsed. 2

जहा णं समणे भगवं महावीरे वासाणं स-वीसइ-राए मासे विइक्कंते वासावासं पज्जोसवेइ तहा णं गणहरा वि वासाणं स-वीसइ-राए मासे विइक्कंते वासावासं पज्जोसविंति। ३

Just as Śramaṇa Bhagavân Mahâvîra performed the *parjuṣaṇā* rites during the monsoon sojourn after the expiry of one month and 20 nights of the rainy season, so did the *gaṇadharas* perform the *parjuṣaṇā* rites on the expiry of one month and 20 nights of the rainy season. 3

जहा णं गणहरा वि वासाणं स-वीसइ-राए मासे विइक्कंते वासावासं पज्जोसविंति तहा णं गणहर-सीसा वि वासाणं स-वीसइ-राए मासे विइक्कंते वासावासं पज्जोसविंति । ४

Just as the *gaṇadharas* performed the *parjuṣaṇā* rites during the monsoon sojourn after the expiry of one month and 20 nights of the rainy season, so did the *gaṇadhara* disciples perform the *parjuṣaṇā* rites during the monsoon sojourn after the expiry of one month and 20 nights of the rainy season. 4

जहा णं गणहर-सीसा वि वासाणं स-वीसइ-राए मासे विइक्कंते वासावासं पज्जोसविंति तहा णं थेरा वि वासाणं स-वीसइ-राए मासे विइक्कंते वासावासं पज्जोसविंति । ५

Just as the *gaṇadhara* disciples performed the *parjuṣaṇā* rites during the monsoon sojourn after the expiry of one month and 20 nights of the rainy season, so did the senior monks, the *sthaviras*, perform the *parjuṣaṇā* rites during monsoon sojourn after the expiry of one month and 20 nights of the rainy season. 5

जहा णं थेरा वि वासाणं स-वीसइ-राए मासे विइक्कंते वासावासं पज्जोसविंति तहा णं जे अज्जत्ताए समणा णिग्गंठा विहरंति एए विय णं वासाणं स-वीसइ-राए मासे विइक्कंते वासावासं पज्जोसविंति । ६

And just as the senior monks, the *sthaviras*, performed the *parjuṣaṇā* rites during the monsoon sojourn after the expiry of one month and 20 nights of the rainy season, so all the monks, *śramaṇa-nirgranthas*, to this day have been performing the *parjuṣaṇā* rites during their monsoon sojourn after the expiry of one month and 20 nights of the rainy season. 6

जहा णं जे अज्जत्ताए समणा णिग्गंठा विहरंति वासाणं स-वीसइ-राए मासे विइक्कंते वासावासं पज्जोसविंति तहा णं अम्हं आयरीया उवज्झाया स-वीसइ-राए मासे विइक्कंते वासावासं पज्जोसविंति । ७

Just as the *śramaṇa-nirgranthas* to this day have been performing the *parjuṣaṇā* rites during their monsoon sojourn after the expiry of one month and 20 nights of the rainy season, so do our preceptors and teachers, *ācāryas* and *upādhyāyas*, perform the *parjuṣaṇā* rights during their monsoon sojourn after the expiry of one month and 20 night of the rainy season. 7

जहा णं ग्रम्हं पि ग्रायरिया उवज्झाया वासाणं स-वीसइ-राए मासे विइक्कंते वासावासं पज्जोसविंति तहा णं ग्रम्हे वि वासाणं स-वीसइ-राए मासे विइक्कंते वासावासं पज्जोसवेम । ग्रंतरा वि य से कप्पइ पज्जोसवित्तए णो से कप्पइ तं रयणिं उवायणावित्तए । ८

Just as the preceptors and teachers perform the *parjuṣaṇā* rites during their monsoon sojourn after the expiry of one month and 20 nights of the rainy season, so do we perform the *parjuṣaṇā* rites after the expiry of one month and 20 nights of the rainy season. (The commencement of) *parjuṣaṇā* rites is permitted prior, but not posterior, to that night. 8

वासावासं पज्जोसवियाणं कप्पइ णिग्गंठाण वा णिग्गंठीण वा सव्वग्रो समंता स-कोसं जोयणं उग्गहं ग्रोगिण्हित्ता णं चिट्ठिउं ग्रहा-लंदं[43] ग्रवि उग्गहे । ९

Monks and nuns performing the *parjuṣaṇā* rites during their monsoon sojourn are permitted to regard their residence as extending over a *krośa* (about 2 miles) added to a *yojana* (about 3 miles) all around. For depositing excfeta, they are permitted to move as far as may be necessary. 9

वासावासं पज्जोसवियाणं कप्पइ णिग्गंठाण वा णिग्गंठीण वा सव्वग्रो समंता स-कोसं जोयणं भिक्खायरियाए गंतुं पडिणियत्तए । १०

On the whole, monks and nuns, performing the *parjuṣaṇā* rites during their monsoon sojourn, are permitted to go and come back, for the sake of begging, upto a *krośa* added to a *yojana* all around. 10

जथ्थ णं णइ णिच्चोयगा णिच्च-संदणा णो से कप्पइ सव्वग्रो समंता स-कोसं जोयणं भिक्खायरियाए गंतुं पडिणियत्तए । ११

If there is (in their way) a river with perennial water supply and perennial flow, then they are not allowed to go and come back, for the sake of begging, as far as a *krośa* added to a *yojana* all around. 11

एरावई[44] कुणालाए जथ्थ चक्किया सिया एगं पायं जले किच्चा एगं पायं थले किच्चा एवं चक्किया ण्हं कप्पइ सव्वओ समंता स-कोसं जोयणं भिक्खायरियाए गंतुं पडिणियत्तए । १२

But if the river is like Irâvati near Kunālā which has a (shallow) bed that may be crossed with one leg in the water and another on the land, then they are permitted to go and come back, for the sake of begging, as far as a *krośa* added to a *yojana* all around. 12

एवं णो चक्किया एवं से णो कप्पइ सव्वओ समंता स-कोसं जोयणं भिक्खायरियाए गंतुं पडिणियत्तए । १३

But where the river bed is not like this, then they are not permitted to go and come back, for the sake of begging, as far as a *krośa* added to a *yojana* all around. 13

वासावासं पज्जोसवियाणं अथ्थेगइयाणं[45] एवं वुत्त-पुव्वं भवइ: दावे भंते ! एवं से कप्पइ दावित्तए णो से कप्पइ पडिगाहित्तए । १४

If the *ācārya* supervising the performance of the *parjuṣaṇā* during the monsoon sojourn says first, '*dāve bhante*', and then giving is permitted, but not taking. 14

वासावा सं पज्जोसवियाणं अथ्थेगइयाणं एवं वुत्त-पुव्वं भवइ: पडिगाहे भंते ! एवं से कप्पइ पडिगाहित्तए णो से कप्पइ दावित्तए । १५

If the *ācārya* supervising the performance of the *parjuṣaṇā* during the monsoon sojourn says, '*padigāhe bhante*' then taking is permitted, but not giving. 15

वासावासं पज्जोसवियाणं अथ्थेगइयाणं एवं वुत्त-पुव्वं भवइ: दावे भंते ! एवं से कप्पइ दावित्तए पडिगाहित्तए वा । १६

If the *ācārya* supervising the performance of the *parjuṣaṇā* during the monsoon sojourn says, '*dāve bhante, padigāhe bhante*', then are permitted both giving and taking. 16

वासावासं पज्जोसवियाणं णो कप्पइ णिग्गंठाण वा णिग्गंठीण वा हट्ठाणं आरोग्गाणं बलीय-सरीराणं इमाओ णव-रस-विगईओ अभिक्खणं आहारित्तए। तं जहा: खीरं दहिं णवणीयं सप्पिं तेल्लं गुडं मच्छं मज्जं मंसं। १७

In the course of the *parjuṣaṇā* during their monsoon sojourn, monks and nuns, who are healthy, who are without physical ailments, and are strong, are not permitted to take frequently these nine items that may cause disorder. They are :

milk, curd, fresh butter, clarified butter, oil, jaggery, honey, wine and meat. 17

वासावासं पज्जोसवियाणं अथ्थेगइयाणं एवं वुत्त-पुव्वं भवइ: अट्ठो भंते! गिलाणस्स? से य वएज्जा: अट्ठो: से य पुच्छेयव्वे—केवइएणं अट्ठो? से य वएज्जा: एवइएणं अट्ठो गिलाणस्स। जं से पमाणं वयइ से पमाणे ओघेत्तव्वे। से य विण्णवेज्जा से य विण्णवेमाणे लभेज्जा से य पमाणपत्ते: होउ! अलाहि! इ इ वत्तव्वं सिया। से किमाहु भंते? एवइएणं अट्ठो गिलाणस्स। सिया णं एणं वयंतं परो वएज्जा: पडिगाहेहि अज्जो! तुमं पच्छा भोक्खसि वा पाहिसि वा। एवं से कप्पइ पडिगाहित्तए णो से कप्पइ गिलाणस्स णीसाए पडिगाहित्तए। १८

The following submission is first made to the *ācārya* supervising the performance of the *parjuṣaṇā* during the monsoon sojourn : —'*Bhante* ! Are the aforesaid items necessary for the sick people ?'

He (the *ācārya* says)—'Yes, they are.'

Then (he) is to be asked—'How much is necessary' ?

He will say—'So much is necessary for the sick people'.

The quantity mentioned by him has to be accepted. He will communicate it to the householder, and having communicated, he will obtain the same. Having obtained the requisite quantity he will say, —'Thank you. No more.'

(If the householder says)—'*Bhante*! Why do ye say so ?'

—'Because this much is necessary for the sick people.'

If on this the fellow says—'*Ārya* ! It behoves thee to accept, which ye may afterwards eat and drink,' then acceptance is permitted, but not on the pretension that the thing is needed for the sick. 18

वासावासं पज्जोसवियाणं अथ्थिणं थेराणं तह-प्पगाराइं कुलाइं कडाइं पत्तियाइं थेज्जाइं वेसासियाइं संमयाइं बहुमयाइं अणुमयाइं भवंति जथ्थ से णो कप्पइ अदक्खु वइत्तए : अथ्थि ते आउसो ! इमं वा इमं वा ? किमाहु भंते ? सड्ढी गिही गिण्हइ वा तेणियं पि कुज्जा । १९

The *ācārya* or the senior monk supervising the performance of the *parjuṣaṇā* during the monsoon sojourn permits, sanctions and allows begging from such households which are inhabited by people who are initiated, faithful, firm and trust-worthy. But the monks are not permitted to ask for things that are not visible (saying)—'Oh long-lived one ! Have you this? Have you that ?'

—'*Bhante* ! Why has this been said ?'

—'(Then) a devoted householder may buy or steal (for serving the monk with).' 19

वासावासं पज्जोसवियस्स णिच्च-भत्तिस्स भिक्खुस्स कप्पइ एगं गोयर-कालं गाहावइ-कुलं भत्ताए वा पाणाए वा णिक्खमित्तए वा पविसित्तए वा । णण्णथा आयरिय-वेयावच्चेण वा एवं उवज्झाय तवस्सि-गिलाण-वेयावच्चेण वा खुड्ड-खुड्डियाए एवं अवंजण-जायएणं । २०

A *bhikṣu* performing the *parjuṣaṇā* rites during the monsoon sojourn will daily take one meal, and it is proper to go only once to the householders' residence for begging food and drink and return therefrom at a fixed hour. Permitted exceptions (about taking food more than once) are : if and when the *bhikṣu* is nursing the *ācārya*, or if and when he is employed to nurse the teacher, monk or some ailing person, or if he (or she) has not yet developed the mark of a mature age. 20

वासावासं पज्जोसवियस्स चउथ्थ-भत्तियस्स भिक्खुस्स अयं एवइए विसेसे जं से पाओ णिक्खम्म पुव्वामेव वियडगं भोच्चा पच्छा पडिग्गहं संलिहिय संपमज्जिय से य संथरिज्जा कप्पइ से तद्दिवसं तेणेव भत्तट्ठेणं पज्जो-सवित्तए । से य णो संथरिज्जा एवं से कप्पइ दोच्चं पि गाहावइ-कुलं भत्ताए वा पाणाए वा णिक्खमित्तए वा पविसित्तए वा । २१

If, in the course of the *parjuṣaṇā* during the monsoon sojourn, a *bhikṣu* takes his meal after a gap of a day, then, for him, there is a special prescription to the effect that he should go out in the morning, and at first take his meal, and thereafter clean his begging bowl. If that meal be enough for the day, then with that much intake, he should participate in the performance of the *parjuṣaṇā* rites; but if the meal be not sufficient, then, for begging food and drink for a second time, he is permitted to enter into the residence of the householder and emerge out therefrom. 21

वासावासं पज्जोसवियस्स छट्ठ-भत्तियस्स भिक्खुस्स कप्पंति दो गोयर-काला गाहावइ-कुलं भत्ताए वा पाणाए वा णिक्खमित्तए वा पविसित्तए वा। २२

वासावासं पज्जोसवियस्स अट्ठम-भत्तियस्य भिक्खुस्स कप्पंति तओ गोयर-काला गाहावइ-कुलं भत्ताए वा पाणाए वा णिक्खमित्तए वा पविसित्तए वा। २३

If, in the course of the *parjuṣaṇā* during the monsoon sojourn, a *bhikṣu* takes his meal every third day, then, for his food and drink, two begging times are permitted for his going to the householder's residence and emerging out therefrom. 22

If, in the course of the *parjuṣaṇā* during the monsoon sojourn, a *bhikṣu* takes his meal every fourth day, then, for his food and drink, three begging times are permitted for his going to the householder's residence and emerging out therefrom. 23

वासावासं पज्जोसवियस्स विगिट्ठ-भत्तियस्स भिक्खुस्स कप्पंति सव्वे वि गोयर-काला गाहावइ-कुलं भत्ताए वा पाणाए वा णिक्खमित्तए वा पविसित्तए वा। २४

If in the course of the *parjuṣaṇā* during the monsoon sojourn a *bhikṣu* takes his meal after a prolonged and extended fast, then for his food and drink, he is permitted any number of begging times for his going to the householder's residence and emerging out therefrom. 24

वासावासं पज्जोसवियस्स णिच्च-भत्तियस्स भिक्खुस्स कप्पंति सव्वाइं पाणगाइं पडिगाहित्तए। वासावासं पज्जोसवियस्स चउथ्थ-भत्तियस्स कप्पंति तओ पाणगाइं पडिगाहित्तए। तं जहा—उस्सेइमं वा संसेइमं वा चाउलोदगं वा। वासावासं पज्जोसवियस्स छट्ठ-भत्तियस्स भिक्खुस्स कप्पंति तओ पाणगाइं पडिगाहित्तए। तं जहा—तिलोदगं वा तुसोदगं वा जवोदगं वा। वासावासं पज्जोसवियस्स अट्ठम-भत्तियस्स भिक्खुस्स कप्पंति तओ पाणगाइं पडिगाहित्तए। तं जहा—आयामं वा सोवीरं वा सुद्धवियडं[46] वा। वासावासं पज्जोसवियस्स विगिट्ठ-भत्तियस्स भिक्खुस्स कप्पइ एगे उसिण-वियडे पडिगाहित्तए से वि य णं असिथ्थे णो वि य णं स-सिथ्थे। वासावासं पज्जोसवियस्स भत्तपडियाइक्खियस्स[47] भिक्खुस्स कप्पइ एगे उसिण-वियडे पडिगाहित्तए से वि य णं अ-सिथ्थे णो वि य णं स-सिथ्थे से वि य णं परिपूए णो चेव णं अपरिपूए से वि य णं परि-णिमिए णो चेव णं अ-परिणिमिए से य णं बहु-संपण्णो णो चेव णं अ-बहुसंपुण्णे। २५

In the course of the *parjuṣaṇā* during the monsoon sojourn, a *bhikṣu* who takes his meal once a day is permitted to accept all (permitted) drinks.

In the course of the *parjuṣaṇā* during the monsoon sojourn, a *bhikṣu* who takes his meal once every alternate day is permitted to accept three types of drink, which are, water passed through flour, water passed through sesamum and water passed through rice.

In the course of the *parjuṣaṇā* during the monsoon sojourn, a *bhikṣu* who takes his meal every third day is permitted to accept three types of drink, which are, water passed through sesamum, water passed through half-broken rice/chaff and water passed through barley.

In the course of the *parjuṣaṇā* during the monsoon sojourn, a *bhikṣu* who takes his meal every fourth day is permitted to accept three types of water, which are, boiled water, sour water and pure water.

In the course of the *parjuṣaṇā* during the monsoon sojourn, a *bhikṣu* who takes his meal after a prolonged and extended fast is permitted to accept only boiled water (water in which rice has been boiled, according to some), free from particles of the grain, and not water with particles of the grain.

In the course of the *parjuṣaṇā* during the monsoon sojourn, a *bhikṣu* who has totally renounced the intake of food, is permitted to take only one drink, which is boiled water (water in which rice has been boiled, according to some), free from particles of the grain, and not with particles of the grain, duly filtered and not unfiltered, in a limited quantity and not unlimited, (but) sufficient and not insufficient. 25

वासावासं पज्जोसवियस्स संखा-दत्तियस्स[48] भिक्खुस्स कप्पंति पंच दत्तीओ भोयणस्स पडिगाहित्तए पंचपाणगस्स अहवा चत्तारि भोयणस्स पंच पाणगस्स अहवा पंच भोयणस्स चत्तारि पाणगस्स। तथ्थ एगा दत्ती लोणा सायण-मित्तं अवि पडिगाहिया सिया। कप्पइ से तद्दिवसं तेणेव भत्तट्ठेणं पज्जोसवित्तए। णो से कप्पइ दोच्चं पि गाहावइ-कुलं भत्ताए वा पाणाए वा णिक्खमित्तए वा पविसित्तए वा। २६

In the course of the *parjuṣaṇā* during the monsoon sojourn, a *bhikṣu*, who is permitted to accept a certain number of offers, may accept food from five (households) and drink from five, or food from four and drink from five, or food from five and drink from four. Besides, he may take in another offer as much salt as may be necessary to impart taste to his food. That food and that drink he has to accept as enough for the day's intake during the *parjuṣaṇā*, and his going to, and coming back from, the householder's residence for a second time for food and drink are not permitted. 26

वासावासं पज्जोसवियाणं णो कप्पइ णिग्गंठाण वा णिग्गंठीण वा जाव... उवस्सयाओ सत्त-घरंतरं संखडि संणियट्ट-चारिस्स इत्तए। एगे एवमाहंसु णो कप्पइ जाव...उवस्सयाओ परेणं सत्त-घरंतरं संखडि[49] संणियट्ट-चारिस्स इत्तए। एगे पुण एवमाहंसु : नो कप्पइ जाव...उवस्सयाओ परंपरेणं सत्त-घरंतरं संखडि संणियट्ट-चारिस्स इत्तए। २७

A monk or a nun is not permitted in the course of the *parjuṣaṇā* during the monsoon sojourn to go to a household where a feast is being prepared, if the house be beyond the seventh house from the monk's residence. According to some, a monk or a nun is not permitted to go to a household where a feast is being prepared, if it be beyond the seventh house excluding the monk's/

nun's abode; but according to others, a monk or a nun is not permitted to go to a household where a feast is being prepared, if it be beyond the seventh house including the monk's/nun's abode. 27

वासावासं पज्जोसवियाणं णो कप्पइ पाणि-पडिग्गहियस्स भिक्खुस्स कणग-फुसिय-मित्तम् अवि वुट्ठि-कायंसि गाहावइ-कुलं भत्ताए वा पाणाए वा णिक्खमित्तए वा पविसित्तए वा । २८

In the course of the *parjuṣaṇā* during the monsoon sojourn, a *bhikṣu*, who uses the hollow of his palm as his begging bowl, the prescription for him is that he is not to enter into, or emerge from, for the purpose of begging food and drink, from the residence of householders even in a very mild shower. 28

वासावासं पज्जोसवियस्स पाणि-पडिग्गहियस्स भिक्खुस्स णो कप्पइ अगिहंसि पिंडवायं[50] पडिगाहित्ता पज्जोसवित्तए । पज्जोसवेमाणस्स सहसा वुट्ठि-काए णिवएज्जा देसं भोच्चा देसमादाय से पाणिणा पाणिं परिपिहित्ता उरंसि वा णं णिलिज्जिज्जा कक्खंसि वा णं समाहडिज्जा अहाछण्णाणि वा लेणाणि वा उवागच्छिज्जा रुक्ख-मूलाणि वा उवागच्छिज्जा जहा से पाणिंसि दए वा दग-रए वा दग-फुसिया वा णो परियावज्जइ । २९

In the course of the *parjuṣaṇā* during the monsoon sojourn, a *bhikṣu*, who uses the hollow of his palm as his begging bowl, is not permitted to stay on (after begging) outdoors; for, while he is performing the *parjuṣaṇā* rites, it may suddenly start raining. (In case it starts raining), (he) should eat a portion and cover the remaining portion in one hand by another hand and shelter it under the breast, or in the arm-pit, or he should take shelter in a place properly covered, or in a cave, or he should come at the foot of a tree, so that no water, drop of water or dew-like spray of water may fall on his hand. 29

वासावासं पज्जोसवियस्स पाणि-पडिग्गहियस्स भिक्खुस्स जं किं चि कणग-फुसिय-मित्तं पि णिवडइ णो से कप्पइ भत्ताए वा पाणाए वा णिक्खमित्तए वा पविसित्तए वा । ३०

In the course of the *parjuṣaṇā* during the monsoon sojourn, a *bhikṣu*, who uses the hollow of his palm as his begging bowl, for him the prescription is that he is not permitted to enter into, or emerge from, for the purpose of begging food and drink, the residence of householders, if there is either a shower, or even a drizzle. 30

वासावासं पज्जोसवियस्स पडिग्गह्-धारिस्स भिक्खुस्स णो कप्पइ वग्घारिय वुट्ठि-कायंसि गाहावइ-कुलं भत्ताए वा पाणाए वा णिक्खमित्तए वा पविसित्तए वा। कप्पइ से अप्प-वुट्ठि-कायंसि संतरुत्तरंसि[51] गाहावइ-कुलं भत्ताए वा पाणाए वा णिक्खमित्तए वा पविसित्तए वा। ३१

In the course of the *parjuṣaṇā* during the monsoon sojourn, a *bhikṣu* who uses a begging bowl, — for him the prescription is that in case of incessant shower, he is not permitted to enter into or emerge from, for the purpose of begging food and drink, the residence of householders; but in case of light shower, he is permitted to enter into, or emerge from, the residence of the householders by covering himself both by an under-garment and by an upper-garment. 31

वासावासं पज्जोसवियस्स णिग्गंठस्स य गाहावइ-कुलं पिंडवाय-पडियाए अणुपविट्ठस्स णिगिज्झिय णिगिज्झिय वुट्ठि-काए णिवइज्जा कप्पइ से अहे आरामंसि वा अहे उवस्सयंसि वा अहे वियड-गिहंसि[52] वा अहे रुक्ख-मूलंसि वा उवागच्छित्तए। ३२

In the course of the *parjuṣaṇā* during the monsoon sojourn, if, after the monk has entered into a householder's residence, there are showers with break, then the monk will take shelter in a park, in a monks' abode, in a water-store (village assembly hall, according to Jacobi) or at the foot of a tree. 32

तथ्थ से पुव्वागमणेणं पुव्वाउत्ते[53] चाउलोदणे पच्छाउत्ते भिलिंग-सूवे कप्पइ से चाउलोदणे पडिगाहित्तए णो से कप्पइ भिलिंग-सूवे पडिगाहित्तए। ३३

If, before the coming (of the monk), rice is being cooked, and the cooking of the pulse-soup begins thereafter, then rice is permitted for acceptance, but not the soup. 33

तथ्थ से पुव्वागमणेणं पुव्वाउत्ते भिलिंग-सूवे पच्छाउत्ते चाउलोदणे कप्पइ से भिलिंग-सूवे पडिगाहित्तए णो से कप्पइ चाउलोदणे पडिगाहित्तए। ३४

If, before the coming, pulse-soup is being cooked, and the cooking of rice begins thereafter, then pulse-soup is permitted for acceptance, but not rice. 34

तथ्थ से पुव्वागमणेणं दो वि पुव्वाउत्ताइं वट्टंति कप्पंति से दो वि पडिगाहित्तए। तथ्थ से पुव्वागमणेणं दो वि पच्छाउत्ताइं णो से कप्पंति दो वि पडिगाहित्तए। जे से तथ्थ पुव्वागमणेणं पुव्वाउत्ते से कप्पइ पडिगाहित्तए। जे से तथ्थ पुव्वागमणेणं पच्छाउत्ते णो से कप्पइ पडिगाहित्तए। ३५

If, before the coming, both are being cooked, then both are permitted for acceptance. If the cooking of both starts afterwards, then none is permitted for acceptance. That what is being cooked before the coming is permitted for acceptance; that what is being cooked after the coming is not permitted for acceptance. 35

वासावासं पज्जोसवियस्स णिग्गंठस्स गाहावइ-कुलं पिंडवाय-पडियाए पविट्ठस्स णिगिज्झिय णिगिज्झिय वुट्ठिकाए णिवइज्जा। कप्पइ से अहे आरामंसि वा अहे उवस्सयंसि वा अहे वियड-गिहंसि वा अहे रुक्ख-मूलंसि वा उवागच्छित्तए। णो से कप्पइ पुव्वगहिएणं भत्तपाणेणं वेलं उवायणावित्तए। कप्पइ से पुव्वामेव वियडगं भोच्चा पच्छा पडिग्गहं संलिहिय संलिहिय संपमज्जिय संपमज्जिस एगाययं भंडगं कट्टु सावसेसे सूरिए। जेणेव उवस्सए तेणेव उवागच्छित्तए। णो से कप्पइ तं रयणिं तथ्थेव उवायणावित्तए। ३६

In the course of the *parjuṣaṇā* during the monsoon sojourn, if after his arrival at the householder's residence there are showers with break, then the monk is permitted to take shelter in a park, in a monks' abode, in a water store or at the foot of a tree; but he is not allowed to pass the day there by holding on the food and drink already collected. He is permitted to take the staff collected, clean the vessels before the sun is down, and then putting his things together, he should move in the direction of his abode before sun-set; permitted is not he to spend the night there. 36

वासावासं पज्जोसवियस्स णिग्गंठस्स गाहावइ-कुलं पिंड-वाय-पडियाए अणुपविट्ठस्स णिगिज्झिय णिगिज्झिय वुट्ठिकाए णिवइज्जा कप्पइ से अहे आरामंसि वा अहे उवस्सयंसि वा अहे वियड-गिहंसि वा अहे रुक्खमूलंसि वा उवागच्छित्तए। ३७

In the course of the *parjuṣaṇā* during the monsoon sojourn, if after his entering into the householder's residence there are showers with break, then the monk is permitted to take shelter in a park, in a monks' abode, in a water store or at the foot of a tree. 37

तत्थ णो कप्पइ एगस्स णिग्गंठस्स एगाए णिग्गंठिए एगयओ चिट्ठित्तए।
तत्थ णो कप्पइ एगस्स णिग्गंठस्स दुण्ह य णिग्गंठीणं एगयओ चिट्ठित्तए।
तत्थ णो कप्पइ दुण्हं णिग्गंठाणं एगाए निग्गंठीए एगयओ चिट्ठित्तए।
तत्थ णो कप्पइ दुण्हं णिग्गंठाणं दुण्ह य णिग्गंठीणं एगयओ चिट्ठित्तए।
अत्थि य इत्थ केइ पंचमे खुड्डए वा खुड्डिया वा अण्णेसिं वा संलोए स-पडिदुवारे,[54] एव ण्हं कप्पइ एगयओ चिट्ठित्तए। ३८

There it is not permitted that a monk and a nun stay together; nor a monk and two nuns are permitted to stay together: nor two monks and a nun are permitted to stay together; nor two monks and two nuns are permitted to stay together. If there is a fifth person — even a lay follower, male or female — and if the place is visible to others, and if the doors open on it, then is permitted their staying together there. 38

वासावासं पज्जोसवियस्स णिग्गंठस्स गाहावइ-कुलं पिंडवाय-पडियाए अणुपविट्ठस्स णिगिज्झिय णिगिज्झिय वुट्ठि-काए णिवइज्जा कप्पइ से अहे आरामंसि वा अहे उवस्सयंसि वा अहे वियड-गिहंसि वा अहे रुक्खमूलंसि वा उवागच्छित्तए। तत्थ णो कप्पइ एगस्स निग्गंठस्स एगाए अगारीए एगयओ चिट्ठित्तए। एवं चउभंगो। अत्थि य इत्थ केइ पंचमे थेरे वा थेरिया वा अण्णेसिं वा संलोए स-पडिदुवारे एवं कप्पइ एगयओ चिट्ठित्तए। एवं चेव णिग्गंठीए अगारस्स य भाणियव्वं। ३९

In the course of the *parjuṣaṇā* during the monsoon sojourn, if after his entering into the householder's residence, there are showers with break, then the monk is permitted to take shelter in a park, in a monks' abode, in a water store or at the foot of a tree. But there a monk is not permitted to stay with a female householder; and all the forms as aforesaid are to be repeated. If there is a fifth person — a senior monk or nun — and if the place is visible to others, and if the doors open on it, then their staying together there is permitted. The perscription is the same for a male householder and a nun. 39

वासावासं पज्जोसवियाणं णो कप्पइ णिग्गंठाण वा णिग्गंठीण वा अपरिण्णएणं अपरिण्णयस्स अट्ठाए असणं वा पाणं वा खाइमं वा साइमं वा पडिगाहित्तए। ४०

से किमाहु भंते? इच्छापरो अपरिण्णए भूंजिज्जा इच्छापरो ण भूंजिज्जा। ४१

In the course of the *parjuṣaṇā* during the monsoon sojourn, unless specifically requested, a monk or a nun is not permitted to receive food or drink, dainties or dry fruits for another unless he has himself informed him (about his collecting these for him). 40

— '*Bhante* ! why has it been said like that?

Because (one who has not been informed already) he may eat if he likes, (but) may not eat if he does not like. 41

वासावासं पज्जोसवियाणं णो कप्पइ णिग्गंठाण वा णिग्गंठीण वा उद-उल्लेण वा स-सिणिद्धेण वा काएणं असणं वा पाणं वा खाइमं वा साइमं वा आहारित्तए। ४२

से किमाहु भंते? सत्त सिणेहाययणा पण्णत्ता तं जहा—पाणी पाणि-लेहा णहा णहसिहा भमुहा अहरोट्ठा उत्तरोट्ठा। अह पुण एवं जाणिज्जा विगओदए से काए छिण्ण-सिणेहे एवं से कप्पइ असणं वा पाणं वा खाइमं वा साइमं वा आहारित्तए। ४३

In the course of the *parjuṣaṇā* during the monsoon sojourn, a monk or a nun is not permitted to take food or drink, dainties or dry fruits when his/her body is wet or moist. 42

— '*Bhante* ! 'Why has this been said like that ?

— Seven places are stated to shelter moisture : the hands, the lines in the hands, the nails, the tips of the nails, the brows, the lower lip and the upper lip. Only when the body is free from water or moisture, is he/she permitted to take food and drink, dainties and dry fruits. 43

वासावासं पज्जोसवियाणं इह खलु णिग्गंठाण वा णिग्गंठीण वा इमाइं अट्ठ सुहुमाइं,[55] जाइं छउमत्थेणं णिग्गंठेण वा णिग्गंठीए वा अभिक्खणं अभिक्खणं जाणियव्वाइं पासिव्वाइं पडिलेहियव्वाइं भवंति तं जहा—पाण-सुहुमं पणग-सुहुमं बीय-सुहुमं हरिय-सुहुमं पुप्फ-सुहुमं अंड-सुहुमं लेण-सुहुमं सिणेह-सुहुमं ।

In the course of the *parjuṣaṇā* during the monsoon sojourn, particularly for one not yet advanced, for such a monk or a nun it is necessary to know, see and imprint in mind all the while these very diminutive forms of life which are :

minute beings, minute insects (mildews), minute life in seeds, minute life in sprouts, minute life in flowers, minute life in eggs, minute shelters/layers (built by small insects), and minute life in moisture.

से किं तं पाण-सुहुमे ? पाण-सुहुमे पंचविहे पण्णवत्ते । तं जहा—किण्हे णीले लोहिए हालिद्दे सुकिल्ले । अत्थि कुंथू अणुद्धरी णामं जा ठिया अचल-माणा छउमत्थाणं णिग्गंथाण वा णिग्गंथीण वा णो चक्खु-फासं हव्वमागच्छइ जा छउमत्थेणं णिग्गंथेण वा णिग्गंथीए वा अभिक्खणं अभिक्खणं जाणियव्वा पासियव्वा पडिलेहियव्वा भवइ । से तं पाण-सुहुमे । ४४

—What are these minute beings, pray ?

The minute beings have been stated to be of five types, which are black, blue, red, yellow and white. There is an insect called *anuddhari*, which, when not moving, is not generally visible to a monk or a nun, who is not yet advanced, (but) which a monk and a nun, not yet advanced, should always, and at all times, know, see and imprint in mind. Such are the diminutive forms of living beings. 44

से किं तं पणग-सुहूमे ? पणग-सुहुमे पंचविहे पाणत्ते तं जहा—किण्हे णीले लोहिएं हालिंद्दे सुकिल्ले । अथ्थि पणग-सुहुमे तदव्व-समाण-वण्णए णामं पण्णत्ते जे छउमथ्थेणं णिग्गंथेण वा णिग्गंथीए वा अभिक्खणं अभिक्खणं जाणियव्वे पासियव्वे पडिलेहियव्वे भवइ । से णं पणग-सुहुमे ।

—And what are these minute insects, pray ?
Minute insects have been stated to be of five types which are : black, blue, red, yellow and white. There are minute insects which are stated to take the hue of the things (on which they thrive), and which a monk as well as a nun, not yet advanced, should always, and at all times, know, see and imprint in mind. Such are the minute insects.

से किं तं बीय-सुहुमे ? बीय-सुहुमे पंचविहे पण्णत्ते तं जहा—किणहे णीले लोहिए हालिद्दे सुकिल्ले । अथ्थि बीय-सुहुमे कणिया-समाण-वण्णए णामं पण्णत्ते जे छउमंथ्थेएां णिग्गंथेण वा णिग्गंथीए अभिक्खणं अभिक्खणं जाणियव्वे पासियव्वे पडिलेहियव्वे भवइ । से तं बीयसुहुमे ।

—And what is this minute life in seeds ?
Minute life in seeds is stated to be of five types which are : black, blue, red, yellow and white. There is a minute seed which is stated to have the same hue as the grain, and this a monk as well as a nun, not yet advanced, should always, and at all times, know, see and imprint in mind. Such is minute life in seeds.

से किं तं हरिय-सुहुमे ?[56] हरिय सुहुमे पंचविहे पण्णत्ते तं जहा—किणहे णीले लोहिए हालिद्दे सुकिल्ले । अथ्थि हरिय-सुहुमे पुढ़वी-समाण-वण्णए णामं पण्णत्ते जे छउमथ्थेणं णिग्गंथेण वा निग्गंथीए वा अभिक्खणं अभिक्खणं जाणियव्वे पासियव्वे पडिलेहियव्वे भवइ । से तं हरिय-सुहुमे ।

— And what about the minute life in sprouts ?
Minute life in sprouts is stated to be of five types which are : black, blue, red, yellow and white. There is minute life in sprouts which is stated to take the hue of the earth, and which a monk as well as a nun, not yet advanced, should, always, and at all times, know, see and imprint in mind. Such is minute life in sprouts.

से किं तं पुप्फ-सुहुमे ? पुप्फ-सुहुमे पंचविहे पण्णत्ते तं जहा—किण्हे णीले लोहिए हालिद्दे सुकिल्ले। अत्थि पुप्फ-सुहुमे रुक्ख-समाण-वण्णए णामं पण्णत्ते जे छउमत्थेणं णिग्गंथेण वा णिग्गंथीए वा अभिक्खणं अभिक्खणं जाणियव्वे पासियव्वे पडिलेहियव्वे भवइ। से तं पुप्फ-सुहुमे।

And what is the minute life in flowers ?
Minute life in flowers is stated to be of five types which are : black, blue, red, yellow and white. There is minute life in flowers which is stated to take the hue of the tree, and which a monk as well as a nun, not yet advanced, should always, and at all times, know, see and imprint in mind. Such is minute life in flowers.

से किं तं अंड-सुहुमे ? अंडसुहुमे पंचविहे पण्णत्ते तं जहा—उद्दंसंडे उक्कलियंडे पिपीलियंडे हलियंडे हल्लोहलियंडे जे छउमत्थेणं णिग्गंथेण वा णिग्गंथीए वा अभिक्खणं अभिक्खणं जाणियव्वे पासियव्वे पडिलेहियव्वे भवइ। से तं अंड-सुहुमे।

—What is the minute life in eggs ?
Minute life in eggs is stated to be of five types which are : eggs of biting insects, eggs of spiders, eggs of ants, eggs of drones (lizards or wasps ?) and eggs of lizards (chameleons ?), and these a monk as well as a nun, not yet advanced, should always, and at all times, know, see and imprint in mind. Such is minute life in eggs.

से किं तं लेण-सुहुमे[57] ? लेण-सुहुमे पंचविहे पण्णत्ते तं जहा—उत्तिगलेणे भिगुलेणे उज्जुए वालमूलए संबुक्कावट्टे णामं पंचमे जे छउमत्थेणं णिग्गंथेण वा णिग्गंथीए वा अभिक्खणं अभिक्खणं जाणियव्वे पासियव्वे पडिलेहियव्वे भवइ। से तं लेण-सुहुमे।

—And what is this minute life in shelters/layers. These are stated to be of five types which are: layers of insects of the asinine variety, drone hives, straight holes, cavities as those widening at the bottom as in the stem of a palm tree and hollows for the snails, and these a monk as well as a nun, not yet advanced, should always, and at all times, know, see and imprint in mind. Such is minute life in shelters/layers.

मे किं तं सिणेह-सुहुमे ? सिणेह-सुहुमे पंचविहे पण्णत्ते तं जहा—उस्सा हिमए महिया करए हर-तणूए जे छउमथ्थेणं णिग्गंथेण वा णिग्गंथीए वा अभिक्खणं अभिक्खणं जाणियव्वे पासियव्वे पडिलेहियव्वे भवइ। से तं सिणेह-सुहुमे। ४५

—And what is minute life in moisture ?

Minute life in moisture is stated to be of five types which are : snow, dew, fog, hail-stone and damp, and these a monk as well as a nun, not yet advanced, should always, and at all times, know, see and imprint in mind. Such is minute life in moisture. 45

वासावासं पज्जोसविए भिक्खु य इच्छिज्जा गाहावइ-कुलं भत्ताए वा पाणाए वा णिक्खमित्तए वा पविसित्तए वा णो से कप्पइ अणापुच्छित्ता आयरियं वा उवज्झायंवा थेरं[58] पवत्ति गणि[59] गणहरं गणावच्छेययं[60] जं वा पुरओ-काउं विहरइ। कप्पइ से आपुच्छिउं आयरियं वा उवज्झायं वा थेरं पवत्ति गणि गणहरं गणावच्छेययं जं वा पुरओ-काउं विहरइ—इच्छामि णं तुब्भेहिं अब्भणुण्णाए समाणे गाहावइकुलं भत्ताए वा पाणाए वा णिक्खमित्तए वा पविसित्तए वा। ते य से वियरेज्जा एवं से कप्पइ गाहावइ-कुलं भत्ताए वा पाणाए वा णिक्खमित्तए वा पविसित्तए वा। ते य से णो वियरेज्जा एवं से णो कप्पइ गाहावइ-कुलं भत्ताए वा पाणाए वा णिक्खमित्तए वा पविसित्तए वा। से किमाहु भंते ? आयरिया पच्चवायं जाणंति। ४६

In the course of the *parjuṣaṇā* during the monsoon sojourn, if a *bhikṣu* desires to go to the residence of a householder for begging food and drink, then, he is not permitted to go out for begging without obtaining the permission of the preceptor, teacher, *sthavira, gaṇi, gaṇadhara,* head of a *gaṇa* division or any other holding a superior rank. To his preceptor, teacher, *sthavira, gaṇi, gaṇadhara,* or head of a *gaṇa* division or any one who is his superior, he submits as follows :

—'Sir, if you be pleased to permit, I desire to go to, and come back from, the residence of householders for the purpose of begging food and drink.'

If permitted by him, he is allowed to enter into, and come back from, the residence of a householder for the purpose of begging food and drink; but if he is not permitted, then he is not allowed to enter into and come back from the residence of the householder for begging food and drink.

—'*Bhante* ! Why has it been said like that ?'

Because the preceptor alone knows the wrongs and remedies thereof. 46

एवं विहारभूमिं वा वियारभूमिं वा अण्णं वा जं किंचि पओयणं एवं गामाणुगामं दूइज्जत्तए। ४७

Identical prescription (regarding seeking permission) for repairing to the place of study/spiritual practices or to the place for depositing excreta or to any other (for any other purpose); and not dissimilar (is the prescription) for wandering from village to village. 47

वासावासं पज्जोसविए भिक्खू य इच्छिज्जा अण्णयरिं विगइं आहारित्तए णो से कप्पइ अणापुच्छित्ता आयरियं वा उवज्झायं वा थेरं पवत्तिं गणिं गणहरं गणावच्छेययं वा जं वा पुरओकाउं विहरइ। कप्पइ से आपुच्छित्ताणं आयरियं वा उवज्झायं वा थेरं पवत्तिं गणिं गणहरं गणावच्छेययं वा जं वा पुरओ-काउं विहरइ—इच्छामि णं भंते! तुब्भेहिं अब्भणुण्णाए समाणे अण्णयरिं विगइं आहारित्तए तं जहा—एवइयं वा एवइ-खुत्तो वा। ते य से वियरेज्जा एवं से कप्पइ अण्णयरिं विगइं आहारित्तए। से किमाहु भंते! आयरिया पच्चवायं जाणंति। ४८

In the course of the *parjuṣaṇā* during the monsoon sojourn, if a *bhikṣu* desires to take/use another medicine, then he is not permitted to do so without obtaining the permission of the preceptor, teacher, senior monk, *sthavira*, *gaṇi*, *gaṇadhara*, head of a *gaṇa* division or any other who is superior in rank. To the preceptor, teacher, *sthavira*, *gaṇi*, *gaṇadhara*, head of a *gaṇa* division or any other who may be holding a superior rank, he submits, 'Sir', if you permit, I wish to use/take a new medicine—so much and so many times.' If he agrees, then he may use the new medicine; but in case he does not approve, then he will not be able to use the new medicine.

—'*Bhante* ! Why has it been said like that ?'

Because the preceptor alone knows about the wrongs and remedies thereof. 48

वासावासं पज्जोसविए भिक्खू य इच्छिज्जा अण्णयरिं तेइच्छिं आउट्टित्तए, णो से कप्पइ अणापुच्छित्ता आयरियं वा उवज्झायं वा थेरं पवत्ति गणि गणहरं गणावच्छेययं जं वा पुरओ-काउं विहरइ। कप्पइ से आपुच्छिउं आयरियं वा उवज्झायं वा थेरं पवत्ति गणि गणहरं गणावच्छेययं वा जं वा पुरओ-काउं विहरइ—इच्छामि णं तुब्भेहिं अब्भणुणाए समाणे अण्णयरिं तेइच्छिं आउट्टित्तए तं जहा—एवइयं वा एवइखुत्तो वा। ते य से वियरेज्जा एवं से कप्पइ अण्णयरिं तेइच्छिं आउट्टित्तए। ते य से णो वियरेज्जा एवं से णो कप्पइ अण्णयरिं तेइच्छिं आउट्टित्तए। से किमाहु भंते ? आयरिया पच्चवायं जाणंति। ४९

In the course of the *parjuṣaṇā* during the monsoon sojourn, if a *bhikṣu* desires to undergo another medical treatment, then he is not permitted to do so without obtaining the permission of the preceptor, teacher, *sthavira*, *gaṇi*, *gaṇadhara*, head of a *gaṇa* division or any other person who is entrusted with the supervision. To the preceptor, teacher, *sthavira*, *gaṇi*, *gaṇadhara*, head of a *gaṇa* division or any other person holding a superior rank, he submits, 'Sir', if you permit, I wish to undergo another medical treatment—this much and for so many times.' If he approves, then he is permitted to undergo it; but in case he does not approve, then he will not be able to undergo it.

—'*Bhante* ! Why has it been said like that ?

Because the preceptor alone knows about the wrongs and remedies thereof. 49

वासावासं पज्जोसविए भिक्खू य इच्छिज्जा अण्णयरं ओरालं तवोकम्मं उवसंपज्जित्ता णं विहरित्तए। णो से कप्पइ अणापुच्छित्ता आयरियं वा उवज्झायं वा थेरं पवत्ति गणि गणहरं गणावच्छेययं वा जं वा पुरओ-काउं विहरइ। कप्पइ से आपुच्छिउं आयरियं वा उवज्झायं वा थेरं पवत्ति गणि गणहरं गणावच्छेययं वा जं वा पुरओ-काउं विहरइ—इच्छामि णं तुब्भेहिं अणुण्णाए समाणे अण्णयरं ओरालं तवोकम्मं उवसंपज्जित्ताए। तं जहा-एवइयं एवइखुत्तो वा। ते य उवसंपज्जित्ताए। ते य से णो वियरेज्जा एवं से णो से वियरेज्जा। एवं से कप्पइ अण्णयरं ओरालं तवोकम्मं कप्पइ अण्णयरं ओरालं तवोकम्मं उवसंपज्जित्ताए। से किमाहु भंते ? आयरिया पच्चवायं जाणंति। ५०

In the course of the *parjusaṇā* during the monsoon sojourn, if a *bhikṣu* desires to perform some exalted penance, then he is not permitted to do so without obtaining the permission of the preceptor, teacher, *sthavira*, *gaṇi*, *gaṇadhara*, head of a *gaṇa* division, or any other holding a superior rank. To such one (repeat as before), he submits, 'Sir, if you permit, I wish to undertake and complete an exalted penance. This is so much and so many times'. If he permits, then he is allowed to undertake it; but not if he does not permit.
—'*Bhante*! Why has it been said like that?'
Because the preceptor alone knows about the wrongs and remedies thereof. 50

वासावासं पज्जोसविए भिक्खू य इच्छिज्जा अपच्छिममारणंतिय-संलेहणा-जोसणा-जुसिए[61] भत्त-पाण-पडियाइक्खिए पाओवगए[62] कालं अणवकंखमाणे विहरित्तए वा णिक्खमित्तए वा पविसित्तए वा असणं वा पाणं वा खाइमं वा साइमं वा आहारित्तए वा उच्चारं वा पासवणं वा परिट्ठावित्तए सज्झायं वा कारित्तए धम्म-जागरियं वा जागरित्तए णो से कप्पइ अणापुच्छित्ता आयरियं वा उवज्झायं वा थेरं पवत्ति गणि गणहरं गणावच्छेययं वा जं वा पुरओ-काउं विहरइ। कप्पइ से आपुच्छिउं आयरियं वा उवज्झायं वा थेरं पवत्तिं गणिं गणहरं गणावच्छेययं वा पुरओ-काउं विहरइ—इच्छामि णं तुब्भेहिं अब्भणुण्णाए समाणे अपच्छिमजाव... जागरित्तए। ते य से वियरेज्जा एवं से कप्पइ अपच्छिम जाव...जागरित्तए। ते य से णो वियरेज्जा एवं से णो कप्पइ जाव...जागरित्तए। से किमाहु भंते ? आयरिया पच्चवायं जाणंति। ५१

In the course of the *parjuṣaṇā* during the monsoon sojourn, if a *bhikṣu* desires to keep waiting for his last moment by performing the penance named *apaścima-māraṇāntika saṃlekhaṇā*, or by giving up food and drink, or by staying motionless like a tree, or desires to go out for food and drink, dainties and dry fruits, or for depositing excreta, or for studying spiritual texts, or for fulfilling the vow of 'spiritual-vigil', then he cannot perform (any one of these) without obtaining the permission of the preceptor, teacher, *sthavira*, *gaṇi*, *gaṇadhara*, head of a *gaṇa* division or any other holding a superior rank. To such one (repeat as before), he submits, 'Sir, if you permit, I wish to wait for my last moment by performing the penance of *apaścima-māraṇāntika-samlekhaṇā*, to give up food and drink, to stay motionless like a tree, to go out for food and drink, dainties and dry fruits, for depositing, excreta, for studying spiritual texts or I wish to fulfil the vow of spiritual-vigil.' If he allows, then he is permitted to perform/undergo any one of these; but not if he is not allowed to perform/undergo any one of these.

—'*Bhante* ! Why has it been said like this?'

Because the preceptor alone knows about the wrongs and remedies thereof. 51

वासावासं पज्जोसविए भिक्खू य इच्छिज्जा वत्थं वा पडिग्गहं वा कंबलं वा पायपुछंणं वा अण्णयरं वा उवहिं आयावित्तए वा पायावित्तए वा[63] । णो से कप्पइ एगं वा अणेगं वा अपडिण्णवित्ता गाहावइ-कुलं भत्ताए वा पाणाए वा णिक्खमित्तए वा पविसित्तए वा असणं वा आहारित्तए बहिया वियार-भूमिं वा विहार-भूमिं वा सज्झायं वा करित्तए काउस्सग्गं वा ठाणं वा ठाइत्तए । अत्थि य इत्थ केइ अहा-सण्णिहिए एगे वा अणेगा वा कप्पइ से एवं वदित्तए —इमं ता अज्जो ! मुहुत्तगं जाणाहि जाव ताव अहं गाहावइ-कुलं भत्ताए वा पाणाए वा णिक्खमित्तए वा पविसित्तए वा असणं वा आहारित्तए बहिया वियारभूमिं वा विहार-भूमिं वा सज्झायं वा करित्तए काउस्सग्गं वा ठाणं वा ठाइत्तए । से य से पडिसुणिज्जा एवं से कप्पइ गाहावइ-कुलं तं चेव । से य से णो पडिसुणिज्जा एवं से णो कप्पइ गाहावइ-कुलं जाव काउस्सग्गं वा ठाणं वा ठाइत्तए । ५२

In the course of the *parjuṣaṇā* during the monsoon sojourn, if a *bhikṣu* desires to dry or warm his robe, begging bowls, blanket, duster for cleaning legs, or any other object, then he is not permitted to do so without informing one or many; and so (i.e., without informing one or many), he is not permitted to enter into, and emerge from, the residence of the householder for the purpose of begging food and drink, to eat food, to go to the place of study or for depositing excreta, to commence study or study of spiritual texts, or to attain an altitude for the practice of *kāyotsarga* meditation. Whoever, one or more, that may be available in close proximity to him to them he is required to say, '*Ārya* ! May I have your attention for a moment. I intend to go to, and emerge from, the householder's residence for the purpose of begging food and drink, (or) to eat this food, to move to a place of study or to a place for depositing excreta, to commence studies, to attain an altitude for the practice of *kāyotsarga* meditation.' If he or they listen to him (i.e., permit him), then he is permitted to visit the householder's residence and/or do the rest; but if he or they do not listen, then he is not permitted to visit the householder's residence, ...till attain an altitude for the practice of *kāyotsarga* meditation. 52

वासावासं पज्जोसवियाणं णो कप्पइ णिग्गंथाण वा णिग्गंथीण वा अणभिग्गहिय-सेज्जासणिएणं होत्तए आयाणमेयं—अणभिग्गहिय-सेज्जासणियस्स अणुच्चा-कुइयस्स अणट्ठाबंधिस्स अमियासणियस्स अणाताबियस्स असमियस्स अभिक्खणं अभिक्खणं अपडिलेहणा-सीलस्स अपमज्जणा-सीलस्स तहा तहा णं संजमे दुराराहये भवइ । ५३

In the course of the *parjuṣaṇā* during the monsoon sojourn, a monk as well as a nun must have his bed and cushion; not having (them) is not approved. Such is the accepted prescription (for monks as well as nuns) : one who has not taken a separate bed and cushion, whose spinal chord is not straight, who is not established on a spiritual seat with his eight limbs duly fixed, who has not borne the trouble of undergoing a penance, who has not made a formal acceptance of a vow, who is not used to frequently recollecting his own lapse, and who is not used to inspect and clean things of his own use, for such one, restraint is impossible to practise. 53

अणायाणमेयं अभिग्गहिय-सेज्जासणियस्स उच्चा-कुइयस्स अट्ठा-बंधिस्स मियासणियस्स आयावियस्स समियस्स अभिक्खणं अभिक्खणं पडिलेहण-सीलस्स पमज्जण-सीलस्स तहा तहा णं संजमे सुआराहए भवइ । ५४

Contrariwise, he who has taken a separate bed and a separate cushion, who has a straight spinal chord, who is established on a spiritual seat with his eight limbs duly fastened, who has exposed himself to the rigours of penance, who has made a formal acceptance of a vow, who is used to recollecting his lapses very often, and who is accustomed to inspecting and cleaning things of his use, for such one restraint is easy to attain. 54

वासावासं पज्जोसवियाएां कप्पइ णिग्गंथाण वा णिग्गंथीण वा तम्रो उच्चार-पासवण-भूमीम्रो पडिलेहित्तए। ण तहा हेमंत-गिम्हासु जहा णं वासासु। से किमाहु भंते ? वासासु णं म्रोसण्णं पाणा य तणा य बीया य पणगा य हरियाणि य भवंति। ५५

In the course of the *parjuṣaṇā* during the monsoon sojourn, if not so much in summer and winter, for a monk as well as a nun, there must be three places fixed for depositing excreta.

—'*Bhante* ! Why do ye say like that ?'

Because during rainfall season, many small insects, grass, seeds, weevils, sprouts and moss shoot up. 55

वासावासं पज्जोसवियाणं कप्पइ णिग्गंथाण वा णिग्गंथीण वा तत्त मत्तगाइं[64] गिण्हित्तए तं जहा—उच्चार-मत्तए पासवण-मत्तए खेल-मत्तए। ५६

In the course of the *parjuṣaṇā* during the monsoon sojourn, a monk as well as a nun must have three pots—one for stool, one for urine, one for phlegm. 56

वासावासं पज्जोसवियाएां णो कप्पइ णिग्गंथाण वा णिग्गंथीण वा परं पज्जोसवणाम्रो गो-लोम-प्पमाण-मित्ता वि केसा तं रयणिं उवायणावित्तए म्रज्जेणं खुर-मुंडेण वा लुक्कसिरएण वा होयव्वं सिया। पक्खिया म्रारोवणा[65] मासिए खुरामुंडे म्रद्ध-मासिए कत्तरि-मुंडे छम्मासिए लोए संवच्छरिए वा थेर-कप्पे। ५७

In the course of the *parjuṣaṇā* during the monsoon sojourn, a monk or a nun has on the head hair even of the length of the cow's fur; then, after the *parjuṣaṇā*, he or she is not allowed to keep in that state even for a single night. It is necessary for an *Ārya* to have his head cleaned by a razor or by a tonsure. Daily tending, fortnightly scissoring, monthly razoring, and tonsure in six months or a year—such are the prescriptions of the senior monks. 57

वासावासं पज्जोसवियाणं णो कप्पइ णिग्गंथाण वा णिग्गंथीण वा परं पज्जोसवणाम्रो म्रहिगरणं वइत्तए। जे णं णिग्गंथो वा णिग्गंथी वा परं पज्जोसवणाम्रो म्रहिगरणं वयइ से णं म्रकप्पेणं म्रज्जो ! वयसि त्ति वत्तव्वे

सिया । जे एां णिग्गंथो वा णिग्गंथी वा परं पज्जोसवणाओ अहिगरणं वयइ
से णं णिज्जूहियव्वे सिया । ५८

Having practised *parjuṣaṇā* during the monsoon sojourn, a monk or a nun should not use harsh words after the *parjuṣaṇā.* A monk or a nun using harsh words after the *parjuṣaṇā* has to be told, '*Ārya*', You speak unpermitted words. A monk or a nun who still speaks harsh words after the *parjuṣaṇā* has to be turned out of the church. 58

वासावासं पज्जोसवियाणं इह खलु णिग्गंथाण वा णिग्गंथीण वा अज्जे व कक्खडे कडुए विग्गहे समुप्पज्जिज्जा सेहे राइणियं खामिज्जा राइणिए वि सेहं खामिज्जा । खमियव्वं खमावियव्वं उवसमियव्वं उवसमावियव्वं सम्मुइ-संपुच्छणा-बहुलेण होयव्वं । जो उवसमइ तस्स अत्थि आराहणा । जो ण उवसमइ तस्स णत्थि आराहणा । तम्हा अप्पणा चेव उवसमियव्वं । से किमाहु भंते ? उवसम-सारं खु सामण्णं । ५९

Having practised *parjuṣaṇā* during the monsoon sojourn, a monk as well as a nun should at once give up contemptuous exchange of words. The disciple should forgive the senior, as the senior should forgive the disciple. It is necessary to forgive, to be forgiven, to appease, to be appeased, to ask often very many pleasant questions. He who is appeased is effective in control; he who is not appeased is not effective in control. So try to be appeased by your own effort.
—'*Bhante* ! Why has it been said like this?'
Because appeasement is the essence of *śramaṇa* monkhood, 59

वासावासं पज्जोसवियाणं कप्पइ णिग्गंथाण वा णिग्गंथीण वा तओ उवस्सया गिण्हित्तए । तं वेउव्विया पडिलेहा साइज्जिया पमज्जणा[66] । ६०

In the course of the *parjuṣaṇā* during the monsoon sojourn, a monk or a nun should have three abodes. They have to be visited frequently and cleaned regularly. 60

वासावासं पज्जोसवियाणं कप्पइ णिग्गंथाण वा णिग्गंथीण वा अण्णयरिं दिसिं वा अणुदिसिं वा अवगिज्झिय अवगिज्झिय[67] भत्तपाणं गवेसित्तए । से किमाहु भंते ? ओसण्णं समणा भगवंतो वासासु तव-संपउत्ता भवंति । तवस्सी

दुब्बले किलंते मुच्छिज्ज वा पवडिज्ज वा तामेव दिसिं वा अणुदिसिं वा समणा भगवंतो पडिजागरंति[68] । ६१

In the course of the *parjuṣaṇā* during the monsoon sojourn, a monk as well as a nun is required to indicate, as he/she proceeds, the direction and subdirection whither he/she repairs for begging food and drink.
—'*Bhante*! Why has it been said like that?'
Because the revered monks (also nuns) often practice hard penances during the monsoons. Being weak or exhausted, such a penancing monk drops down or becomes senseless on the way; then other monks keep their eyes in that direction or subdirection (to help him). 61

वासावासं पज्जोसवियाणं कप्पइ णिग्गंथाणं वा णिग्गंथीण वा जाव. ..चत्तारि पंच जोयणाइं गंतुं पडिणियत्तए अंतरा वि य से कप्पइ वत्थए णो से कप्पइ तं रयणिं तत्थेव उवायणावित्तए । ६२

In the course of the *parjuṣaṇā* during the monsoon sojourn, a monk or a nun may walk over a distance of four or five *yojanas* (12 to 15 miles) and return; but he/she is not permitted to pass the night there. 62

इच्चेयं संवच्छरियं थेर-कप्पं अहा-सुत्तं अहा-कप्पं अहा-मग्गं अहा तच्चं सम्मं काएण फासित्ता पालित्ता सोभित्ता तीरित्ता किट्टित्ता आराहित्ता आणाए अणुपालित्ता अत्थेगइया समणा णिग्गंथा तेणेव भव-ग्गहणेणं सिज्झंति बुज्झंति मुच्चंति परिणिव्वइंति सव्व-दुक्खाणं अंतं करेंति अत्थेगइया दोच्चेणं भवग्गहणेणं सिज्झंति बुज्झंति मुच्चंति परिणिव्वइंति सव्वदुक्खाणं अंतं करेंति अत्थेगइया तच्चेणं भवग्गहणेणं सिज्झंति बुज्झंति मुच्चंति परिणिव्वइंति सव्वदुक्खाणं अंतं करेंति सत्तट्ठ भव-ग्गहणाइं णाइक्कमंति । ६३

By following throughout the year this text which is meant for the senior monks, by adhering to prescriptions, by traversing on the right path, by knowing the true fundamentals, by practising them in their own person, by obeying them, by arranging decently all the sacred rites, by singing in praise of religion, and by following all the rules as per sacred texts, many *ācāryas* and monks have in this very life attained perfection, enlightenment and liberation—total liberation terminating all misery; and some in two or three lives; but none has to wait (for liberation) in any case beyond the seventh or eighth birth. 63

तेणं कालेणं तेणं समएणं समणे भगवं महावीरे रायगिहे णगरे गुणसिलए चेइए बहूणं समणाणं बहूणं समणीणं बहूणं सावयाणं बहूणं सावियाणं बहूणं देवाणं बहूणं देवीणं मज्झ-गए चेव एवम् आइक्खइ एवं भासइ एवं पण्णवेइ एवं परूवेइ पज्जोसवणा-कप्पं[69] णाम अज्झयणं स-अट्ठं स-हेउयं स-कारणं स-सुत्तं स-उभयं स-वागराणं भुज्जो भुज्जो उवदंसेइ । त्ति बेमि । ६४

In that period, at that time, Śramaṇa Bhagavān Mahāvīra had, while staying at the Guṇaśilaka *caitya* in the city of Rājagṛha, in the midst of many monks, many nuns, many male and female followers, many gods and goddesses, explained again and again this chapter entitled '*pajjuṣaṇākappa*' with object, with logic, with history, with import, with the text and its meaning, with an analysis of import and etymology, expressed it in words, made it known, and demonstrated its methodology by practising it himself. So say I. 64

पज्जोसवणा-कप्पो समत्तो ।
Parjuṣaṇā-kalpa ends.

Appendix

Alternative reading on *Sūtras* 33-46

1. तए णं सा तिसला खत्तियाणी इक्कं च णं महं पंडरं धवलं सेयं संखउल-विमल-दधि-घण-गो-खीर-फेण-रय-णिकर-पयासं थिर-लट्ठ-पउट्ठ-पीवर-सुसिलिट्ठ-विसिट्ठ-तिक्ख-दाढा-विडंबिय-मुहं रत्तोप्पल-पत्त-पउम-णिल्लालियग्ग-जीहं वट्ट-परिपुण्ण-पसत्थ-णिद्ध-महु-गुलिय-पिंगलक्खं पडि-पुण्ण विउल-सुजाय-खंधं णिम्मल-वर-केसर-धरं सोसियसुणिम्मिय-सुजाय-अप्फोडिय-लंगूलं सोमं सोमाकारं लीलायंतं जंभायंतं गगण-तलाओ उवयमाणं सीहं अभिमुहं मुहे पविसमाणं पासित्ता णं पडिबुद्धा। ३३

1. Then kṣatriyāṇī Triśalā saw a noble, calm, moon-like, playing, roaring, pale, bright and white lion come down from the sky, jumping towards her and enter into her mouth, seeing which she woke up. His complexion was like that of a heap of conches or fresh curd or thick cow-milk, or foamy flow of water; his mouth set with sharp teeth, steady, beautiful, excellent, thick, well-arranged and attractive; his tongue like the petal of a red lily or even lotus, with saliva at the tip; his eyes round, full, broad, placid, like small honey-balls, and yellow; his shoulder well-developed and well-formed; his mane pure and excellent; and his tail lifted, well-placed, well-formed and developed. 33

2. एक्कं च णं महं पंडरं धवलं सेयं संखउल-विमल-सण्णिकासं वट्ट-पडिपुण्ण-कण्णं पसत्थ-णिद्ध-महु-गुलिय-पिंगलक्खं अब्भुग्गय-मल्लिया-धवल-दंतं कंचण-कोसी-पविट्ठ-दंतं आणामिय-चाव-रुइल-संविल्लियग्ग-सोंडं अल्लीण-पमाण-जुत्त-पुच्छं सेयं चउद्दंतं हत्थि-रयणं सुमिणे पासित्ता णं पडिबुद्धा। ३४

2. (Triśalā woke up on seeing) a gem among elephants, noble, golden, bright, white, four-tusker; his complexion pure and bright like conches; his ears round and lovely; his eyes placid, like small honey-balls, and yellow; his tusks stretching out, and white like *mallika* flower, set in a gum of gold; his trunk slightly bent, bow-like, bedecking the face; his tail withdrawn, of standard size and fixed (with the body). 34

3. एक्कं च णं मह्ं पंडुरं धवलं सेयं संखउल-विउल-सण्णिकासं वट्ट-पडिपुण्ण-कंठं-वेल्लिय कक्कडच्छं विसमुण्णय-वसुहोट्ठं चल-चवल-पीण-ककुहं ग्रल्लीण-पमाण-जुत्त-पुच्छं सेयं धवलं वसह् सुमिणे पासित्ता णं पडिबुद्धा। ३५

3. (Triśalā woke up on seeing) an ox, noble, golden, bright and white; his appearance like a huge (pile of) conches; his neck round and developed: his eyes like a trembling crab; his lips strong and steep; his hump restless, thick and fleshy; his tail withdrawn, of a measured size and fixed with the body. 35

4. एक्कं च णं महं सिरियातिमसेयं सुमिणे पासित्ता णं पडिबुद्धा। ३६

4. (Triśalā woke up on seeing) the anointment of the noble goddess Śrī. 36

5. एक्कं च णं महं मल्लदामं विविह्-कुसुमोवसोहियं सुमिणे पासित्ता णं पडिबुद्धा। ३७

5. (Triśalā woke up on seeing) a garland, noble and made of sundry flowers. 37

6-7. एक्कं च णं चंदिम-सूरिम-गणं उभग्रो पासे उग्गयं सुमिणे पासित्ता णं पडिबुद्धा। ३८-३९

6-7. (Triśalā woke up on seeing) on each side a noble lunar family and a noble solar family. 38-39

8. एक्कं च णं महं महिंदज्झयं अणेक-कुडभि-सहस्स-परिमंडियाभिरामं सुमिणे पासित्ता णं पडिबुद्धा। ४०

8. (Triśalā woke up on seeing) the most beautiful and noble banner named Mahendra surrounded by several thousand small flags. 40

9. एक्कं च णं महं महिंद-कुंभंवर-कमल-पइट्ठाणं सुरहि-वर-वारि-पुण्णं पउमुप्पल-पिहाणं आविद्ध-कंठ-गुणं सुमिणे पासित्ता णं पडिबुद्धा। ४१

9. (Triśalā woke up on seeing) a noble jar named Mahendra, which contained inside the best of lotuses, and the best and most fragrant water, with lotuses and lilies serving as its cover, with a (holy) thread tied round its neck. 41

10. एक्कं च णं महं पउमसरं बहुप्पल-कुमुय-णलिण-सयवत्त-सहस्सवत्त-केसर-फुल्लोवचियं सुमिणे पासित्ता णं पडिबुद्धा। ४२।

10. (Triśalā woke up on seeing) a noble lotus lake, whereon were deposited the pollens of lilies, lotuses, *nalina*, *śatapatra*, *sahasra-patra*, and many other flowers all in blossom. 42

11. एक्कं च णं सागरं वीची-तरंगं उम्मी-पउरं सुमिणे पासित्ता णं पडिबुद्धा। ४३

11. (Triśalā woke up on seeing) a noble ocean full of waves, wavelets and ripples. 43

12. एक्कं च णं महं विमाणं दिव्वं तुडिय-सद्द-संपण-द्दियं सुमिणे पासित्ता णं पडिबुद्धा। ४४

12. (Triśalā woke up on seeing) a noble celestial abode with a din of sound from (the musical instrument) *tritika*. 44

13. एक्कं च णं महं रयणुच्चंयं सव्व-रयणमयं सुमिणे पासित्ता णं पडिबुद्धा। ४५

13. (Triśalā woke up on seeing) a noble pile of gems containing gems of all varieties. 45

14. एक्कं च णं महं जलण-सिहिं णिद्धुमं सुमिणे पासित्ता णं पडिबुद्धा। ४६

14. (Triśalā woke up on seeing) a noble flame, smokeless. 46

Notes and Comments

[Abbreviations used : S for Sūtra, T for Therāvalī and P for Parjuṣaṇā]

1. अरिहंताणं—सर्वज्ञो जितरागादिदोषस्त्रैलोक्यपूजितः ।
   यथास्थितार्थवादी च देवोऽर्हन् परमेश्वरः ॥

   According to the commentator, three implications of the word are as follows :

   देवादिभ्योऽतिशय-पूजा-वन्दनाद्यर्हत्वाद् अरहंताणं, तथा कर्मारि-हननाद् अरिहंताणं, कर्मबीजाभावे भवेऽप्ररोहाद् अरुहंताणं इति पाठ-त्रयम् । S. 1.

2. आयरियाणं—आचार्यः सूत्रार्थं व्याख्याता दिगाचार्यो वा, उपाध्यायः सूत्राध्यापकः —टीकाकार समयसुन्दर

   cf. Manu (२।१४१)

   एकदेशं तु वेदस्य वेदांगान्यपि वा पुनः ।
   योऽध्यापयति वृत्त्यर्थम् उपाध्यायः स उच्यते ॥ S.1.

3. उवज्झायाणं—See (2) S. 1.

4. काल, समय — काल is an eternal flow, like the current of the river, while समय is a point in time when an event is taking place. Thus समय is a minutest division of काल । In the Jaina view, it may be as short as the twinkle of the eye, or equivalent to the time taken to pierce a piece of rotten cloth or pluck a petal from the lotus.

Innumerable units of समय	= 1 आवलिका
16777216 आवलिका	= 1 मुहूर्त
	= 48 minutes
30 मुहूर्त	= 1 day-night
Innumerable years	= 1 पल्योपम
10 crores × 10 crores of पल्योपम	= 1 सागरोपम । S.1.

5. अणंते अणुत्तरे णिव्वाघाए णिरावरणे कसिणे पडिपुण्णे केवल-वर-णाण-दंसणे समुप्पण्णे ।

   According to the commentator,

अनन्तम् अनन्तार्थ-विषयत्वात्; अनुत्तरम् सव्वोत्तमत्वात्; निर्व्याघातं कटकुट्यादिभिर् अप्रतिहतत्वात्; निरावरणं क्षायिकत्वात्; कृत्स्नं सकलार्थग्राहकत्वात्; पडिपुन्ने प्रतिपूर्णं सकल-स्वांशसहितत्वात्; केवलम् अतएव वरं ज्ञानं दर्शनं च ततः प्राक् पदाभ्यां कर्मधारयः; तत्र ज्ञानं विशेषावबोध रूपं दर्शनं सामान्यबोधरूपम्। S.1.

6. परिणिव्वुए — This word has been confused by some with another परिणिव्वुडे (Sū. 118). But the two do not give identical meaning. The root in the first word is 'वा' but in the second word, it is "वृ।" The first means 'to enter into liberation', while the second means 'to derive great pleasure. S. 1.

7. अट्ठमे पक्खे आसाढ सुद्धे—bright half of the month of Āṣāḍha, which is the eighth fortnight of summer. In the Jaina view, there are three seasons in the year, summer, rains and winter, each of the duration of four months. S.2.

8. महाविजय-पुप्फुत्तर-पवर-पुंडरीयाओ महाविमाणाओ—महान् विजयो यत्र तथाविधं च तत् पुष्पोत्तर-संज्ञकं च तदेव प्रवरेषु श्रेष्ठेषु पुंडरीकं विमानानां मध्ये उत्तमत्वात्।

It may be useful to give here the outline of Jaina cosmology, with description of inhabitants in different spheres. In the Jaina view, the entire cosmos looks like the English letter 'X' at the centre of which is तिर्यग्लोक or the world of animals, human beings, with hells underneath, and the heavens or celestial spheres in the upper portion. There are three broad types of heavens called देवलोक, ग्रैवेयक and अनुत्तर-विमाण and beyond them, and not touched by them, is the abode of the perfected-liberated-enlightened beings called सिद्धसिला। The beings in the lower sphere are as follows :

(i) Devas, viz., Amba, Ambarasa, Rudra, Sāma, Sabaḷa, Mahārudra, Kāla, Mahākāla, Ashipāta, Dhanu, Bālu, Betarani, Khara-svara, Mahāghoṣa. These chastise the sinners in diverse ways.

(ii) Ten Bhavanapatis of the netherworld : Asura-kumāras, Nāgakumāras Suvarṇakumāras, Vidyutkumâras, Agnikumâras, Dvipakumâras, Udadhikumâras, Diśâkumâras, Vâyukumâras and Stanitkumâras.

(iii) Vyantaras of the nether world : Piśâca, Bhūta, Yakṣa, Râkṣasa, Kinnara, Kiṁ-puruṣa, Mahoraga, Gandharva.

(iv) Vâṇavyantara Devas : Ânapanni, Pânapanni, Iśivâyi, Bhutavâyi, Kandiya, Mahâkandiya, Kohanda and Pahanga.

In the upper sphere, the Devas are :

(i) Jyotiṣkas or planetary bodies like the sun, the moon, the stars, the planets, the comets, etc.

(ii) The dwellers of Vimânas or *kalpas*, which fall into three species as follows :

(a) In the Devaloka live the denizens of the *vimānas* / *kalpas* called Sudharmâ, Îśâna, Sanatkumâra, Mâhendra, Brahma, Lāntaka, Mahâsukra, Sahaṣâra, Ânata, Prāṇata, Ārana and Acyuta.

(b) In the Graiveyakas live Bhadra, Subhadra, Sujāta, Sumânasa, Priyadarśana, Sudarśana, Amoga, Supratibhadra and Yaśodhara.

(c) The five Anuttara Vimānas, viz., Vijaya, Vaijayanta, Jayanta, Aparâjita and Sarvārthasiddha, are occupied by the Indras.

There are a few other species of gods who work as valets or errand boys. They are : Kilvisiyas, Tiryak-jṛmbhakas, Lokāntikas.

The seven hells are : Ratnaprabhā, Śarkarāprabhā, Balukāprabhā, Paṅkaprabhā, Dhūmraprabhā, Tamaḥ-prabhā, Tamaḥ-tamaḥ-prabhā.

Beneath all these there is a hell, the severest of all, called, Nigoda.

At the centre of the figure, which is the thinnest, is located the Tiryag-loka with its two and a half isles or continents, each one of which has a secret region called Mahāvideha. The inhabitants of Mahâvideha may, if they strive, earn liberation. S. 2.

9. ओसप्पिणी – This is the down-phase of the Jaina time-cycle, of which there are six parts as follows: exceedingly bracing, bracing, bracing-unbracing, unbracing-bracing, unbracing, exceedingly unbracing. The up-phase called उस्सप्पिणी has also six parts, with the previous six reversed, viz., exceedingly unbracing, unbracing, unbracing-bracing, bracing-unbracing, bracing, execedingly bracing. For bracing the word is सुसमा, for unbracing दुस्समा. S. 2.

10. अद्ध– This word is used to denote deficiency by half, e.g.,
अद्धुट्ठम् $=4-\frac{1}{2} = 3\frac{1}{2}$,
अद्धट्ठम् $=8-\frac{1}{2} = 7\frac{1}{2}$,
अद्धनवम् $= 9-\frac{1}{2} = 8\frac{1}{2}$. S. 2

11. गइ–The word is used here to mean 'pace'. In the Jaina literature, the word has a special meaning, which is the 'state of existence' that a soul attains. It is another name for what has been called '*nāmakarma.*' There are four states of existence—as infernal beings, as non-human (animal) beings, as human beings and as celestial beings. S. 5

12. कट्टु–Although the word may be written in Sanskrit as कर्तुम् and कृत्व, it is not always in this sense that the word has been used in the Sūtra. A few instances are cited below :
तं पि देवाणंदाए···कुच्छिंछसि · साहराविात्तए त्ति कट्टु एवंसंपेहेइ ।
ओराला णं तुमे···सुमिणा दिट्ठ त्ति कट्टुभुज्जो भुज्जो अणुवूहइ ।
दसणहं मथ्थए अंजलिं कट्टु । S. 5

13. अट्ठ, अथ्थ-Although ordinarily these two words are used as synonyms, there is difference in their meaning. When it implies 'meaning' in dictionary sense, it is अथ्थ; but when it indicates desire, motive, inclination, necessity or cause, it is अट्ठ । S. 8

14. धम्मवर-चाउरंत-चक्कवट्टीणं—धर्मवर चातुरन्त चक्रवर्तिम्यः त्रयः समुद्राः चतुर्थो हिमवाण् एते चत्वारः पृथिव्या अन्ताः । तेषु भवाः स्वामितयेति चातुरन्ताः ते च चक्रवर्तिणः । धर्मेषु वरः श्रेष्ठो धर्मवरः । तत्र विषये चातुरन्त-चक्रवर्तिन इव धर्मवर-चातुरन्त-चक्रवर्तिनः । S. 6

15. पोग्गल This is one of the five items called *ajīva* or non-soul by the Jainas. Atoms or molecules of matter coming together give rise to *pudgala*. It has colour, taste, smell

and touch. It is with the help of a particular variety of *pudgala* that the physical body is formed round the soul. S. 27

16. विव्वोयण etc.—The word is an amalgam of affection and pride. A more appropriate meaning with reference to the context would be विलासोद्दीपक ।
The commentator has, however, adopted a roundabout way to explain the word. Compare : सालिंगनेत्यादि । सहालिंगनवर्त्या शरीर-प्रमाण-गन्डोपाधानेन यत् तत् सालिंगनवर्त्तिकं तस्मिन् । उभयतः उभौ शिरोस्तपादान्तावाश्रित्य । विव्वोयणेत्ति । उपाधाने गन्डके यत्र तत् तथा । क्वचित् पन्नत्तगविव्वोयणि त्ति दृश्यते तत्र च सुपरिकर्मित-गन्डोपाधाने इत्यर्थः । S 32

17. लडह—According to the commentator, लटभा सुविशाला । In Sanskrit, however, the word has been used to signify beauty or grace. Hence the commentator's meaning is not appropriate. It does not fit in with the context either which is रोमराइं । S. 36

18. कोउय—कौतुकानि माषतिलकादीनि । S. 61

19. सण्ह—सण्ह-पट्ट-भत्ति-सह-चित्त-ताणं । S. 63

20. आछावेर—According to Jacobi, the Sanskrit equivalent of the word is आकर्षयति । But this does not seem to be correct. It should be आस्थापयति । S. 63

21. कुण्डधारिणे—कुण्डमायत्ततां धारयन्ति ये ते । According to Jacobi आज्ञां धारयति । S. 89

22. जंभग—तिर्यग्लोक-वासिनो देवा जृम्भकाः । S. 89

23. उप्पिजलग, उप्पिजलजमान—उत्पिजलो भृशमाकुलः स इवाचरतीत्याचार-क्विपि शतरि च; शत्रानशः (हेमचन्द्र ३-१८१) इति प्राकृतलक्षणेनः माणादेशे उप्पिजलमाणि त्ति सिद्धम् तद् भूताभूत शब्दस्योपमा र्थत्वाद् उत्पिजलन्तीति वा ।—सन्देह विषौषधि टीका । S. 97

24. उल्लोइय—The meaning given by the commentator is somewhat confused. According to him, ला-उल्लोइय-महियं-लाइयं छागनादिना भूमौ लेपनं । उल्लोइयं सटिकादिना कुटयादिषु धवलनम् ताभ्यां महितं पूजितं तैरेव वा महितं पूजनं यत्र तत् तथा । अन्येतु: लिप्तम् उल्लोचितम् उल्लोचयुक्तं महितं चेति व्याचक्षते ।—सन्देह विषौषधि टीका । S. 100

Actually, two things are implied, viz, scattering of fried rice (लाज) and hanging of the canopy (उल्लोच)।

25. लासग—According to the commentator, लासका रासकान् ददति जयशब्दप्रयोक्तारो वा। This is not correct. If read as रासक it should mean a small dance-drama. The word means a dancer; Feminine लासिका। S. 100

26. ठिइ-पडिया It is a ceremony at child birth which lasts for 10 days. Jacobi's rendering of it as स्थिति पतिता does not lead anywhere. Of six ceremonies prescribed for the Jaina householders, viz., इज्या, वार्ता, दत्ति, स्वाध्याय, संयम and तपः, इज्या stands first. This is propitiation of deities, spiritual master and scriptures. स्थिति is span of life. The word पडिया has been used in the Sūtra is another connection. (see 50) S. 102

27. परीसह—Hardship. Hardship is deliberately courted and borne to terminate *karma* bondage. Twenty-two hardships have been named as follows :
hunger, thirst, cold, heat, insect bite, clothing, residence, celibacy, wandering, living at places avoided by others, bed, spite, torture, begging, indifference to disappointment in begging, disease, thorn, dirt, indifference to fame and insult, giving up pride of learning or of shame for ignorance, equanimity which means not losing faith in Jainism. S. 108

28. इरिया-समिति—*Samiti* means precaution. Five precautions are part of 57 *saṁvaras* which are intended to prevent fresh influx of *karma* matter. Five precautions are as follows : (i) precaution regarding movement, sleeping, standing, lying, etc., (ii) precaution regarding the use of words or speech, (iii) precaution in the course of begging, (iv) keeping things in the monk's use perfectly clean and dust-free, (v) precaution in depositing excreta, unused food, etc. S. 118

29. अणासवे—without *āsrava*. *Āsrava* refers to inlet of fresh fetters generated by pious and impious *karma* that bind the soul. Compare :

Āsravas are 42 in number, of which the principal ones are 17 as follows :

Pleasures to five organs of senses—5

Passions, viz., anger, pride, attachment and greed— 4

Non-fulfilment of 5 great vows — 5

Activities of body, mind and speech — 3 S. 118

30. कंस-पाइ—The word पाइ is particularly deserving of note. This is in feminine gender, and not in neuter gender. It seems that in olden times, pots of certain size / measure used for eating, cooking or storing food were called पात्रिक, of which the feminine form would be पात्रिकी, Prakrit पाई । S. 118

31. लेसा—Subjective inclination that induces the soul to activity and imparts to the soul a certain tinge. Six tinges have been named as black, blue, ash, red, pink and white. This is in ascending order of purity, 'black' being the worst and 'white' being the best. The idea is illustrated as follows with the help of an example. Six persons with these six tinges desire to eat the fruits of a tree. How would they behave ? The person with black tinge will cut the tree at the very root. The one with blue tinge will chop its branches. The one with ash tinge will cut one branch only, bearing fruit for his consumption. The one with red tinge will pluck all the fruits, green as well as ripe. The one with pink tinge will pluck only the ripe fruits. The one with white tinge will take only those ripe fruits that have dropped on the ground, but will not touch the tree. S. 118

32. अट्ठियग्गाम—name of a town. So goes the story that this town sprang up on a pile of bones of animals and human beings whom a *yakṣa* killed and devoured. It was located somewhere in Rāḍhā (modern West Bengal). S. 122

33. अंतरावास—stay/sojourn in between summer and winter, or in between ceaseless wanderings. From this, it follows that the monk should stay at one place during the rainy season. It does not mean a 'rainy night', as interpreted by Jacobi. S. 122

34. अंतक(ग)डे—Termination implied here is that of *karma* which go out at death, viz., name, lineage, etc., after which one is entitled to full liberation. S. 124

35. पाराभोय—To see from a distance the end of earthly life. As used in the *Sūtra*, it is a ceremony at the passing away of Śramaṇa Bhagavān Mahāvīra. In this connection, the following description may be interesting :
अमावस्यायां तस्यां पारं पर्यन्तं भवस्य आभोगयति पश्यति यः स पाराभोगः संसार-सागरपार-प्रापण-प्रवणम् तम् । अथवा, पारं पर्यन्तं यावद् आभोगो विस्तारो यस्य स पाराभोगः अष्टप्राहरिकः प्रभात-कालं यावत् सम्पूर्ण इत्यर्थः तथाविधं पौषधोपवासं पौषधयुक्तोपवासं पोट्ठविसु त्ति प्रस्थापितवन्तः कृतवन्तः । केचित् च वाराभोए इति पठन्ति द्वारम् आभोग्यतेऽवलोक्यते यैस्ते द्वारा भोगाः प्रदीपाः तान् कृतवन्तः आहारत्याग पौषध-रूपम् उपवासं चाकर्षुरिति च व्याचक्षते (इति वृद्ध व्याख्या) एतदर्थानुपात्येव चोत्तरसूत्रम् । S. 128

36. अज्ज-चंदणा—She was the leader of a community of 36,000 nuns. She was the daughter of Cetaka, king of Vaiśāli. In another view, she was the daughter of Dadhivāhana, king of Campā. So goes the story that she became a captive in the hands of a soldier and suffered enormous torture in his hands, but she remained steadfast in her chastity. S. 135

37. अइसेसपत्ताणं—Those who have arrived at the last limit. The limit implied here is that of knowledge, from which it follows 'masters of *avadhi* knowledge'. S. 139

38. अड्ढा इज्जेसु दीवेसु—2½ isles or continents. For details, see (8) above. S. 142

39. संपलियंक—सम्पर्यंकः संगतपर्यंकः पद्मासनं तत्र निषन्न उपविष्टः । According to another explanation
एकं पादमथैकस्मिन् विन्यस्योरौ तु संस्थितम् । इतरस्मिंस्तथैवोरुं वीरासनमुदाहृतम् ॥ S. 47

40. गणहर—Direct disciples of a Tīrthaṅkara. Each Gaṇadhara was the head of a community of monks. From these communities later branched out *kulas* and *śākhās*. S. 160

41. अकंपिए—name of a senior monk. He was the third brother of Indrabhūti Gautama, and had 300 monks in his group. Certain Jaina sects consider him to be the friend of Gautama. Th 1

42. अभिण्णाया— Its Sanskrit form is अभिन्नात्मा, not अभिज्ञातः, as rendered by Jacobi. Th 5

43. अहा-लंदं—as far as is necessary to deposit excreta. The meaning of the commentary given below is not clear: तत्रोदकार्द्रः करो यावता शुष्यति तावान् कालो जघन्यं लंदम् । उत्कृष्टं पंचाहोरात्रास्तयोरन्तरं मध्यम् । P 9

Jacobi's translation as follows is based on a confusion : "Monks or nuns during the *Pajjuṣanā* are allowed to regard their residence as extending a Yojana and a Krośa all around, and to live there for a moderate time." Hermann Jacobi, *Ibid.* p. 297.

44. एरावई—name of a river. Its use with another word Kunāla gives the impression to some that it was not a river but an outlet of dirty water. It is more appropriate to take Kunāla as the name of a town by which the river flowed. P 12

45. अथ्थेगइयाणं–अथ्थेगइया आयरिया इत्युक्तम् अथ्थं भासेइ आयरिओ इति वचनात् ।

According to सन्देहविषौषधि टीका :—

अस्त्येतद् यद् एकेषामाचार्याणामिदमुक्तम् भवतीति एवं व्याख्येयम् । तत्र षष्ठी तृतीयार्थे ततश्चाचार्येरिदमुक्तं भवति । P 14

46. सुद्ध-बियडं—शुद्ध-विकटम् उष्णोदकम् उसिण-वियडे इति उष्ण-जलम् ।

There is, however, a controversy as to whether this means pure hot water, or hot water in which rice has been boiled. The former appears more appropriate. P 25

47. भत्तपडियाइक्खियस्स—One who has given up the intake of food. During the *Prajuṣaṇā*, some monks, and some householders too, undergo a prolonged fast for the whole period, or even thereafter. During this period, the only intake is that of boiled water. It is perhaps not the practice during this prolonged fasting to take water in which rice has been boiled. P 25

48. संखा दत्तियस्स—दत्ति is offer. In this case, the monk restricts the number of houses which he should visit for purposes of begging. According to the commentator : P 26

संख्ययोपलक्षिता दत्तयो यस्येति संख्यातदत्तिकस्तस्य । दत्तिपरिमाणवत्ता इत्यर्थः ।

49. संखडि— cooked food. According to the commentator, संखण्ड्यंते विराध्यन्ते प्राणिनो यत्र सा संखडी since the process of cooking kills many living beings. P 27

50. पिंडवाय-पडियाए—The begging cloth in which the vessels containing food are carried. P 29

51. संतरुत्तरंसि—ग्रान्तर: सौत्रकल्प: उत्तर श्रौर्णिक: ताभ्यां प्रावृतस्य अल्पवृष्टौ गंतुं कल्पते ।

According to the writer of the *Cūrni* : ग्रन्तरं रयहरणं पडिग्गहो वा उत्तरं पाउरणकप्पो तेहिं सह त्ति । P 31

52. वियड-गिहंसि—water-store. The meaning given by the commentator is : विकटगृहे ग्रास्थानमंडपिकायां यत्र ग्राम्य-पर्षदुपविशति। Accordingly Jacobi has translated it as 'assembly-hall of the village'. P 32

53. पुव्वाउत्त—According to the commentator, पूर्वं साधु-रागत: पश्चाद् दायको राद्धुं प्रवृत्त: इति पूर्वागमनेन हेतुना पूर्वायुक्त: तन्डुलोदन: कल्पते पश्चादायुक्त: भिलिंगसूपो न कल्पते । तत्र पूर्वायुक्त: साध्वागमनात् पूर्वमेव स्वार्थं गृहस्थै: पक्तुमारब्ध: ।

The stand is not very clear. The monk should share a morsel from the householder's food which has been prepared or is already in the process of preparation. This does not put him to the trouble of cooking extra food. P 33

54. सपडिदुवारे—Jacobi's rendering of it is स-प्रतिद्वारे, i.e., 'doors open on it'. P 38

55. ग्रट्ठ-सुहुमाइं—eight very minute types of life which have been identified as minute beings, insects, seeds, sprouts, flowers, eggs, mildew and mist. P 44

56. हरिय-सुहुमं—Sprouts. According to the commentator, नवोद्भिन्नं पृथिवीसमवर्णं हरितं तच्चाल्प-सहननत्वात् स्तोकेनापि विनश्यते । P 44

57. लेण-सुहुमं—insects that live in some shelter, in the hollow of a tree or crevice on the earth, e.g., mildew. लयण is the place of hiding. P 44

58. थेर—senior monk. Compare : स्थविरो ज्ञानादिषु सीदतां स्थिरीकर्त्ता उद्यतानाम् उपबृंहकश्च । P 46

59. गणी–teacher of the *ācārya*. Compare : यस्य पार्श्वे आचार्याः सूत्राद्यभ्यस्यन्ति गणिणो वाऽन्ये आचार्याः सूत्राद्यर्थम् उपसम्पन्नाः । P 46

60. गणावच्छेयय—Compare : यः साधून् गृहीत्वा बहिः क्षेत्रे आस्ते गच्छार्थम्; क्षेत्रोपधिमार्गणादौ प्रधावनकर्त्ता सूत्रार्थोभयवित्; यं वा स्पर्धकाधिपत्येन सामान्यसाधुमपि पुरस्कृत्य विहरति । P 46

61. अ-पच्छिमं-मारणांतिय-संलेहण-जूसणा-जूसिए— Compare : अपश्चिम मारणांतिकी सा चासौ संलेखना तस्या जूसणत्ति सेवा तया जूसिए त्ति क्षपितशरीरोऽतएव प्रत्याख्यात-भक्तपानः ।
The word जूसण in dictionary sense means 'service' and जूसिए 'with body exhausted'. In the present context, the word should, however, mean 'a vow'. The whole thing would thus mean : "one who is resolved to court death by giving up food and drink." P 51

62. पाओवगए (प्रायोपगमणम् प्रायोपवेशनम्)—The commentator's meaning पादपोपगतः कृतपादपोगमन, which has influenced Jacobi, whose translation of the word is 'remaining motionless like a tree', does not give the correct sense. The word given in its Sanskrit form within brackets simply means 'sitting motionless by giving up food to court death'. P 51

63. आयावित्तए वा पायावित्तए वा—According to the commentator : आतापयितुम् एकवारम् आतपे दातुम्; प्रातापयितुम् पुनः पुनः आतपे दातुम् । P 52

64. मत्तगाइं—The comment by the writer of the *Cūrṇi* is as follows : बाहिं तस्स गुम्मियादिगहणं तेण मत्तए वोसिरित्ता बाहिं नित्ता परिट्ठवेइ पासवणे वि अभिग्गहितो धरेइ तस्स सइ जो जाहे वोसिरइ सो ताहे धरेइ न निक्खिवइ सुवंतो वा उच्छंगे ठितयं चेव उवरिं दंडाए वा दोरेण बंधति गोसे असंसत्तियाए भूमीए परिट्ठवेइत्ति । P 56

65. पक्खिया आरोवण—fortnightly arranging. Various meanings have been given to this. According to some, the word

preceding सिया means 'bed'. Therefore, it is the fortnightly arranging/checking of the bed. Some have also added the checking of the wicker-work or basket every fortnight. According to others, there should be a fortnightly atonement for lapses. The commentator Samaya Sundara says that these words are not connected with those preceding or following, and their deeper significance (*paramārtha*) should be learnt from a well-instructed brother. According to Jacobi, and also according to B.K. Chattopadhyaya, this implies the arranging of hairs in the form of a braid by the nuns every fortnight. This meaning would be correct on the assumption that the nuns were permitted to grow long hairs. P 57

66. तं वेउव्विया पडिलेहा साइज्जिया पमज्जण—The two words वेउव्विया and साज्जिया respectively imply 'frequently' and 'again and again'. The commentator's meaning is not clear. Compare :

वेउव्विया पडिलेहा क्वचिच्च वेउट्टिया पडिलेहा इति दृश्यते । उभयत्रापि पुनः पुनः इत्यर्थः । साइज्जिया पमज्जणा इति आर्षे—"जे भिक्खु हत्थकम्मं करेइ करितं वा साइज्जइ" त्ति वचनात् । साइज्जि धातुरास्वादने वर्त्तते । तत उपभुज्यमानो य उपाश्रयः स, कयमाणे कडे त्ति न्यायात् साइज्जिउ त्ति भण्यते । तत् सम्बन्धिनी प्रमार्जना साइज्जिया । यस्मिन् उपाश्रये स्थितास्तं प्रातः प्रमार्जयन्ति, भिक्षागतेषु साधुषु, पुनः मध्याण्हे, पुनः प्रतिलेखनाकाले तृतीय प्रहरान्ते, इतिवार-चतुष्टयं प्रमार्जयन्ति वर्षासु, ऋतुमध्ये त्रिः । अयं च विधिरसंसक्ते संसक्ते तु पुनः पुनः प्रमार्जयन्ति, शेषोपाश्रयद्वयं तु प्रतिदिनं लिखन्ति प्रत्यवेक्षन्ते । मा कोऽपि तत्र स्थास्यति ममत्वं वा करिष्यति इति । तृतीय दिवसे पादप्रोञ्छनकेन प्रमार्जयन्ति । अत उक्तम्—वेउव्विया पडिलेह त्ति क्वचित् साइज्जिया पडिलेह त्ति दृश्यते । तत्रापि प्रतिलेखना प्रमार्जनयोरैक्य विवक्षया स एवार्थः ।

Elsewhere—

स्वादनीयाः; साइज्जि धातुरास्वादने वर्त्तते । तत उपभुज्यमाणो य उपाश्रयः स कयमाणे कडे त्ति न्यायात् साइज्जिउ त्ति भण्यते । तत्संबंधिनी प्रमार्जना साइज्जिया । यस्मिन्नुपाश्रये स्तिथास्तं प्रातः प्रमार्जयन्ति, भिक्षागतेषु साधुषु पुनर्मध्याण्हे, पुनः प्रतिलेखनाकाले तृतीय

प्रहरान्ते, इति वारचतुष्टयं प्रमार्जयन्ति वर्षासु, ऋतुमध्ये त्रिः । श्रयः च विधिरसंसक्ते संसक्ते तु पुनः पुनः प्रमार्जयन्ति शेषोपाश्रयद्वयंतु प्रति-दिनं प्रतिलिखन्ति प्रत्यवेक्षन्ते: मा कोऽपि तत्र स्थास्यति ममत्वं वा करि-ष्यति इति । तृतीय दिवसे पादप्रोंञ्छनकेन प्रमार्जयन्ति । अत उक्तम्: वेउव्विया पडिलेह त्ति क्वचित् साइज्जिया पडिलेह त्ति दृश्यते तत्रापि प्रतिलेखना प्रमार्जनयोरैक्यविवक्षया स एवार्थः । P 60

67. अवगिज्झिय—Compare : अवगृह्योद्दिश्याऽहम् अमुकां दिशं अनुदिशं वा यास्यामीत्यन्यसाधुभ्यः कथयित्वा ।–सन्देहविषौषधिटीका । P 61

68. पडिजागरंति—According to the commentator : तवस्सो दुब्बले किलंते मुच्छिज्ज वा पवडिज्ज वा ताम् एव दिसिं वा अनुदिसिं वा समणा भगवन्तो पडिजागरंति । P 61

69. पज्जोसवणा-कप्प—spiritual practices during a part of the rainy season. The text gives details of these practices to be observed by the monks. The text is also called '*Sāmācārī*'. It is stated to be the practice that on first night of the *Parjuṣaṇā*, the whole of the *Kalpa Sūtra* is read at a congregation and this has to be organised by some well-to-do person. Even now the practice is in vogue with minor changes. P 64

INDEX

The figures indicate the number of Sūtra where the name first occurs. For Part VI, list of senior monks, the Sūtra number is preceded by 'Th' and for Part VII on Parjuṣaṇā, by 'P'.